The Guitar
and the
New World

SUNY series in Italian/American Culture
Fred L. Gardaphe, editor

The Guitar and the New World

A Fugitive History

JOE GIOIA

excelsior editions
State University of New York Press
Albany, New York

Cover images courtesy of the Library of Congress Prints and Photographs Division

Published by State University of New York Press, Albany

For information, contact State University of New York Press, Albany, NY
www.sunypress.edu

Excelsior Editions is an imprint of State University of New York Press

Production by Diane Ganeles
Marketing by Kate McDonnell

Library of Congress Cataloging-in-Publication Data

Gioia, Joe, 1955–
  The guitar and the new world : a fugitive history / Joe Gioia. — Excelsior editions.
      pages cm. — (SUNY series in Italian/American culture)
  Includes bibliographical references and index.
  ISBN 978-1-4384-4617-2 (hardcover : alk. paper)
  1. Music—Social aspects—United States—History. 2. Guitar makers—United States. 3. Italian Americans. 4. Blues musicians—United States. 5. Pan-American Exposition (1901: Buffalo, N.Y.) I. Title.

  ML3917.U6G65 2012
  780.973'0904—dc23   2012017398

10 9 8 7 6 5 4 3 2 1

to

Rosalie and Joe

⤳

Sicily, that America of antiquity.

—Giuseppe di Lampedusa

And isn't one of the implicit functions of the American frontier to encourage the individual to a kind of dreamy wakefulness, a state in which he makes . . . rash efforts, quixotic gestures, hopeful testings of the complexity of the known and the given?

—Ralph Ellison

Hell yeah, I play guitar! You know who taught me how to play? Charlie Patton! Charlie Patton was an Indian and he was the baddest motherfucker in the world.

—Howlin' Wolf

You know, time is the root of music.

—Ishmon Bracey

Contents

Introduction

After three years of looking, I found the guitar in a small vintage instrument shop on Hertle Avenue in Buffalo, New York—the city where it had been made over sixty years before. It was listed on the Internet and, after a call, I drove from Chicago to get it. Even for Buffalo, the day was unseasonably cold for early June, more like the western New York Octobers I remembered growing up: windy, with rows of crenulated clouds, slate gray and bruised purple in their deeper recesses, rolling east from Lake Erie.

If the past lingers anywhere it is in places like the old frame house on a worn commercial avenue—with a rectangular storefront probably added in the late forties—where Scott Freilich keeps his vintage instrument business. A sign in the window led me to a side door, where Freilich appeared; the visit was by appointment and I was his only customer. He led the way up two flights of creaking backstairs to the attic.

A fraction of daylight slanted through small windows in the eaves and an overhead bulb glowed enough to push the larger shadows under the eaves of a ceiling which sloped steeply along the roof line. At least a dozen old guitar cases lay handles up, like luggage in a forgotten lost and found, with a few others in stacks of two or three. Freilich, a husky man in his late fifties, in jeans and plaid shirt, sorted among several, looking at their tags, and drew out a battered black case with corroded brass locks and a handle made from several loops of strong white cord. A light smell of mildew drifted into the air.

The guitar, Freilich explained, was part of a consignment from the estate of a local collector—sadly, a personal friend—

who'd recently died. He raised up a big, warm-toned sunburst archtop, with an elegantly inlayed mother-of-pearl headstock and an elaborate, elongated hourglass figure under the manufacturer's name, GUGINO, rendered in bold pearl letters with a flourished underline.

Its neck, back, and sides were densely grained maple, which had an onyx glow; the spruce top, balanced with two f-shaped sound holes, bulged slightly, a straw-toned center—the so-called sunburst—merging to brown edges. Its neck, fashioned from three lengths of wood fit seamlessly together, felt solid as an ax handle. The cream-colored plastoid binding sealing the fret board to the neck had shrunk slightly over decades, raising slight bumps at each metal fret and giving it, as I ran my left hand down its length, the feeling of vertebra.

Its strings were shiny, but dead, old without ever being played. They were heavy, too, thicker than what my fingertips were used to, and didn't sound like much when I plucked them. Freilich handed me a hard pick. When it hit the strings, the guitar sounded like it had been switched on.

The truth of the matter is that I had no real business wanting such an elegant, vintage instrument. By then I'd been playing guitar only about four years, and owned two very nice flat-top guitars, a jumbo Gibson and a dreadnought Guild, both of which rang like bells and were rather better than my skills justified. No, I wanted the Gugino since the night I found out, over dinner with my late father's older brother, that it had been made by their maternal uncle, my great-uncle, Carmelo Gugino—who died a decade before I was born—who once built stringed instruments, mainly mandolins and guitars, in his very active factory/workshop.

This was news to me, delivered only after I'd mentioned to my uncle that I was learning how to play guitar. It turned out that music ran a bit in the family.

I knew little of Uncle Carmelo; Dad occasionally mentioned him with something like an embarrassed pride. "He swore he'd make a million dollars, and he did!" he told me once. "And he spent every dime." Carmelo was seventeen years older than my grandmother, so as to be of nearly a different generation, and I came to fill in his outline—who he was and how he came to manufacture high-end guitars—by looking in old newspaper files and talking to distant cousins, several in their nineties.

The guitar in Freilich's shop dated from 1945, the year before Carmelo died, at seventy-seven. With one significant difference, it was a twin to the Gibson model L5, one of the most advanced and desirable acoustic guitars ever made. The L5 was the largest and, for its size, lightest model available in its time, broader and thinner than the standard flat-top—designed before there were amplifiers to be loud enough to play in dance bands. From the 1930s through the '50s, luthiers like Carmelo, and the New York City master John D'Angelico, produced archtops exquisitely refined from the Gibson model.

Born in 1868 into a stubbornly feudal Sicilian society, Carmelo came to America at twenty with his younger brother Natale. He thrived in several businesses—construction, real estate, banking—before losing nearly everything in the Crash of 1929 and the Great Depression that followed. It was then, at sixty-five, that Carmelo started his guitar company, driven by a vision (he patented a unique design in 1935) and probably something like love.

Though Carmelo might have seen it differently, I think he invested everything he felt about America in his guitars. The archtop was the most modern stringed instrument imaginable at the time, embraced by jazz musicians and recording artists. It was beautiful, loud, and it did not look back.

Sturdy as they may feel, acoustic guitars are essentially fragile things: thin shells of stressed wood held together by snug joints and a little glue, braced only enough to endure the colossal implosive tug of their strings, to vibrate harmonically under the implicit promise of coming apart. Eventually they do. Guitars tend to have a human lifespan. Though they gain riches with age, very few survive to reach ninety.

Which is why, I think, they tend to capture our imaginations more than, say, trumpets and clarinets, why they are better companions than pianos. A certain sympathetic magic exists in even the cheapest guitar. A lot of diverse ideas and fugitive emotions can rest in their long necks and hourglass shapes.

Carmelo, apparently with the help of a couple assistants, turned out an estimated three hundred archtops in a little over ten years, along with an unknown number of flat-back mandolins—another Gibson company innovation—and ornate mandocellos, as well as a steady stream of stringed experiments. Freilich, after I mentioned the family connection, said he'd seen a lot of Carmelo's work over the years. "He tried a lot of different designs," he said, not all successful. "Some of them sound like they were made out of cardboard."

My archtop was not one. Back in Chicago, with a new set of strings, the sixty-year-old Gugino sounded as loud as a train, twangy, and bluesy as hell.

In searching out Uncle Carmelo's life and work, wider aspects quickly intruded: questions regarding Buffalo and western New York. If Sicilians were part of the third wave of immigrants there, what about the first two, and, then, the original inhabitants whom those people displaced? Soon enough I had to account for the transits of these associated cultures—what was lost, what was passed along in the process—nothing less than the forming of America: broadly speaking, those matters having to do with the guitar and the New World.

This was because it became pretty clear early on that though the modern acoustic guitar had its roots, like Uncle Carmelo— like me—in an ancient Mediterranean culture, it was as much an American invention as jazz or the ice cream cone. The small, flat-backed, hollow-shelled four-paired stringed instrument carried on the first Atlantic voyages by Spanish and Italian sailors—a polite, courtly thing meant to be plucked for love ballads—was shortly thereafter transmogrified into something big and loud, with five single strings, meant to be thrashed in rhythms to accompany the violent new dances which also came back with the ships from the New World.

Gradually the outlines of a kind of fugitive history presented itself, something outside the lines of a standard account, one in which songs and family memories could weigh as much as old newspaper stories and the conflicting reports of books. Something unique appeared among Americans some time ago; it has not gone away, and might still be found, I submit, anywhere you care to search. The following relates what I eventually discovered, in Buffalo and elsewhere, among my folk and many others.

Mascalzoni

In early spring of 2003, after years of indecision, I bought my first guitar. I was living in Minneapolis, somewhat adrift after a failed marriage. Many nights, after work at a small theater, I'd walk past a vintage guitar shop on Lyndale Avenue, its window displaying a row of old National steels. It was there, on a bright and snowy day, I got a classical six-string secondhand, following the advice of a musician friend.

The classical style guitar, for those unfamiliar, uses mainly nylon strings on a fingerboard wider than the one standard on American-style flat-top guitars, which have metal strings. These make the American guitar louder and brighter-sounding than the classical model, and also much harder for a novice to play. Nylon strings are easier on the fingertips, and a wide fingerboard, however much a challenge, leaves some extra room for the ignorant hand to form chords.

There were a lot of reasons why, after forty-five years, I decided to get my own guitar, just as there were a lot of reasons why I was still living in Minneapolis, after moving from New York for a marriage that, even by modern standards, ended quickly. One reason was that my mother died not long after my divorce, leaving me pretty tired of enormous change. Furthermore, she had left me an amount of money, my share of my late father's estate, considerable enough so that I would not have to work to support myself in a low-overhead locale, which Minneapolis—Bohemian, remote, and cold—very much was.

A lot of my friends in town were guitar players and getting free lessons wasn't hard. The city was a wellspring of live music.

My local bar was, in the words of one regular, a Minneapolis musicians' graveyard: Jayhawks, Son Volts, Soul Asylums, mainly polite, quiet drinkers who kept to themselves. Then there's the sad fact that my ex left me for a guitar player—and I know what you're thinking. Still, I'm not sure that had much to do with my decision to learn how to play. I had wanted to for a long time.

Getting the guitar was something of a turning point and in fact reflected deeper changes. Within three months I'd left Minneapolis for Chicago, where my life quieted down considerably. I mainly stayed home, read a lot, and practiced guitar. I began taking classes at the Old Town School of Folk Music, and met a lot of musicians. My net worth declined steadily, but at a rate that would still last for years, and I modulated my unease over this with the satisfaction of knowing how furious it would have made my father had he'd known how I reckoned my portion of *his* father's not insubstantial fortune. I had reasoned that, by diving again into the life of a big city, I would somehow gain a purpose, find work. What happened was the writing of this book.

Work and family duty largely formed the world in which I was born. As a consequence, I was at a loss talking to most of my relatives after I quit regular employment. Though I didn't need to justify myself to my late parents or to my two sisters, there were always moments during dutiful, nostalgic trips to Rochester to visit relatives when I felt something akin to a familial exasperation with myself as I attempted to account for my apparently aimless days.

One evening I had dinner with my father's older brother Nino and his wife, Gloria, at their club, an old-money bastion downtown which once existed precisely as a social barrier to wealthy self-made men like my immigrant grandfather, Alfonso. But times, of course, change. Now Nino and Gloria, handsome and gregarious in their eighties, were themselves a bastion of a certain American postwar order, one where adults were expected to dress up when they went out at night, and were expected to go out a lot. They were regulars at the club, a place my father never belonged to nor had any use for.

Over an excellent dinner in a quiet dining room which indicated nothing so much as how far we'd come from rural Sicily in a hundred years, I decided to admit the truth of my days and frankly admitted I really wasn't doing much outside of learning how to play the guitar, something I very much enjoyed.

Nino was more enthused than I expected. "Oh," he said, "There's a family connection."

A connection? I asked.

"Our Uncle Carmelo in Buffalo made guitars and mandolins. They're collectors' items now."

I was speechless. Carmelo was little more than a name, one of my grandmother's older brothers, a man who died long ago. No one ever bothered mentioning I'd been born into a musical family, and I had a good idea why. Carmelo and Natale Gugino, my grandmother's charming older brothers, were "gay blades," as Dad once called them (employing the older sense of the word). "It was wine, women, and song with those guys." Over dinner, Nino recalled them more succinctly.

"They were *mascalzoni*," he said fondly.

Mascalzoni? I asked.

Aunt Gloria translated.

"Rascals!" she said.

I gradually pieced together a portrait of Carmelo's life and times from stories his grandchildren, the youngest nearly seventy, told me and from old Buffalo newspaper articles. One of the earliest was an 1891 feature in the Buffalo *Express,* noting some ten thousand Italians settled in the city. While it judges those who arrived first to be mainly respectable citizens, the Sicilians, "members of the lowest classes," now arriving in droves, were clearly cause for concern.

The story notes the new arrivals' endemic laziness, and skill as "natural scavengers":

> Just as you inevitably presume that a negro is a waiter or a Chinamen [sic] is the proprietor of a laundry,

so, unless you have knowledge to the contrary, you unhesitatingly size up an Italian for a rag picker, cigar stump collector, or a gatherer of junk.

The article avers that the favored pastimes of Sicilian men are louse racing and stiletto throwing, and finishes by observing their "un-American habit of herding together" in their ghetto. On summer evenings along Mechanic Street, a thoroughfare of houses and factories near the lake docks, the article noted a Sicilian fondness for "mooning and guitar music and serenades."

Carmelo had come to Buffalo with his brother in 1888 from Valledolmo, Sicily, a fairly large but very rural town, and, I discovered, became as prominent there as any Italian of his time; nothing I found out about Dad's uncles sounded especially rascally, either on paper or in the admiring recollections of their grandchildren. In fact, once established as a construction contractor, Carmelo appears in newspaper accounts as a genuine role model. He founded one of the first macaroni companies in the country, opened a bank for Italian immigrants, and owned a farm; in short, a widely respected, successful businessman when Alfonso Gioia—my future self-made grandfather, twelve years his junior—was still selling fruit from a cart.

Valledolmo sits on a hill some forty miles southeast of Palermo, above wheat fields and the flaming silhouettes of cypress trees. A ruined train station in the valley four miles from town is still a stop on the Palermo line, and was once the departure point of a voyage that took three of my grandparents, and hundreds of their neighbors, to the western reaches of New York State.

By Sicilian standards, Valledolmo is itself very new, built in the early seventeenth century by a Genoese count on part of his estate, near ruins of a Norman castle, itself the site of a Saracen fort. The Duke of Palma put up a church and a palace and named the surrounding town for the old elm (*olmo*) tree at its heart and the valley below. Valledolmo grew as a market center for semolina wheat, which is the main ingredient of dried macaroni, and for the fabrication of furniture.

In October 1885, some forty-five men from the town, a few with wives and children, arrived in Buffalo following an expedition of five Valledolmese who arrived there by freight train two years before. One of the five, Frank Barone, opened a bar in the city, while the others headed to Fredonia, a farm town in the vineyard belt fifty miles south—famous, if that is the right word, for having been the first municipality in the nation to have its streets lit by gas.

The size of the Valledolmo diaspora in the following twenty years is breathtaking. Dr. Charles Borzilleri, the son of another freight-car arrival, told a reporter in 1903 that of the Sicilian town's population of twelve thousand, three-quarters now lived in Buffalo. (Italian census numbers instead show a 40 percent population loss in Valledolmo between 1881 and 1900—which is impressive nevertheless and a number that probably accounts for almost all men between eighteen and fifty.)

"It is almost like the removal of a city from Italy to Buffalo," Borzilleri said.

Most of those in the second wave were friends or relatives of Barone, among them one Antonio Gugino, possibly a relative of Carmelo and Natale (the name means *cousin* and is common to the district). The new settlers inhabited a neighborhood of run-down mansions between the old canal port and the train yard, a slum filled with shanties assembled in the former gardens of the departed rich, by then mainly populated by the Irish.

While the official family story of Carmelo and Natale's voyage to America has them fleeing military conscription (Carmelo was twenty and Natale two years younger), they may have been escaping their father, an olive-oil dealer who considered music a frivolous pursuit. The story goes that the two boys, mandolin and guitar players, had to practice their instruments at their grandmother's house. Musicianship aside, the brothers became apprentice woodworkers.

So Carmelo and Natale may have fled the military, or their father, or here perhaps a shadow passes over their tale. Around this time, their youngest brother Francesco drowned, the family story goes, trying to cross a flooded river on horseback; his body was never found.

Now, no one familiar with Sicily's long and frightful history can hear that story and accept it at face value. Kidnapping children for ransom was a widespread Mafia practice, as was murdering anyone, including children, who might testify about a crime. So many have vanished without trace or for any particular reason in Sicily for so long that a folklore of loss, a legacy of deep silences, has stained—if only slightly—the spirit of everyone related to that beautiful and awful place. Nothing is as it seems there, and few witnesses are reliable. Indeed, Sicily has no history, only stories.

So let us consider why the two surviving sons of a Sicilian olive-oil dealer might want to leave for a distant land, and immediately celebrate their freedom. Apparently, Carmelo and Natale spent their travel money while still in Naples (one suspects on wine, women, and song) before their boat departed, arriving in New York destitute. An aunt in Buffalo wired them train fare.

In America, Sicilians tended to settle around fellow-townsmen. In New York City, whole villages moved to single streets. The Valledolmese populated Buffalo and Fredonia, where Oratzio Gioia, a farmer and my great-grandfather, arrived with his family around 1890.

In Buffalo, the Gugino brothers were probably delighted to discover that the nation's eighth-largest city had a vibrant and abiding musical culture, with opera, classical orchestras, marching bands, mandolin ensembles, and ragtime piano players performing in dozens, if not hundreds, of venues—theaters, restaurants, bars, clubs, and recital halls.

Harold Arlen, arguably America's greatest songwriter, was born there in 1905, and started performing locally at age fifteen. Fifty years earlier, Buffalo had been home of George Christy's first blackface minstrel troupe, whose wildly popular revues introduced the songs of Stephen Foster. The musician Henry Worrall, who emigrated from Liverpool with his parents in 1835, lived in Buffalo for nearly twenty years before publishing his bestselling, and highly influential, guitar songbook, *The Eclectic Guitar Instructor*, in Cincinnati. (Worrall's composition "The Siege of Sebastapol" would find its way, its name changed to "Vestapol," into the repertory of the first blues guitarists.)

Italian musicians were quick to find work in local ensembles, both pop and classical. A residential block near Mechanic St., that locus of Italian life mentioned in the 1891 *Express* story, was home to so many musicians, one resident recalled a half-century later, that when one started practicing, others in earshot would join in.

Buffalo's great 1901 Pan American Exposition gave several Italian musicians a chance to perform for mainstream Americans at the Venice in America concession. A guidebook to the fair offers a more positive view of what had been condemned a decade earlier as "mooning and guitar music and serenades":

> Not even the clearest, softest note from the silvery throat of the most celebrated contralto can equal the lustrous diapason of delicious melody that floats . . . free and languorous from the lips of those Venetian boatmen and laughing soubrettes . . . [B]oatloads of people [glide] through the luminous water to tinkling guitars and clattering castanets [while] buxom girls in blue dance [a] blithsome tarantella.

A photo of the "Venice" string band shows young men in white pants and shirts, dark sashes around their waists, and white broad-brimmed hats holding guitars and mandolins. Two stand in rather more medieval costume; two others wear band uniforms with big plumes in their hats, blowing trumpets. Most are smiling, though a couple regard the camera with a smoldering romantic intensity. Their names include at least two Valledolmo families: a La Duca—the maiden name of Carmelo's mother—and another Gugino.

Shortly thereafter, the suspicion and ill-will that newspapers directed at "the wily sons of the land of Macaroni" (this from September 1901) went away. A January 4, 1903, *News* feature story noted the local Italian population had grown by some seven percent the previous year, totaling in excess of twenty thousand, and deemed it a community well-suited to social progress, industry and agriculture:

> Italians are forming a large colony in Fredonia and Dunkirk and other sections of the neighboring grape belt. Many of those in Fredonia already own their homes and small farms . . . [Buffalo has] three maccaroni [*sic*] factories, several importers, three physicians, two druggists, two lawyers, two bands of music—In fact Italians are pretty nearly in every business.

One of the macaroni factories was Carmelo's. According to Natale's daughter Frances, the two brothers returned to Valledolmo in the summer of 1901 to tell their parents, then in their early fifties, that unless they moved to America with them, they would never see each other again. It was persuasive. The brothers, their parents, and their sisters, Providenza (thirteen) and my grandmother, Antonetta (fifteen), returned that autumn. The ship manifest on file at Ellis Island shows the Guginos traveling with Valledolmo neighbors, Lo Ducas and Barones, also bound for Buffalo. The manifest also shows that Carmelo, Natale, and their father carried some $3,200 between them, a *very* tidy sum at the time. Carmelo was also bringing back macaroni machines he bought in Termini, south of Naples.

In retrospect, Carmelo's ambitions and accomplishments seem part of a more gallant place—in some ways more serious, in others more devil-may-care—than what America was becoming. He called his new business the People's Macaroni Co. (Natale stayed in the building trade) and, following World War I, sent two ships filled with food to Sicily for hunger relief. Italy's King

Umberto II knighted him for the gesture, granting Carmelo the title *Cavalere*, a rare honor for an Italo-American.

None of Carmelo's obituaries noted his guitar business, though one mentioned that he was "a lover of music," and said that, "during a visit here by the late Enrico Caruso, Mr. Gugino accompanied the famous singer on a tour of the Niagara Frontier." One cannot imagine a higher status for an immigrant Italian of that place and time.

By 1923, a three-part series in the *Buffalo Courier* noted that the local Italian population had reached nearly fifty thousand, some 10 percent of the city's total. The series retold the story of the immigrant settlement and singled out many men for praise, including the successful construction contractor and macaroni manufacturer, Chevalier Carmelo Gugino, knighted the previous winter by the king of Italy for "raising large sums of money for the Red Cross and Italian relief."

In September 1927, the *Buffalo Times* ran another long feature on the Italian community. Again Carmelo figured prominently. He had by then been the sole Italo-American appointed to the board of the Peace Bridge Authority, a binational agency that constructed the first bridge for motor traffic between Canada and the United States, which had opened to great fanfare in June of that year. The story recalled his knighthood and declared his macaroni company was "one of the largest in America." What's more, it related confidently, "Gugino's wealth is estimated all the way from one half to one million dollars."

And here you should know that seeing that bit of news in the public press would have made any sensible Sicilian's blood run cold. Even I, reading it off microfilm at the Buffalo public library eighty years later, gasped out loud.

For, as any will explain, it is *no one's* business—*especially* tens of thousands of strangers—how much money you have in the bank. Such a thing not only attracts the envy and calculation of others—far worse, it is an insane invitation to the baleful attentions of Fate, whose slightest stirrings Sicilians feel in their marrow.

And Fate accepted the invitation which that poor knight of Italy had so heedlessly extended.

Two months after the story appeared, fire swept the People's Macaroni plant. Three months after that, Carmelo's wife Francesca, who had been ill with a heart condition for some time, died unexpectedly of a stroke.

"The building and equipment were underinsured," writes Carmelo's youngest son, Carmelo Jr., in some brief biographical notes for his grandchildren. "This fact and the severe 1929 Depression contributed to the ultimate demise of the company." Young Carmelo also noted that, "In the prosperous 1920s my father invested heavily in the stock market." The Great Crash "created severe financial problems."

What the memoir neglects to mention was that Carmelo had been accused of arson by one De Santis—a Neapolitan, judging by his name—a blackmailer, whom my great uncle refused to pay. There was a trial; Carmelo was acquitted. He was on his farm when the fire started; and his modest insurance coverage probably mitigated the decision in his favor as well. De Santis was jailed for perjury.

The balance of Carmelo Jr.'s memoir is taken up with his mother, who died when he was twelve, and fond recollections of family parties, the food and music. "Bessie [his older sister] played the piano, papa and Uncle Natale played mandolins and guitars."

I asked my ninety-year-old cousin Frances, a piano teacher for forty years who eventually replaced cousin Bessie in the family rhythm section, what sort of musicians her father and uncle were. "They played by *ear*," was her dismissive reply.

After People's Macaroni went under, in 1933, Carmelo, at age sixty-five, turned part of the former macaroni plant, located on Mechanic Street, into a lutherie. He hired assistants and commenced the production of guitars, mandolins, and ornate mandocellos, which occupied him until death claimed that gallant knight in 1946.

It is noteworthy that Uncle Carmelo kept his name off of every professional endeavor of his life except the last. Each instrument from his factory had a florid *Gugino* set in mother of pearl at the head.

Beginning my research I called Carmelo's grandson, my second cousin Frank Gugino, at his home in a Buffalo suburb. I got the impression that, though proud of Carmelo's guitar works, his grandchildren considered it to be little more than the pastime of a retired businessman who had been a craftsman in his youth. Property income, it seems, had kept Carmelo afloat in his final decade.

A few weeks later, I drove to Buffalo to meet Frank, who was exceptionally gracious and generous with his time. He had two of Carmelo's instruments, both beautiful, high-end pieces clearly beyond the aims of a mere hobbyist. One was an ornately inlayed mandocello (a mandolin with a guitar-length neck that uses four pairs of strings). The other was an archtop that sounded fine regardless of its ancient strings, which Frank kept (he does not play) leaning against a wall in his living room.

He also had pictures of Carmelo, whose likeness I'd never seen before. The oldest of them, an oval-shaped portrait, showed a natty, bow-tied young man with sandy hair, a fierce look in his eyes, and a vulpine sweep to his mustache and beard—clearly someone at home in a world defined more by honor than mere commerce.

In a photo made ten years later, Carmelo sits on a dark bobtailed horse, his fierceness now swaddled in a respectable rotundity. It was some formal occasion, for he's in a long black coat, black top hat, with what looks like a sash on his sleeve. His face is slightly blurred (the lens was not sharp), so it is hard to tell if he still had his mustache, though his jaw and cheeks are clean-shaven. There might be a short cigar in the left corner of his mouth. By then People's Macaroni was a thriving concern.

Two other pictures from the era show the macaroni works, a four-story brick warehouse, with the employees assembled on a long loading dock, the company name painted across the building above the second-floor windows. The other picture shows the interior: a line of men in work clothes next to two vats, presumably where the pasta dough was mixed. With them is a smiling mustached man in a three-piece suit, very likely Carmelo, though the negative has been so poorly exposed that his face is almost completely obscured.

Two studio portraits (in a 1920s style) show a prosperous businessman. By then Carmelo was director of a small bank he had started, and had a truck farm near Lockport. Beardless now, in a sober suit and a dark tie, he wears the rimless spectacles that were then the epitome of municipal respectability. One looks in vain for any sign of the fierce young man.

In only one photo is Carmelo unposed. He stands with several others on a raised platform, unaware of the camera, seen above several heads in a crowd. He and the other men have their jackets and ties off, their collars open. It might be a political picnic (he once ran for selectman). Carmelo grips a heavy microphone stand, perhaps addressing the crowd. His mouth is open.

And here something in the tilt of his head and the seriousness of his expression indicate an attention to the matter at hand which looked very familiar. In fact, the resemblance is uncanny. That photo of Carmelo could pass as a likeness of my father.

Taking dad's envious appraisal at face value, Carmelo and Natale seem less libertines than unashamed remnants of an Italian culture distinctly at odds with the prevailing moral and professional requirements abroad in early twentieth-century America. Alfonso Gioia, my grandfather, understood these requirements keenly, however, and passed them, with no kidding around, to his sons. It is easy to see why those boys idolized their two uncles, perhaps the only men they knew who took pleasure as seriously as work.

The archtop is the last iteration of the acoustic guitar in America, created about 1901 by the visionary luthier Orville Gibson, a shoe-store clerk and amateur musician, who created hand-carved arched tops meant to mimic the sound dynamics of violins. Gibson had earlier produced a line of unique, flat-backed mandolins in his Kalamazoo, Michigan, workshop, which sold so well that, in 1902, several local businessmen backed a company in Gibson's name.

A national mandolin craze had been in full swing for over a decade by then. Most towns had mandolin clubs, which gave recitals, the musicians often dressing in elaborate oriental costume. (A photo exists of young Orville with one of his mandolins, looking a bit like Aladdin.) There is some question as to Gibson's mental stability at the time (he died in an asylum in 1918). He was a very minor shareholder in the company that bore his name and left it after only a few months, mainly over fights about his new guitar.

Gibson's innovation was to make his mandolins like violins and his guitars like his mandolins, with tops hand-carved to thin concavities from single pieces of spruce. His beautiful 1902 Style O archtops, though fancifully designed, mainly resembled standard guitars, with an oval sound hole centered under the strings and a glued-on bridge. Their construction, which Gibson refused to compromise, was too exacting to produce economically. Gibson did not have a prayer of competing with the huge Chicago instrument companies.

In 1924, the Gibson Company produced the first L5 model archtop (the L stood for its designer, Lloyd Loar), one of the most expensive guitars then made. Loar defined the broad and shallow lower bout, and designed a machine-milled top with a pair of f-shaped holes balanced under the strings that, as on a violin, vent sound in all directions. Loar anchored the strings to a hinged metal tail piece fixed to the lower bout, which holds them in great tension, passing their vibrations mainly through the bridge onto the convex top. The L5 was embraced by such diverse performers as jazz innovator Eddie Lang and the groundbreaking country player Maybelle Carter, who played her L5 for nearly fifty years.

While changing the strings on my Gugino, I saw a small label through one of the f-holes, brown with age, pasted inside the body. It was a patent notice and certificate of workmanship. Inked in a tidy hand that must have been Carmelo's own, were the guitar's number, 183, and model type, GC 2. Printed underneath was:

GUARANTEE

This instrument is guaranteed to be absolutely perfect in workmanship and material. Distortion of neck or body absolutely impossible.

Should it, with proper care and usage develop any imperfections, the manufacturer agrees to repair same at the factory free of charge or replace it with another instrument of the same style or value.

Cav. Carmelo Gugino
Manufacturer of musical instruments
Buffalo, New York U.S.A.

A quick online search revealed a copy of patent number 2113446, filed in 1935 and granted two years later, for a stringed musical instrument "of the guitar or mandolin type in which the construction is composed of a sound box, a neck and strings under relatively great tension connecting the extremities of the neck and the sound box."

What follows are two-and-a-half pages, in two justified columns, of careful prose outlining first the problems inherent in guitar design, followed by Carmelo's solutions to them.

It is hard to say how much of the elegantly worded patent declaration, which tends towards run-on sentences, was Carmelo's own way of expressing himself. But he was clearly an educated man who'd thought long and hard about the innate vagaries of guitar design.

"With instruments such as guitars or mandolins," the second paragraph begins,

> where a relatively large number of strings are under a comparatively high tension, the tension of the strings tends to bend the neck upwardly and to distort the sound box. As this occurs the strings gradually move away from the fingerboard and render the instrument more and more difficult to play since the performer is required to use a great deal more finger pressure in fingering the strings and also is required to move them a greater distance to engage the frets of the fingerboard.

There is, to my ear anyway, a distinct measure of a player's aggravation in the above, while "more and more difficult" and "required to move them a greater distance" indicate something more than an academic understanding of the problem. The vexations continue:

> The tonal qualities of the instrument are also adversely affected by the distortion of the instrument and with the abnormally high strings, of course, it is impossible to finger the instrument correctly.

(Oh, the exasperation behind that "impossible"!)

> In addition to this, the accuracy of each individual note played upon the strings is impaired due to the fact that each string is put under excessive tension and its pitch thereby considerably changed when the

player moves said string laterally an inordinate distance into contact with the desired fret.

Carmelo goes on to note that other manufacturers attempted to remedy this by strengthening the neck and by making it adjustable. However, "none of these means have been wholly satisfactory and, moreover, such means have greatly increased the cost of the instruments."

In exacting prose and three pages of precise diagrams the rest of the patent outlines Carmelo's ideas on how to construct a stronger, less expensive guitar. His two main ideas were for a neck attached to a rectangular metal frame, into which the sound box was inserted sideways and fixed. The other main idea, and the one on which my GC 2 was based, was for the neck to extend the length of the guitar. In both cases, "The strings are connected at their opposite ends to a single member which extends the full length of the neck and sound box."

His archtops differed from others in three distinct ways. The neck fits into the soundbox through a square channel, not a dovetail joint. A maple louver, two inches broad and a half-inch deep, then extends from the bottom of the fingerboard through the length of the guitar. The steel carriage holding the strings is attached to the lower end, stretching them end-to-end as if on a bow. The Gugino design keeps all tugging of the strings off the archtop body and prevents any bending of the neck away from it. The compressed force of the strings pushes down only on the bridge.

The pick guard, a stout plastic wing meant to protect the top from the downstroke assaults of picks and fingernails, is held by two steel slats, resembling popsicle sticks, that fit into the fingerboard extension. Standard archtops attach pick guards with a brace at the neck and another—placed rather indelicately—into the side.

The main problem with Carmelo's design, as Freilich pointed out in an article he wrote for a collectors' magazine, was that by "eliminat[ing] all of the compression on the instrument's body . . . it also eliminated most of the sound." (Had Carmelo been an electrician, and thought to add pickups to the strings, he might have done away with the soundbox completely and invented the solid body electric guitar years before Les Paul.)

The metal frame design seems to have been discarded fairly early. But the body-length neck was better suited to archtops anyway, designed by Loar so the strings anchored into the hinged tail piece screwed to the bottom of the instrument instead of a bridge glued to its top.

All immigrants work to bring their selves and their new country into some kind of concord. By making a guitar that would not warp, it strikes me that Carmelo was addressing, however obliquely, certain inherent flaws, the constant stresses that characterized his life in the United States. Perhaps after his other businesses failed, he began making guitars less for solace than to offer a solution to the times, something practical to his life and symbolic to America. To improve the guitar is, in no small way, to improve the world.

Cousin Frank told me that shortly after Carmelo died, a big order for guitars came in from Chicago, but though there were a couple luthiers working there, the company closed. The building and workshop was locked for fifteen years. Around 1960, the old warehouse neighborhood around Mechanic St. was purchased by the state and leveled. The old streets vanished under parking lots and a hotel resembling a bunker. A large concrete fountain shoots seven jets of water out of a shallow pool on the proximate spot of Carmelo's factory.

Frank recalled little of his grandfather's shop, though remembered that a guitar maker from Rochester, he didn't know the name, came and bought the whole inventory—tools and instruments, finished and not—before the factory was torn down.

A search for Rochester luthiers revealed only one who had been in business that long. When I called, a very surprised Dave Stutzman told me that his father, who died long ago, indeed bought the contents of the Gugino shop, and that he still kept "a slew of wacky guitars" in various stages of construction. He sounded delighted to hear from someone interested in them.

Dave said that he once had his own brand of guitars, Acousteck, himself, making a couple thousand instruments before a health crisis in 1995 prompted him to simplify his life. Now, fully recovered, he mainly does repairs and builds a small number of instruments on his own. He gave the impression that Carmelo was one of his heroes.

"He had a lot of strange ideas: strange sound holes, oval and teardrop, and guitars with holes in the back and sides. I don't know if there was a standard model that came out of his shop."

I was able to fill in some biographical details for Dave, mostly about Carmelo's other businesses, and his early training as a woodworker in Sicily. Dave felt Carmelo must have had some familiarity in making instruments. "He had to have had some experience to carve those tops, especially at that time. I envision someone who was a good woodworker who wanted to experiment. He had a lot of ideas ahead of his time, and may not have been accepted as a result of it." Aside from owning the world's largest collection of Guginos, Dave said he's seen a few for repair. "They're certainly the equal of anything Gibson and Epiphone made," he told me. "They're really good." He promised to show me his collection next time I was in town.

Several Saturdays later, I drove out to Stutzman's Guitars, conspicuous in an old white farmhouse in the path of an expanding six-lane stretch of strip malls and car dealerships on Rochester's northwest side—his parents' former home, Dave said. He hews to the classic guitar-shop standard: two small showrooms—one for acoustics, the other for electrics—a counter, and a crammed workspace in the back. A back hall contains a pocket museum of nineteenth- and early twentieth-century fretted instruments.

A slim man in blue jeans, plaid shirt, and spectacles, Dave had the practical, mildly amused air of a person who's made a living doing something he loves, in his own name, for about forty years. He was shorthanded that day, he explained. Two clerks had recently left to start their own store, and Saturday morning was a busy time as clients, all men, came by to look at, trade and buy instruments, and pick up repairs.

In between attending to those customers his two remaining employees could not, Dave had a look at my Gugino and showed me one of his, a sunburst model made the same year and slightly more elaborate than mine, with two five-pointed stars added to the headstock design and a grander tail piece. If you removed all the strings, he explained, and took out a screw at the bottom of the neck slat, the whole neck would slide entirely out of the body. While the engineering daring behind this was clear, the practical application of it (interchangeable bodies? easier storage?) was not.

Dave remarked that my guitar's bluesy twang was not because of the patented neck design, but came from the particular top bracing Carmelo used to accommodate it. There were interesting similarities, he said, between the Gugino instruments and the more conventional archtops made by Epiphone at the time. Dave wondered if maybe an Epiphone luthier came to work for Carmelo.

While I trust Dave's instinct, I prefer to think of my great uncle working steadily at his own refinements. A constant experimenter, the Guginos got better as he went along.

Dave pointed to an oval-shaped, guitar-sized Gugino instrument resembling a short oar. "I don't even know what *that* is." It had no waist and the sound hole was carved into the side rather than the top. Lacking strings, there was no clue as to how it might sound.

"You see guitar designs now, where people think they're all innovative because they put the sound hole in the side," Dave said. "What's really the case is that there's nothing new."

Not unlike some families, the modern guitar is a collection of many cultures; no instrument has evolved more rapidly, and spread more widely, in the last five centuries. What was once considered the Spanish guitar evolved from Roman and North

African instruments, and was produced in Naples and Palermo just as in Seville. Taken on the first New World voyages, the Spanish guitar changed even faster.

What left Spain with four pairs of strings was soon simplified to four single ones. (A fifth string, a bass, was added on some models sometime in the sixteenth century.) The guitar thereafter was an instrument meant to be strummed vigorously to accompany dancers instead of plucked sweetly for singing. Wild new folk dances, called *chaconnes*, and *passacaglias* ('street walks,' in both Spanish and Italian), were introduced to Spain and Italy by soldiers and sailors returning from the Americas, all based on what they witnessed among the indigenous people and African slaves in South America and the Caribbean.

The new dances applied heavy bass rhythms to lewd—for Christians, anyway—body movements and rude lyrics, the first American dance craze to sweep the world. For the next three hundred years, the guitar was mainly scorned by polite society and professional musicians for its vulgar appeal. It was, in fact, a sure sign of low company. But the new music was, of course, a popular hit from the start.

> Italian books [of the era] offer a number of dances only, simply presented as a progression of chords to be played in a rasqueado [strumming] technique, the right hand varying the up and down strokes according to the directions given . . . [These] Italian publications of strummed dances reveal more than anything else the true nature of the sixteenth-century life of the guitar.

In the 1630s one indignant French lute player described the go-go action that had spread to Paris. Spaniards, he said, "know how to play [the guitar] more madly than any other nation," and

> with a thousand gestures and body movements which are so grotesque and ridiculous that their playing is

bizarre and confused. Nevertheless even in France one finds courtesans and ladies who turn themselves into Spanish monkeys trying to imitate them . . . there are some in our nation who leave everything behind in order to take up and study the guitar.

Is this, the writer frets, because the guitar is so much easier to play than the lute? "Or is it," he asks, "because it has a certain something that is feminine and pleasing to women, flattering their hearts and making them inclined to voluptuousness?" The answer to both of the aggravated lutist's questions is, of course, yes.

Washington Irving's 1829 travel memoir, *The Alhambra*, gives an account of a folk dance at the old Moorish palace in Grenada. His description has a distinct hot-cha-cha air, and gives a good idea of what the guitar had been up to for three centuries:

> The guitar passed from hand to hand, but a jovial shoemaker was the Orpheus of the place . . . he touched the guitar with masterly skill, and sang little amorous ditties with an expressive leer at the women, with whom he was evidently a favorite. He afterwards danced a fandango with a buxom Andalusian damsel, to the great delight of the spectators.

Later in the book, Irving lays out the details of nightfall in the village next to the Alhambra's wall.

> Now break forth from court, and garden, and street and lane, the tinkling of innumerable guitars . . . blending at this lofty height in a faint and general concert.

Which sounds remarkably like a typical summer evening around Mechanic St. in Buffalo, circa 1901.

By Irving's time, as his witness shows, the guitar became a central object of the Romantic movement, and returned to America with the enormous German migration of the 1840s. German luthiers, most notably C. F. Martin, whose family company still makes premium guitars, began building them for the growing US market.

In the United States, by the late nineteenth century, a heavy sixth string, an earlier Italian innovation allowing even deeper bass notes, became standard on what already was a recognizable American-style guitar. It was bigger and stronger than the European model, meant to support the stresses of long-distance shipping by hazardous means across a rough landscape. The bigger guitars were naturally louder than the European type, and became even more so after 1900, when metal strings, an idea borrowed from mandolins, began to replace ones made from livestock intestines.

Metal guitar strings were promoted by the giant Chicago musical instrument companies, which were by then selling and shipping tens of thousands of guitars across the country every year, most of them for just a few dollars. By 1904, what we would recognize as a distinctly American guitar was fully formed and loud enough to play alongside fiddles and banjos in front of a crowd.

Though plucked-string instruments are probably older than agriculture, scant proof of a recognizable guitar exists much before 1300. Written accounts mention instruments without bothering to describe what they looked like or how they were tuned. During the Crusades, the milling of armies had the one happy consequence of exchanging stringed instruments between several kingdoms and two distinct cultures.

Varieties of string-and-soundbox instruments came to be called by similar Greek, Latin, and Arabic names. The Moors' *cithera*, or *cithern*, had a vaulted body, five pairs of strings, a long neck, and a large round hole in the center of the sound board. The name came from the Greek *kithera*, generally translated as *lyre*. From cithern came *gittern* (first applied to a small instrument resembling a mandolin, popular in Tudor England) and so *guitar* and *zither.*

This mainly straightforward etymology is complicated by the parallel presence of another recognizable guitar, with a flat back and hourglass shape, called a *vihuela* in Spain, in Italy a *vigola.* This instrument evolved from the Roman *fidicula,* brought to Iberia with the invasion in 206 BCE. Fidicula came from *fides,* Latin for a musical string. (Nero played a fidicula, not a fiddle, as Rome burned.)

Medieval Spain had three kinds of vihuelas, one played with a bow (which became the viola) and another with a quill pick. The third, *vihuela da mano,* had four Maltese-cross-shaped sound holes, one at each quadrant of its top. This one was, per its name, played with the fingers.

No one knows why the vihuela da mano came to be called the *guitarra latina,* or why the cithern became the *guitarra morisca,* the Moorish guitar, but after 1600, etymology merged with design. The round, centered sound hole of the guitarra morisca was combined with the flat back and hourglass shape of the latina, becoming simply the *guitarra* by the eighteenth century. (Something called a vihuela, an enormous, guitar-shaped bass instrument, is still found in Mexican Mariachi bands).

The music historian Harvey Turnbull called the rapid disappearance after 1500 of the vihuela da mano, which had been a refined, widely popular instrument, inexplicable. "Its splendid [published] music makes it difficult to understand why it disappeared in the latter part of the sixteenth century. The facile answer has been that it was replaced by the guitar, but this is no real replacement as the guitar inspired no comparable literature."

Though guitar makers are properly called luthiers, the lute, for centuries Europe's most popular stringed instrument, evolved separately from the *guitarra* family, descending from the *oud* (being the Arabic word for *wood*), which had a pear-shaped body and fretless neck, introduced to Europe by the Moors.

The standard lute had eight courses of strings and a head stock that angled at 45 degrees away from the neck. Tuning the correct pitch on sixteen strings made of dried sheep's intestine, and then keeping them in tune for more than two songs in the prevailing European damp was a maddening task. (One sixteenth-century observer declared lutists spent more time tuning than playing.)

The seventeenth-century English diarist Samuel Pepys, besides being chief secretary of the admiralty, was an avid amateur musician. He met frequently with friends for evenings of song, hired servants on the basis of their singing voices, paid for their music lessons, and played the viol and theorbo, an early bass. However, young Pepys's main joy was his lute, and he mentions playing it early in the morning and late at night. "So staid within," he remarks typically in December 1660, "all the afternoon and evening; at my lute, with great pleasure, and so to bed with great content."

But the lute was already a bit old hat. Perhaps some inkling of this occurred to Pepys when, having gone to Dover with the navy to welcome Charles II home from exile, he was tasked to bring the royal guitar back to London. A little over a year later, he heard a Frenchman, likely Charles's teacher, "play . . . the guitar, most extreme well, though at the best methinks it is but a bawble."

In 1840, Christian Frederick Martin left Germany for New York City to work for a stringed-instrument company run by several countrymen. He soon started his own guitar business there, moving it to the Moravian settlement of Nazareth, Pennsylvania, in 1860, where it has been run by Martin's descendants ever since.

Martin and his New York competitor, William Tilton, began improving the strength of their guitars to make them more durable for long-distance shipping and rough use across a vast rural nation. These structural changes to the guitars—sturdier bracing for the tops, smaller bridges, and heavier necks—also had the desirable consequence of increasing the strength of the instruments' vibrations, making them louder.

By the late nineteenth century there was a boom in facto-ry-made guitars, dwarfing the sales of the craft-made, high-end Martins. By 1900, there were some forty stringed-instrument manufacturers in Chicago, including the giants Lyon & Healy, Kay, Harmony, National, and Maurer, which yearly produced tens of thousands of cheap and sturdy guitars, sold by mail order and shipped nationwide.

The Maurer Company manufactured guitars under half a dozen brand names, like *Prairie State* and *Euphonon*, and is gen-erally considered to have produced in 1904 the first guitar made for steel strings, with a reinforced neck to "resist the problem of warping and twisting from the strain." The American guitar arrived with the American Century.

Flat-top guitars produce sound when the vibrations of a plucked string are transmitted to the sound box through a bridge that's been glued to the top under the sound hole. Because the strings pull at about two hundred pounds per square inch, the bridge tugs up on the lower bout and pushes down on the upper. Wooden struts are glued under the top for strength and to bet-ter transmit across the whole top the mainly lateral vibrations coming from the bridge. A good guitar will vibrate stem to stern, with even the neck adding strength to the sound.

Flat-top sound boards are generally made from two pieces of thin and pliant spruce, glued together edgewise. A hardwood, like maple, is used for the back and sides. Vibrations from the top are then amplified by bouncing off the dense back, exiting the sound hole.

Early plucked-string instruments, like the mandolin and lute, all used proportionally large vaulted sound boxes, resem-bling half moons, to amplify their sound. The volume of these instruments depends entirely on their size. The flat-backed gui-tar, with its relatively small inner chamber, relies on the efficient amplification of string vibration. A variety of subtle structural means enhance this effect and are at the core of the art of guitar making. The design and size of the bridge, the shape and place-ment of the inner braces of the top and back, and the construction of the neck all factor into the force of the sound. A good guitar is a difficult compromise between lightness and strength.

For the last eighty or so years, American style flat-top guitars have used tops milled about one-sixteenth of an inch thick. Even the best guitars are temporary arrangements. A good guitar should last a lifetime, but not two without some repair. As a guitar ages, as the wood dries, the varnish and glue cracks and its own vibrations force the body to loosen and recompose, it takes on characteristics of its own. "A good guitar," the luthier Ken Parker observed, "is in agreement with itself." If long neglected, however, a good guitar will finally pull itself apart.

The C. F. Martin Company was for most of its history a small-output factory, and no one paid much attention to the brand until Jimmie Rodgers, the Yodeling Brakeman, considered to be the father of country music, had one custom-made in the late twenties with his name inlayed along the length of the finger board. Thereafter Martins became prized by country players, beautiful, expensive instruments, the mark of no small achievement, whose bell-like tones set the standard for how flat-top guitars should look and sound.

Martin essentially completed the design of the contemporary American guitar around 1916 by lengthening the necks of its models from twelve to fourteen frets (to accommodate banjo players used to the longer fingerboards), and also by inserting an adjustable steel rod into the necks, allowing them to be narrower and stronger, and making the action—being the distance between the strings and the fingerboard—adjustable.

Martin's third chief innovation was their Dreadnought model, which the company debuted in 1916 to little notice. Reintroduced during the Depression, the Dreadnought (named for the largest existing battleships) became a professional's favorite. The biggest of flat-top guitars, it has a slightly arched back, a broader, deeper body and a flatter bottom-end, with a silhouette closer to a rectangle than an hourglass.

Up to that time, the banjo, which evolved from the African *banjar* in slave communities, had been the most popular American plucked instrument for over a century, and was integral to the first jazz bands—that is, until the advent of a young Italo-American musician from Philadelphia.

Born Salvatore Massaro, Eddie Lang was the son of a mandolin and guitar maker. Though he started playing jazz banjo, by the mid-1920s he had switched to the L5, bringing to jazz arrangements the arpeggios and counterpoint of his classical training. With his childhood friend Joe Venuti on fiddle, Lang changed the tempo of jazz along with the instrumentation of small ensembles. His blazing guitar solos and fills pretty much banished the banjo from jazz bands nearly overnight.

Lang and Venuti are the chief examples of a remarkable musical culture of second-generation Italians that, beginning around 1890, transformed American music.

Though mainly considered a historical fluke, the first band to cut a jazz record, for Victor in February 1917, was a mostly Italo-American outfit from New Orleans, the Original Dixieland Jass Band, led by one Nick LaRocca. The band is dismissed by historians for the relative shallowness of its material, and because it broke up in 1925 after LaRocca's nervous collapse. (LaRocca squandered what credibility he had in several dumb, racist interviews he gave late in life, claiming to have invented jazz.)

Though LaRocca's band is slightly known, hardly mentioned at all is that the first published twelve-bar-blues song, 1908's "I Got the Blues," was composed by one Antonio Maggio, beating W. C. Handy's "St. Louis Blues" by six years.

Maggio passed into history without the temerity to insist that he invented the blues. But, slight as they may be, these firsts cannot be wished away. The best explanation is that young Italian American musicians, unencumbered by the valences of US race relations, were the first white players to implicitly *hear* indigenous American music for what it was, not trash or coon tunes but unique and profound expressions of sorrow and joy. What's more, the music had no trace of Europe, and so exemplified the freedom their parents had come to the new land to find.

Young Massaro (he apparently took the name Eddie Lang from a popular basketball player) was protean in his work and elemental in his contributions. He played and recorded constantly in the ten years before his untimely death, with an assortment of white jazz bands, including those of Paul Whiteman, Bix Beider-becke, Red Nichols, Jean Goldkette, and Adrian Rollini. Using the name Blind Willie Dunn, Lang recorded with black artists too, playing on jazz and blues sides with Joe Oliver, Clarence Williams, Bessie Smith, and Victoria Spivey.

Today, Lang's best-known work is a series of guitar duets he made as Blind Willie with Lonnie Johnson, the best-selling blues artist of the era. In their work together, Lang played nimble rhythm figures behind Johnson's sometimes weepy blues lines, sophisticated recordings that speak more to urban complexities— Johnson was from New Orleans and lived in Chicago—than the stark, small-town tales which Delta blues players were cutting at the same time.

Decades later, Johnson, who made records into the 1960s, did not stint in his praise for Lang: "Eddie could lay down rhythm and bass parts just like a piano. He was the finest gui-tarist I had ever heard in 1928 and 1929. I think he could play anything he felt like."

The writer Richard Hadlock points out that Lang, by work-ing with black musicians, was central in incorporating larger blues forms into mainstream jazz, a movement led by south-ern players like Louis Armstrong and Jack Teagarden: "South-ern blues deliverances soon replaced the more ordered measures of Miff Mole and Bix Beiderbecke in the affections of East [Coast] musicians . . . For Eddie it was easy; he already knew it all."

Lang kicks off the Armstrong band's wonderful 1929 single "Knockin' a Jug," a highlight in the careers of all the musicians involved, and a high-water mark of American musical art. Thanks to his steady work with Bing Crosby, Lang was the highest-paid sideman in the country when he died of a hemorrhage following a routine tonsillectomy in 1934. (Crosby blamed himself, hav-ing told Lang to get his tonsils taken care of before they started movie work together, and supported the guitarist's widow for the rest of her life.)

It is highly likely that affluent, fun-loving Carmelo Gugino would have at least known of the Italian kid who played guitar in Whiteman's band and was in Crosby's movies. Lang's example, if not his memory, may well have inspired Carmelo in the first place.

The fretted fingerboard, often decorated with ornate inlay, evolved as a compromise between purity and necessity. During the Renaissance, natural philosophers finally had to admit what musicians had known for some time: pure musical intervals on fretted instruments did not extend very far past the limits of a single key. To play songs in different keys, or across more than two octaves, lutists and guitarists had to either move the frets, which were also made from gut and tied onto the neck, or use separate courses of strings. Guitars used for dance music needed as few as four frets, but the lute, which remained a singer's instrument, had various sets of frets and strings added over time.

Aristotle insisted that all musical tones existed in perfect intervals from one another, and were therefore purely determined by mathematics. But the inescapable fact was that this was not so—painfully evident when scales played on fretted instruments which divided strings in strict Aristotelean terms quickly lapsed into dissonance after about two octaves. The problem was that the same fret ratio which would, say, render perfect semitones for a G scale would not work for D.

There were several medieval ways of dividing the length of the fingerboard into sections to render perfect Pythagorean tones. One typical method called for the second, fourth, and sixth frets to be set down first, the second fret placed at one-ninth of the length below the nut, which is that bone saddle that separates the strings at the top of the neck. The fourth fret was then placed a ninth of the way below the second and the sixth fret the same proportional distance below that.

The third fret was to be placed one-third of the way down the neck, and the fifth fret at one-quarter. The first fret was put down last, reckoned above the third fret at one-eighth of the distance between the third fret and the bridge. Easy as π, right?

Layouts like this one were based on perfect sections of nines or sevens, and attempted not only to justify a musical system, but the world view behind it, one which insisted, against growing evidence, on a universe of exact proportions made by a perfect God. This image of divine, balanced order began coming undone in the mid-1500s when it was at last understood that, put simply, ascending scales did not link up evenly.

No one discovered why this was until the mid-eighteenth century, when the Swiss mathematician Daniel Bernoulli, whose main work was on fluid dynamics, realized "that the series of overtones resonating above a string's fundamental musical tone extends much farther than anyone suspected." Bernoulli found that pure tones were impossible not only because vibrations on any given string didn't diminish at a constant rate, but that they also varied with mass; that, even in the same key, heavy strings vibrated at a slower frequency than lighter ones. The upshot is that what we consider Harmony is in fact a temporary and situational arrangement. Instead of existing in perfect harmonic ratios, "all vibrating bodies naturally float in an ocean of discord."

Luckily, the problem had been solved for fretted instruments nearly two centuries earlier, by cheating. In 1581, Vincenzo Galilei, a renowned Italian lute player, and Galileo's father, proposed the system of equal temperament (some think his son came up with it), which—with slight tweaking—became the enabling factor of all western music since.

Galilei realized that, since most people don't have perfect pitch, the discordant gap that lies, for example, in the scale between low G and high C could be averaged away bit by bit. His system did exactly that by dividing the eight-step Do-Re-Mi octave into twelve equal intervals. The only perfect interval in Galilei's system was the whole octave, of which the modern standard-tuned guitar has four. This serial tempering, using slightly flat or sharp notes to replace pure intervals, allowed for the invention of a standard keyboard, and so the harpsichord and piano as well as our guitar.

With Galilei's discovery, luthiers were able to set twelve metal frets permanently onto the guitar neck, spaced in a diminishing ratio of one-eighteenths. (The first fret is placed one-eighteenth the distance between the nut and the bridge, the second at one eighteenth the remaining distance, and so on.)

The fret board therefore combines both musical and proportional meanings of the word *scale*, which comes from the Italian word for *stair*. For one of the occult features of the guitar is that the regular shortening of its frets towards a singular point never reached mimics exactly our visual perspective of the world. A guitar fretboard, in a pinch, can be used to measure distant objects.

If the notion of the guitar-as-ordering-measure strikes you as farfetched, consider that, in ancient Rome, the word *fides*, the string of a *fidicula*, also meant *trust, belief, faith, truth*, and *word of honor*. These ideals, which the ancient world prized above all, were literally laced into Apollo's instrument with its strings.

Our guitar then, in its very form, offers a small remedy for the world's chaos, an agreement with the universe, not perfect, but good enough. To consider the ancient Mediterranean world, which produced the *fidicula*, and the *guitarras latina* and *morisca*, is to be presented with a turmoil of centuries, endemic horrors to make our own era appear a place of refuge. Regarding the history of the last five hundred years, in the Old and New Worlds, we will find no less cruelty perhaps compared with ancient times, but something resembling a humane, distinctly freeing spirit gradually taking hold.

While it might sound absurd to credit the guitar for the dawning ideal that humans can in fact repudiate the monstrous and brutal portions of our nature, neither, I think, can the instrument's liberal abilities towards harmonization be casually dismissed. As such it is an avatar of our finest wishes and dreams.

There exists a magnificent grotesque guitar, made in Paris in 1693, now at the Musee de la Musique there, "uniquely

constructed from the entire carapace of a tortoise. Glazed ceram-
ic replicas of the creature's head, tail and feet [were] added to
complete the illusion . . . it was originally set up as a working
guitar with five pairs of strings." Whether its maker realized it
or not, the tortoise-shell guitar is connected to the mythologi-
cal origins of stringed instruments. "Apollo the god of archers,"
Frederic Grunfeld observes, "is also Apollo the god of Music."
Fritz Jahnel, in an archeological study of stringed instruments,
proposed that humans first amplified the twang of a bow-string
by setting the haft of the weapon into the leg holes of an empty
turtle shell.

In *The Greek Myths*, Robert Graves describes the very
thing, when young Hermes, needing to soothe an angry Apollo, stretches strings across the underside of a turtle shell and
"plays such a ravishing tune on it with the plectrum he had also
invented . . . that he was forgiven at once." Tellingly, Apollo just
had to have the instrument, and purchased it from the kid with
a herd of cattle.

Graves viewed the myth as reflective of an arriving Indo-
European civilization appropriating elements of the Creto-Hel-
lenic people around 1700 BCE. Yet even earlier instruments
existed, Grunfeld observes: the Assyrian *chetarah*, "the Hebrew
kinnura . . . the Chaldean *quitra*." The *guitar* logos stretches back
far as ears might hear.

The guitar's first quality, then, may be its ready adaptability,
an ability to please the imagination, the ear, and the eye, a feminine shape formed in the Middle Ages and brought to our day. It
is light, easy to carry and hold; it has a certain psychic buoyancy,
something that might bear a person across roiled waters of the
spirit and times—as the turtle, in several mythologies, carries the
world—a thing verging on grace, beyond words.

We have as evidence two photographs, taken in Oklahoma
in 1939 by Russell Lee, the great documentary photographer
for the Depression-era Farm Securities Administration. General
portraits of rural migration, in particular the photos are about
guitars.

In one, a boy of about thirteen lifts a small flat-top guitar from a nail in a corrugated cardboard wall. Lee noted that the boy's family is moving west, and he probably isn't taking much more than this one prized possession, a cheap, mail-order Maxwell, named perhaps for the street in Chicago (very likely where the instrument was made) that was at the time the focus of black commercial life in the city.

Crucially, the guitar is missing its bridge, and therefore all its strings. The boy is taking something beautiful—maybe the most beautiful thing he knows—but broken, which makes it a promise for later. The guitar can be fixed and he can play it again.

The other Lee photograph shows what looks like a picnic lunch by a migrant couple on their way west. The wife, a plain, glum-looking woman, perhaps in her late twenties, sits in the passenger seat of a rundown Model T, looking with no small amount of worry at a man, probably her husband, in a broad, peak-brimmed hat, sitting on a blanket. He is the main subject of the carefully-composed photo, by all appearances singing and playing a C chord on an inexpensive archtop guitar, again the finest looking thing in sight.

These two black-and-white photos, from the Library of Congress collection, give a good look at how the guitar moved for centuries across the new world. Beauty, portability, companionship, its body something that, Lee implies, one holds onto for dear life.

Those same tremendous forces that formed the guitar from three distinct civilizations formed as surely the Sicilians themselves. Sicily had been the westernmost Greek isle, deeply forested, with thriving cities and beautiful temples, noted for its olives and wine, poets and philosophers. Rome annexed it in the second century BCE Punic wars: "a grisly chronicle of mass executions, public torture, . . . rape, pillage and enslavement, with the Romans as the worst, but by no means the only, habitual offenders."

Roman Sicily was stripped of its forests and its inhabitants sent in slave gangs to the vast wheat fields which replaced the trees. It was, to Cato, "the nurse at whose breast the Roman people is fed." And for the next seven hundred years, Rome exploited Sicily "on a colossal scale."

The island remained Greek in language and habit, never fully integrated into the empire. "For the most part," observed John Julius Norwich, "Sicily bore her sufferings in silence." Absentee landlords, their huge estates managed by way of terror, would be the Sicilian paradigm for the next two thousand years.

Once the Roman Empire collapsed, Vandals ruled the island, as they did Spain, before leaving both to the Ostrogoths, whom the Sicilians, of course, deeply resented. In 535, the Byzantine emperor Justinian sent troops to "liberate" his fellow Greeks, and the Goths left without much of a fight.

Peace, maybe a kind of exhaustion, prevailed for nearly three hundred years. In 827, a deposed Byzantine governor who fancied himself king invited a Saracen invasion from North Africa to help further his royal ambitions. He was disposed of, almost as an afterthought, three years later, and the Arabs ruled the island from Panormus, the principal Roman city, which they renamed Palermo. Though it took them another fifty years to capture a couple stubborn coastal towns, for the next two centuries Sicily was a Muslim land.

The Saracens made substantial improvements to Palermo and the surrounding countryside, building beautiful houses and gardens, watered by new canals and irrigation systems, and introducing cotton, citrus, date, and sugar cane cultivation, as well as dried pasta. Along with the improved infrastructure, the Saracens were remarkably tolerant in religious matters. Latin and Greek culture continued and the island "soon became one of the major trading centers of the Mediterranean, with Christian, Muslim and Jewish merchants thronging the bazaars of Palermo."

The Arabs, resourceful as they were at cultivation and trade, were just as prone to the type of armed feuds that characterized their Greek rivals. In 1035, factions loyal to Palermo's emir and his rival brother took to fighting. The Byzantine emperor saw an opportunity. A mixed force of Greeks, Lombards, Salernitans, Bulgarians, and Normans, mainly an alliance of conniving warlords, drove out the Arabs three years later, and instituted another couple decades of civil war. The eventual winners of their cynical, violent, and shifting political alliances were the ones who had started out with the least to lose—the footloose Normans.

For decades, small Norman cadres had wandered down from northern France, hiring on as mercenaries for the constant Italian ducal spats. Daring fighters, gifted commanders, and exceptional rulers, the Normans consolidated forces in the Italian south and eventually came to be as powerful and calculating as their former employers. By 1061, invading from their armed towns on the peninsula, Sicily was theirs.

A relatively small group, the Normans had no interest in changing Sicilian mores and were as tolerant in matters of trade and worship as the Saracens—troops of whom they kept employed as brutal fixers for any trouble back on the mainland. The first Norman chief, Roger Hauteville, ruled from Palermo and, along with his lieutenants, swanned around the city in Arab kit, some of them, it was reputed, keeping harems. Sicilians to this day are conspicuously fond of the Normans, constantly retelling their tales of conquest in the stories of Orlando Furioso. This is probably because Norman rule was the best the island was to know for centuries to come.

For five hundred years, Saracen-Norman Sicily was a beacon of high culture and trade. Though history has given Spain bragging rights to the invention of the guitar, the Spaniards lacked the accommodating instincts of their future Italian serfs. During the late medieval period, when the Latin and Moorish guitars merged, it seems more likely to have taken place in Sicily, in those portions still culturally Moorish or radiantly Greek, than in ethnically cleansed Spain.

My family tree branches mainly trace this sad history. Names prefixed *Sci-* (which is pronounced *shhh),* like Scinta, my mother's maiden name, are from Arabic and uniquely Sicilian.

The Guginos were a Norman clan (which probably accounts for Uncle Nino's formerly sandy brown hair—the family hair turns snow white in old age) and blue eyes. Gojas came from Spain and settled in Sicily early in the Spanish misrule of that apparently cursed island, becoming Gioias along the way. Spanish monarchs, in one form or another, ruled the south for five hundred years, until Garibaldi finally dispatched the rotten Bourbons shortly before Uncle Carmelo was born.

Toward the end of my research for this book, I was staying at a beach house, high on a big dune in Truro, on Cape Cod, facing Massachusetts Bay. I was by then a compulsive reader of local histories, and found one on a shelf there. In it was an account of what is very likely the first guitar performance, for paying customers, in North America.

In 1603, Martin Pring, an English sea trader, dropped anchor at the mouth of the Pamet River, near what is now Truro, and sent his men ashore to harvest sassafras, then considered a cure for venereal disease. The local Wampanoags, already familiar with Europeans, received Pring's crew with some cheer, exchanging items and indulging in a masculine kidding—neither party understanding the language of the other—that felt a bit menacing.

Published in London in 1605, Pring's account indicates the English did not know quite what to make of the Wampanoags. The sailors built a small palisade on a hill near the shore.

One night the English held a party for the neighbors in their little fort. "We had," Pring wrote,

> a youth in our company that could play upon the git-
> tern, in whose homely music [the Indians] took great
> delight, and would give him many things, as tobac-
> co, tobacco pipes, snake skins six foot long, which
> they used for girdles, fawn skins, and such like, and
> danced twenty in a ring, and the gittern in the midst of
> them, using many savage gestures, singing *Io, Ia, Io,*
> *Ia, Ia Io.*

The nineteenth-century house where I read the above overlooked the very spot, that small hill next to the harbor. And as I considered this first encounter, one which seemed to hold such possibility for American and European alike, it only made the following four hundred years that much sadder to regard, and all the more necessary to account for in some way. (When the Pilgrims landed in 1621, they found the ruins of Pring's fort, but the Wampanoags there had already died off from their first exposure to European germs.)

The crowning coincidence of Pring's narrative came later, when, drifting to sleep that night in the sound of wind and waves, I realized that his transcription of the Indians' singing constituted the last four letters—*Io, Ia*—of my last name, a detail that, coming after three years of some strenuous research on my part, was of vivid interest only to me.

History lodges in our instruments, and in our bones, there whether we feel it or not, covered over as Time carries us away. Very little of what I've been able to record here was given to me without asking, and, of course, a great deal had already vanished forever. None of the people there at the time, who I knew growing up, bothered to tell me much of anything about their lives or the life they saw around them when they were young.

Part of that, certainly, is .that deep silence Sicilians have absorbed from the land around them. One says nothing because, ultimately, there isn't all that much to say. You look after your family, and the day, and hope for the best. Landing in America didn't change that. A big reason why I came to play the guitar was, I suspect, to compensate for my father's silences, the ones he was stuck with, which I eventually found in myself.

My grandmother, Carmelo's much-younger sister Antonetta, whom everyone called Nanetta, never spoke much of the past. She arrived in Buffalo in November 1901, when she was fifteen. Thirteen years later, when Alfonso Gioia, that rising young man, asked permission to marry her sister, Providenza, he was refused. Nanetta, the older daughter, had precedence. And so she and Alfonso were wed.

By the time I knew her, Nanetta was a lovely woman with snow-white hair and an abiding sense of humor, which severe arthritis could not dampen. Though an invalid for her last twenty-five years, she loved music and laughter and lived at home with her widowed daughter Josie. She died at one hundred, surviving her brothers and sister, husband, even her oldest son, by many years. When I'd visit, I'd tell her jokes and we'd listen to opera records. She loved Luciano Pavarotti, said he was as good as Caruso, whom she'd heard sing *Tosca* in New York on her honeymoon. Natale had a beautiful voice too, she said, and would sing "Una furtiva lagrima" to her.

She never spoke about Alfonso. I gather their marriage had not been easy. An elegant, large-format photographic portrait of him, in warm-toned black-and-white, stood in a silver frame on its own table in her living room. For years, it was the only picture of him I ever saw, and even today I know of only four others. In his round, frameless eyeglasses and dark three-piece suit, calmly regarding the camera, hands in his trouser pockets, I now see his resemblance to his older townsman, Carmelo Gugino. Indeed, the two might once have passed for brothers, and my father resembled both.

In her nineties, looking back on the path of her life, considering all the paths of her children and grandchildren, Nanetta one day gave me her final considered judgment of the distances we travel in time and the world. It was very Sicilian, and therefore brief.

"Fate. Destiny," she said in her Italian accent, which over eighty years in America never completely wore away.

"Everything is Destiny."

The Temple of Music

There had never been anything like the Electric Tower; topping four hundred feet, ivory white, and made of huge plates of ornate, weather-resistant plaster bolted to a wood-beam superstructure, it was the central landmark of Buffalo's 1901 Pan-American Exposition. By day it appeared to glow in the lake-humid air. At night, lit up, it could be seen for miles. As colossal as any new skyscraper going up in Chicago or New York City, the baroque Palladian steeple was a temporary advertisement for Progress, built to last about six months.

Though the tower seemed all business, none was conducted inside; its genius lay in the lines of insulated wires, light sockets, and incandescent bulbs that ran along its every outer edge and detail. Every evening that summer, as the light faded over Lake Erie and dark rose up from what had been farm land two years earlier and utter wilderness ninety years before, a man would throw a switch and the Electric Tower would pulse, then snap bright. It was said you could hear thousands gasp at that sight every night, a collective shout of surprise, or possibly fright, for the new century just underway.

The tower rose at the center of a square mile of exhibition pavilions lit at night by some 200,000 bulbs and 900 arc lights, with 94 underwater spotlights that gave the dozens of fountains, reflecting pools, and the sightseeing canal ringing the grounds a full-moon glow. At the tower's peak stood the Goddess of Light, an eighteen-foot tall statue astride a rotating spotlight that shot a broad ray in quick bursts through the damp air to every part of the grounds.

At its base was a huge fountain, a seventy-foot-tall rep-
lica of Niagara Falls (the real falls, twenty miles away, ran the
enormous generators powering the Exposition), which poured
11,000 gallons of water per minute past giant figures of Native
Americans and pioneers in a triumphalist allegory of progress
and domination.

Indeed the exhibition was thick with such symbolism; the
buildings themselves were designed to be vast symbols of racial
superiority, the thematic details of which, at this distance, have
all the marks of a fever dream. Structures at the outer ends of
the Exposition were painted bright colors meant to symbolize
not only the wildness of early human history, but the "primitive" red-, yellow-, olive-, and brown-skinned races. As fairgoers
walked towards the central esplanade, the buildings became
lighter toned, until one finally reached the ivory white Electric
Tower.

Bracketing the tower a short way down the Esplanade were
the paired ornamented domes of the Ethnology Building and the
Temple of Music. The ethnology hall was hung with paintings
depicting the races of mankind and contained cases displaying
tools, weapons, and ritual artifacts grouped geographically. The
pavilion was painted red at its base, gradually merging to blue
across its dome—prompting, according to one newspaper, "the
analogy between it and the ascent of man from savagery to civilization." Ethnology's nearly identical twin, the Temple of Music,
was intended to balance the study of the primitive with almost
hourly expressions of the highest European culture.

The Buffalo Exposition's planners set out deliberately to give
it an identity distinct from the 1893 Chicago fair. Where that
one had been the White City, Buffalo's promoters called theirs
the Rainbow City during the day, and the City of Light at night.
Where Chicago preached a message of classical Apollonian order
and endeavor, Buffalo was meant to celebrate the more recent
imperial Dionysian pleasures of amusement and ease. Even the
Buffalo Exposition's other official name, the Pan, conjured, inten-
tionally or not, the wild Greek demigod of frolic and disorder.

There was something deliberately freakish about the fair, as if it was celebrating something in the wrong way, or honoring something that should not be celebrated at all.

The Pan was at heart how white America viewed itself, broadly inclusive and unashamedly racist, attending to business and addicted to amusement, democratic in ideals and imperial in ambitions. Few at the time noticed the contradictions. Mark Twain, who had briefly lived in Buffalo decades before (and gave its public library his handwritten manuscript of *Adventures of Huckleberry Finn*), had marveled over the Chicago fair eight years earlier. Now, living in New York City, he kept his distance (he had been miserable in Buffalo) and an uncharacteristic silence.

Perhaps because this national schizophrenia was conjured on such a vast stage, the Pan, which began with such optimism, could only end in chaos. Once a symbolic space, crafted so deliberately on such an enormous scale, is opened, there's no telling what will fall into or jump out of it. An overdetermined display of order might allow for unintended, perverse notions to appear—that much more powerful for being unplanned. The Pan's designers had no idea that they might be conjuring something as freakish and uncontrolled as the pagan demigod who the Exposition's nickname so naively invoked.

Though the 1893 Chicago Colombian Exposition is still celebrated, and the 1904 St. Louis World's Fair fondly recalled in song, Buffalo's Pan American Exposition has vanished, for good reason, from the national memory. The American century was launched in Buffalo in a spasm of violence and disorder that is as much a part of America as Chicago's ideal of civic planning and St. Louis's Ferris Wheel.

Nothing marks the center of the Pan now except for a stone with a bronze plaque set off by small American flags. It sits on an ornamental traffic island in a old residential street, commemorating the spot nearby, its exact location now unknown, where that September, at the height of this celebration of the nation's new power and empire, President William McKinley was shot in the Temple of Music, to die eight days later. And if we refuse to accept the possibility that a dark magic was connected to the spilling of the president's blood, we might first have a look at other things that happened that summer around the Temple of Music.

As building contractors, Carmelo and Natale Gugino did well during the rush to build the elaborate fairgrounds. A small army of Italians and other laborers worked constant shifts on 350 acres of farmland for eighteen months to frame, cover, paint, and wire the elaborate buildings. Job done, the two returned to their hometown of Valledolmo, Sicily that summer to fetch their parents and baby sisters: Providenza and my father's mother-to-be, Antonetta. Living in Buffalo too was my mother's father, Antonio Scinta, another Valledolmese who'd been sent to America after his mother died of pneumonia in 1894, when he was five, to be with his father Luigi, a stonemason.

The Pan meant a lot to the city's Italians, for the men who helped build it, and to the men and women who worked at Venice in America, the midway concession that conjured a dream of the old country and employed them as craftsmen, waiters, cooks, strolling singers, and guitar and mandolin players—even gondoliers (some hired from the real Venice) to ferry tourists in a circular canal from one elaborate marvel to another.

Venice in America was one of the most successful concessions at the Pan, a goofy mix of Venetian architecture and Neapolitan fun. The people who worked there apparently had a ball. After nearly twenty years of prejudice, ridicule, and scorn, the concession was the first broadly positive depiction of Italian people and culture, their food and music, for the American public. Its effect, now forgotten, was profound.

Nowhere is that positive effect more apparent than in Buffalo's newspapers, which had up to then mainly depicted Italians, and the Sicilians especially, as dirty and dangerous scavengers. In 1903, a feature story in the city's *News* noted that the local Italian population now totaled in excess of twenty thousand, and called it a community well-suited to developments in social progress, industry, and agriculture.

So maybe the Pan *was* magic. How could an immigrant see it and not be amazed, entranced? But if Buffalo was witnessing the rise of the newest Americans, it also exhibited the fall of the first. Opposite Venice in America on the midway was the enormous gate of the Indian Congress, home that summer to some seven hundred Native American men, women, and children—most notably Geronimo and the great Sioux leader Red Cloud. People from thirty-seven nations (including eleven bands of Sioux and four Apache) were paid to be living relics in the 150,000-square-foot enclosure, mainly in a "village" of tipis, wikiups, and a model pueblo at one end. These people probably looked at the fair a lot differently.

And I, like so many others at the time, after visiting Venice in America, took in the Indian Congress. There I discovered almost by accident something which the attending Indigenous people, and no one else, probably knew—that a great protecting spirit appeared at last to save its suffering people. At least I think it did. That's the problem with magic, it's hard knowing for sure.

The entrance to the Indian Congress was shaped like a mountain peak, three stories tall and a hundred feet across, topped with several larger-than-life Indian figures shown looking into the distance, that being the allegorical past. Inside was a semicircular grandstand, which seated ten thousand, before which the Indians performed, at 2:30, 5, and, under the lights, 9 pm. Booths selling crafts and souvenirs ringed the enclosure. Admission was twenty-five cents.

An irreducible mix of exploitation and admiration, the Congress was the creation of Col. Frederick Cummins, a man of no small mystery, a forty-two-year-old son of an Indian trader from Council Bluffs, Iowa, who rode and hunted with local Omaha bands from an early age. Cummins had been a ranch hand in Montana, and rambled between Helena and the Pine Ridge Sioux reservation. His official biography, published as a program for one of his entertainments in 1912, is hazy about what he did for twenty years, stating only that Cummins—now called Colonel—was a famous scout and friend of the Indians who came to manage the first Indian Congress at Omaha's Trans-Mississippi Exposition in 1898. (An entertainment organized after a Northwest Indian village proved a commercial success on the midway at the 1893 Chicago fair.)

Cummins's publicity presents a man of no small vision, saying that while in Omaha he

> conceived the idea of producing at the remarkable Pan American Exposition, which was to be held at Buffalo, N.Y., in 1901, the greatest gathering of noted Indian chiefs and their tribes that could be segregated in North America. He worked indefatigably to compass this great enterprise and to carry out his effort to present to the people of the world the best representatives of the leaders and chiefs of the fast departing tribes of the aborigines of America.

Looking back eleven years later, Cummins adds: "In this he was remarkably successful."

Hiring Native Americans to perform in popular entertainments had been at first encouraged by the Bureau of Indian Affairs, thinking that such shows would educate the public regarding Indigenous culture and were a good way to bring hard currency to people on the reservations. By 1901, however, after about twenty years of Wild West shows, Buffalo Bill Cody's most notably, official policy had shifted completely.

Though these entertainments presented Indians as simple, fierce, noble, and doomed, they did let them perform traditional songs and dances, race horses, engage in symbolic battles, and allow them an opportunity to see the world—nearly everything, except hunting, harvesting, and freedom, they enjoyed before Europeans arrived. Assimilation had been the government's pol-

icy since the Grant administration, and such broadly respect-
ful displays of traditional aboriginal customs probably annoyed
Washington officials more than the putative exploitation.

One searches in vain for accounts of any ill feelings Indians
held toward their show business bosses. Unlike nearly everyone
of any consequence whom Native Americans encountered in two
hundred years of official misconduct, both Cummins and Cody
respected their culture, honored their people, paid good wages,
were generous with food and clothing, and, best of all, kept their
promises.

The 1901 Congress built on the success at Omaha and
was an unprecedented gathering of representatives of the Plains
and Western tribes. If one includes members of New York's Iroquois nation (which Cummins certainly did in his promotional
literature), it was the widest representation of North America's
Indigenous people ever assembled. Missing were any members
of Northwest nations or those Southern peoples who were then
in the process of losing title to the Oklahoma Territory.

Astonishing to consider now, the stars of the show were the
Apache leader Geronimo, and the great Sioux chief Red Cloud.
Fifteen years earlier, Geronimo, now seventy-two, had been the
last Native American "chief" (followers considered him a medicine man) to give up arms against the US government, and was
still deemed by the government as a prisoner of war. Red Cloud,
who had won treaty concessions from the Grant administration
a quarter-century earlier, was seventy-nine years old and going
blind. To protect his eyes from daylight he wore round, very
dark glasses. In photographs made that summer, he cuts a rather
psychedelic figure, a frail old man in full ceremonial clothing and
headdress, and very hip, round shades.

After Geronimo and Red Cloud, third billing went to Crazy
Snake, a Creek leader arrested for promoting a small insurrection
against the impending Oklahoma statehood the summer before.
Though Creeks had been a farming, once even a slave-holding,
people for over a century, the studio portrait of Crazy Snake

printed in the Congress's program shows a proud young man dressed like a Fenimore Cooper brave. Geronimo's portrait, in contrast, shows him wearing a tie.

Other Congress Sioux chiefs were Shot-in-the-Eye (who helped finish Custer at Greasy Grass), American Horse, Flat Iron, and Little Wound. Also present was Kicking Bear, the medicine man who had been central to the Ghost Dance, the last great spiritual movement of the Plains people which had flared up, and was brutally put down, ten years earlier.

Red Cloud was once the most famous Indian in the United States. In 1868, after a series of raids against illegal army posts along the Bozeman Trail, he led a Sioux delegation to Washington for a formal state reception with the new president, Ulysses Grant, gaining in that visit the only territorial concession ever granted Native Americans by the federal government.

As a homesick, alcoholic lieutenant stationed in the remote Northwest Territory after the Mexican War, Grant was furious to witness the treatment the tribes there received from federal agents, leaving him with a lifelong sympathy for Native people. At Vicksberg, he promoted an engineer named Eli Parker, a Seneca from their reservation near Buffalo, to his staff. Parker wrote out the clear copy of the surrender signed by Lee at Appomattox ("I am glad to see one real American here," Lee said of Eli) and became, in Grant's administration, the first Indigenous American to head the Bureau of Indian Affairs.

Clearly uncomfortable during an awkward meeting with the Native delegation and the full diplomatic corps, the president quickly turned care of the Sioux over to Parker, who shortly thereafter agreed to shut the Bozeman Trail posts and recognized Sioux sovereignty over large parts of what is now South Dakota, Wyoming, and Montana.

The treaty lasted ten years, broken in the wake of Custer's Last Stand. By then, Red Cloud, who had counseled his people to accommodate the whites and, in 1876, stay away from the independent bands gathering at the Little Big Horn, had lost a great deal of influence to the militant Sioux leaders, especially

Sitting Bull and Crazy Horse. Both of them were subsequently murdered while in Army custody, Crazy Horse in 1877, Sitting Bull, following his star turn in Buffalo Bill's Wild West show, in 1890. Red Cloud, though reviled in later years for preaching accommodation, lived long enough to go to Buffalo and, according to the advance publicity, meet another president.

Geronimo's legend, though no less marked by armed resistance, was largely created by the newspapers. He was one of several Apache leaders who opposed civil authority on both sides of the Mexico border, raiding ranches and trading posts and, depending on who was after them, hiding out in Mexico's Sierra Madres or the desert canyons of the Arizona Territory.

Twice Geronimo was persuaded to settle his band in an Arizona reservation, where some Apaches kept ranches. Life was dull there, however, and a rustling trip south, in 1885, left Geronimo's very small band trapped at last between the two armies. An American delegation offered the choice of arrest and imprisonment in the United States, or certain extermination by Mexican troops.

Geronimo probably regretted not choosing the latter. The Apaches, even the ranchers who helped catch Geronimo, were transported to Gulf Coast prisons where hundreds of them died in malarial heat. Some survivors were pardoned and returned to Arizona after a few years. Geronimo and his band were not, eventually taken in by their old enemies, the Comanches, at the Fort Sill reservation. For the rest of his life, Geronimo made paid personal appearances. The Buffalo papers, which mainly referred to him as the Human Tiger, several times reported him selling his hat or demanding money to have his picture taken. The standard fee for both, wordlessly indicated by a raised hand, was five dollars. One 1901 editorial predictably observed that every man now had his price.

Fairgoers would find Geronimo and Red Cloud, and see a variety of dances, for an additional dime, in a theatre at the center of the Indian Congress. It is unclear how long the dances lasted, though they may well have been the main entertainment between the three scheduled exhibitions of riding, dances, and mock battles, and gone on all day.

There was a War Dance, and the Devil Dance, featuring the Messingq, a grotesque figure dressed in a bear skin and wooden mask, whose role was to amuse the adults and frighten little children into minding the grownups. The Messingq, which grunted and gestured strangely, was placated with gifts of tobacco. "It does not represent an evil spirit but is always considered a peacemaker," the program explained.

Cummins called the lavishly photo-illustrated program a *"Libretto."* It related breathless accounts of Indian raids, and exhibited several artful pictures of half-naked girls, while expressing an appreciation of Native American arts and spiritual philosophy rare for the time. Nearly hidden on a rear page is this cry, presumably written by Cummins:

> He who has a more intimate knowledge of Indian character sees only their virtues, their truth, their fidelity to a trust, their simple and innocent sports, and wonders that a morally degenerate, but powerful civilization, should destroy that primitive life.

In repertory also was the Buffalo Dance, in which dancers circled around a kettle of hominy, snorting like buffalo to invoke success in hunting. Here one might wonder if something more than money had drawn the great Sioux leaders to the Pan in their old age. Perhaps the opportunity to appear at a whites' powwow, in a city named Buffalo—a coincidence that apparently never dawned on the men running the show, but something which must have been achingly obvious to the assembled Plains people—was inducement enough.

Certainly when the Sioux got to Buffalo, they would have seen, as one can today, likenesses of the great animal nearly everywhere, on posters, statues, plaques, reliefs, and advertisements. This could only have struck them as promising.

In 1901, Buffalo was within a day's rail travel of 80 percent of the country's population. This centrality made it an ideal location for a national fair mainly sponsored by the railroad trust. Special promotions brought excursion trains from across the country on specific days for citizens to visit their state's own pavilions, which boosted local products, at special rates. Passengers disembarked at a station at the north end of the grounds.

Once in Buffalo, customers were prey to expensive accommodations, high admission fees, pricey food, and souvenirs. Adding to the experience, the summer was unseasonably hot and exceptionally humid (by September the plaster plates on many buildings were crumbling). The style of middle-class dress required men to wear jackets, ties, hats, and long pants. Women wore long dresses, corsets, and hats, and many carried parasols to keep the sun off their skin. Consequently, contemporary accounts detail a particular exhaustion among the fairgoers, though presented mostly as a positive thing—the result of so much to see and do. US government buildings promoted domestic and military hardware, agriculture, and education. International pavilions had trade and cultural displays that mainly touted the virtues of colonial economies, which went quite well with the entertaining ethnic "villages" found along the midway.

Business displays crowded the Manufacture and Graphic Arts pavilions. The Horticulture pavilion, a huge hothouse, was a big draw; as was the Ethnology Building, with artifacts and murals depicting the rise of European civilization. The Temple of Music offered two free orchestra concerts and organ recitals daily. More music was available at two outdoor bandstands, which featured bands playing marches and pop tunes, and in the various international attractions on the nearly mile-long midway which meandered along all of the ground's western edge and half of its northern.

There, notions of exotic pleasure and colonial rule were fully expressed in concessions, each with a separate admission charge, which were intended by the planners to make enough money to pay for the Pan's more edifying cultural and commercial displays.

Its central attraction was a funhouse of mazes, mirrors, and projected images called Dreamland, which people entered under a forty-foot-high relief portrait of a sleeping woman with her eyes shut in ambiguous bliss, called by one magazine an "Anglo-American Buddha."

Handy to Dreamland was the Trip to the Moon, where customers climbed into a closed omnibus and watched as the earth receded outside their portholes while they approached the looming moon. Upon arrival they disembarked in a grotto where strangely dressed midgets led them to meet the giant King of the Moon for a brief reception before heading back.

Elsewhere people could take in a working display of infant incubators, visit the Streets of Mexico and its bullring, and head over to the Streets of Cairo for a camel ride. On the way they would pass the opposing entrances of Darkest Africa and the Old Plantation, the former a model village of people hired from several African nations to dress in costume, perform dances, and create handicrafts, from basket weaving to jewelry making; the latter was, of course, an antebellum fantasy of "Darkie" song and dance. There were Japanese, Philippine, and "Esquimaux" villages, a zoo, and Alt Nuremberg, a tiny re-creation of the German town, with a restaurant and beer garden.

While most of these attractions were little better than human zoos, the best of them exhibited a sincere interest in the cultures displayed, attempting, however crudely, to present them to a curious, and very provincial, American public. To this end, one element all shared was music, which was everywhere that summer—from the Italian singers and string band, to the songs and dances at the Indian Congress, marimba music at the Streets of Mexico, Hawaiian guitar and ukulele playing, African drumming, Japanese dancers and acrobats, spirituals and cakewalks at the Old Plantation.

Pabst's beer garden and the restaurant at Alt Nuremberg had German bands and yodelers, creating a fad for that vocal novelty that went from there straight to vaudeville, and cowboy singing shortly thereafter. Another soon-to-be wildly popular music was presented by the Royal Hawaiian Band at the Hawaiian village. Their unique innovations were close-part harmony singing, and a way to play an open tuned guitar with a metal bar that rendered beautiful sliding tonalities to mimic the human voice.

Open—or what the Hawaiians called "slack key"—tuning lets a guitarist strum a full chord, usually a G or D, without having to press any strings. It appeared first before the Civil War, in popular how-to songbooks which allowed modestly skilled players to pick out simple melodies enhanced by the sympathetic tones of the ringing open strings. Tradition states that Portuguese immigrants, Mexican *vaqueros,* and New England sailors all brought their stringed instruments to Hawaii around that time, where they were avidly taken up by the locals.

Hawaiian singers and players accompanied a theatrical recreation of an eruption of Mount Kilauea at the Chicago Exposition in 1893, and took the act to San Francisco the following year. A picture of the Hawaiians in Buffalo (with John Philip Sousa) shows them holding flutes, fiddles, and mandolins along with their ukes and guitars. They embarked on an extensive vaudeville tour immediately after the fair.

Exactly who came up with the idea of using a smooth metal bar to press guitar strings to create a sliding, weeping sound is much debated, but the beguiling effect was soon adopted by American players, especially down south, where it took on haunting associations quite distinct from sun, surf, and palms.

The sightseeing gondola tours that embarked at Venice in America were expensive, but probably the easiest and coolest way to see the sights. The Edison Company filmed a three-part newsreel shot from the bow of an electric launch as it tours the length of the central canal, which is now archived at The Library of Congress.

The Edison catalogue notes that in the second part of the film, "three of the gondolas contain the Venetian Band and many of the pretty girls of the 'Streets of Venice' [*sic*] all of which attend to make the picture highly interesting." We see one gondola in particular weighted down with passengers, some of whom wave gently at the viewer. (People had yet to learn how to clown for movie cameras, nor does the operator think to direct the lens' gaze anywhere but forward.) One can just make out a figure in the bow of the passing gondola wearing a tasseled beret and playing a small guitar.

At the end of the film the boat glides into Venice in America. The small-scale rendering of a Venetian landing, with its tourists and idlers, probably appears more real now on the old black-and-white film than it ever did in person; and our modern eyes might recognize the fake Venetian square as the first, albeit unintentional, movie set.

We see striped gondola moorings jutting out of the water, and gothic facades. A small Bridge of Sighs passes overhead; beyond it, the boat landing and another covered bridge. People walk along the canal bank, and the bridge's canvas awning flaps in a brisk wind. A woman in a bright dress and large hat looks down at the boat as it passes.

Then the film switches course. Shot in one long take until now, with gaps only where the film was changed in the camera, now it cuts and we are back again at the beginning of the Venice landing, with the camera angled to take in more of the quayside as it sweeps up the canal again.

People are milling around and in the distance a strange figure stands in a boat tied to the canal side, lunging and waving its arms. Closer, we see it's someone in an elaborate, full-body costume: hairy, long-sleeved, and with some kind of broad insignia on the back. In one hand he comically swings what looks like a small pick or hatchet at bystanders. He appears to be wearing big fuzzy boots and a headpiece with apparently two large plumes, a slapstick *opera buffa* figure. As the camera slides by, the clown looks at the camera and for a moment we see two broad reflecting disks covering his eyes.

The Edison catalogue offers no hint as to what the bizarre figure might be. We do know that Exposition planners hired several clowns to dress in costume and wander the grounds to entertain visitors. There was a Yokel, for example, an exaggerated country bumpkin overwhelmed by the surrounding wonders. Presumably, the Venice grotesque was one of those entertainers.

There is something floridly Italian in his gestures, how he waves his arms and lunges with the hatchet without hitting anyone. What is unfamiliar, of course, is the costume. In a striking resemblance to the Messingq figure described in the Indian Congress *Libretto*, it appears to be a parody Indian, an early Chief Wahoo, with tomahawk, moccasins, ornate vest, and headdress. Certainly an odd figure for an Italian clown to have taken up. Especially those disks covering its eyes, which, however, greatly resemble Red Cloud's sunglasses.

That June, local papers noted that Blue Horse, the elderly signatory of every Sioux treaty for the last fifty years, had extended an invitation to President William McKinley to a special performance at the Congress during his eagerly anticipated visit. The invitation, according to one paper, was "inscribed on the face of a button not as large as a dime, taken from the buckskin coat of Blue Horse . . . a wonderful piece of work . . . executed by the chief of the Navajo tribe."

McKinley had been eager to get to Buffalo all summer. Mrs. McKinley, prone to nervous disorders, had not been well for the Pan's opening ceremonies, and so Vice President Theodore Roosevelt had attended for the president. Back in DC, he'd given a typically enthusiastic report of what he'd seen. Plans were made for a presidential visit in September to coincide with the newest national holiday, Labor Day.

His second term just underway, McKinley was the most popular man in the United States, an affable Civil War veteran and ex-schoolteacher with a fine speaking voice who came to political prominence in his native Ohio through the patronage of his former commanding officer, Rutherford Hayes, elected president in 1876, and Mark Hanna, the multimillionaire war profiteer from Cleveland with a notorious skill at winning elections.

A rotund, middle-class Caesar, McKinley in his first term used the occasion of the Spanish-American War to form an American colonial empire in the Pacific, annexing the Philippines after an expeditionary force sent to help Filipino troops oust the remaining Spanish forces (easy enough after Admiral Dewey sank Spain's fleet in Manila Bay) became an occupying army. The mission of empire came to him, McKinley reportedly said, while he was on his knees praying, a divine admonition to spread civilization and Christianity:

> I don't know how it was, but it came . . . There was nothing left for us to do but to take them all, and educate the Filipinos, and uplift and civilize and Christianize them and by God's grace do the very best we could by them as our fellow-men for whom Christ also died. And then I went to bed, and went to sleep, and slept soundly.

(History does not record if anyone mentioned that the Philippines had been Catholic for over three hundred years.)

Anyway, on September 4, President McKinley's entourage left Ohio for Buffalo, where it was met by a crush of well-wishers. The first shadow fell on the occasion as the presidential train was easing into the Pan's station. The concussion from an army honor guard's over-enthusiastic 21-gun salute smashed several train windows. People thought there'd been a bomb; someone screamed "Anarchists!," a pervasive national fear, and the crowd panicked before order was quickly restored.

President and Mrs. McKinley rode a carriage to the grand home of John Milburn, the chief executive of the Exposition, about a mile from the grounds, where they would stay during their visit. That evening the president enjoyed a view of the illuminated Electric Tower from the porch of the Milburn home.

The next day was sweltering, and the McKinleys took a carriage tour of the Exposition, avoiding the midway and whatever welcome the Congress Indians had planned. Though lacking "either the blessing or sanction of the Indian Bureau," the concession still had several men once important enough to meet a president; and all of them, including Geronimo, had extended hands of accommodation, even friendship. To have had Blue Horse's engraved invitation dismissed so casually by the White Chief must have been galling indeed.

Security that day was tight. The McKinleys' passage through the huge crowd was cleared by some fifty mounted police and soldiers. Even so, a madwoman was discovered hiding under the bandstand podium where McKinley addressed a large crowd.

Another Edison newsreel at the Library of Congress shows the opening moments of the address. After entering with his wife and being introduced, McKinley stands, framed by flag bunting; his left hand holds a piece of paper, the right rests casually on the railing in front of him. He is clearly at ease in front of the crowd. Notable also, as he hitches his pants to stand, is his immense, pear-shaped gut. While speaking, he constantly scans the crowd and rocks back and forth in emphasis of his words.

The Buffalo *Times* report noted, "A picturesque figure stood in front of the stand and listened attentively to the President's address—Red Cloud, one of the Seneca nation [*sic*]."

After the speech, it was off to the stadium for a review of the troops, which makes one more Edison movie: officers in high-plumed hats, troops marching past the grandstand presenting arms. McKinley can just be seen doffing his top hat as the colors pass.

After a long lunch and a visit to the US Government building, the president's party left the grounds, returning at nightfall for the "largest pyrotechnical display ever seen" in his honor, designed by the Fire Works King, the famous, and ominously named, Henry Pain.

It was, even by Pain's excessive standards, an orgy of bombardment.

At sunset the exposition grounds were illuminated by fifty powerful fires in five different colors. A large number of lighted balloons were next, followed by the discharge of a hundred three-pound rockets fired simultaneously from different sections of the fairgrounds. Ten batteries of mines were then put in motion. Next came five hundred colored lights discharging electric comets in a continuous stream and a salvo of ten thirty-inch bombs with five colors each.

And on and on.

Revolving fountains . . . Fujiyama rockets . . . shower of pearls prismatic whirlwinds . . . umbrellas of fire . . . triple star candles . . . 100 feet high, triple chrysanthemum bombs . . . Revolving cascade bombs . . . peacock plume bombs . . . Golden Wheel of Prosperity . . . Eruption of Sinbad's jeweled cave, grand deluge of liquid gems.

McKinley watched the thunderous show from a boat in the broad lagoon that took up the lower third of the Exposition grounds. As they disembarked, the Goddess of Light spotlight, sharply defined by air thick with gunpowder smoke, "threw its gleaming light upon the party."

Ten days earlier, Bill Cody had finally brought his Wild West Show for an indefinite engagement. As in Chicago in 1893, when he sold two million tickets, Cody's two enormous tents were pitched outside the Exposition grounds, where their principal attractions were, as always, trick shooting, fancy riding, and a dramatic recreation of Custer's Last Stand, which had once been Sitting Bull's star turn.

Shortly after Cody arrived a newspaper reported:

All of the Indians on exhibition within the Exhibition grounds, anxious to see their red brothers traveling under the banner of Col. Cody, wrapped their most gaudy shawls about them and went on a tour of visitation . . . "How!" said Chief Geronimo of the Exposition Indians. "How!" exclaimed Chief Irontail of the Wild West Show.

That same day, another paper noted reciprocal visits between the two Native American camps, calling it a powwow, and detailing an exchange of gifts, which included some five hundred silver dollars Cody gave his Native associate Irontail to dispense among the Congress.

The Cody show at the time had some seventy-five Sioux (by then the entertainment had come to include veterans of more modern conflicts: Boers, Rough Riders, and British soldiers). Taken in aggregate, and including members of the local Iroquois, once Cody arrived there was in Buffalo an unprecedented colloquy of nearly one thousand Native Americans.

In its way it was the widest convocation of Indigenous people since the Messiah Dance (commonly called "Ghost Dance") movement, when, in 1889, a Paiute medicine man named Wovoka began to preach his visions of the return of the dead and the buffalo, a renewal of the prairies, and the disappearance of the whites. Word of this traveled quickly through the desolated reservations of the Far West, where marathon ceremonies of dancing, drumming, and singing were meant to induce visions of the afterlife. Fueled in large part by war widows, the Messiah Dance was drawn from Christian end-times theology, and Wovoka was considered by some the second coming of the Messiah.

The Sioux medicine man Kicking Bear, who was at the Buffalo congress, went to Utah in the summer of 1890 to meet Wovoka, and afterwards described the Paiute flying above the train back to Nebraska, singing sacred songs. Kicking Bear refined the dance by placing a dead branch, symbolic of the Sioux nation, at the center of its circle, and the ceremony was passionately taken up by the demoralized and divided Sioux.

Another Sioux medicine man, Black Elk, was struck by how the dance resembled his own great vision of Thunder Beings, spirits widely understood by Indigenous Americans to embody the power and mystery of creation, to be living forces of a magnitude just beneath the Great Spirit. Believed by many to dwell in the west, Thunder Beings are terrifying dispensers of sudden death, but are also seen as protectors, and as sources of healing and transforming change. They are manifested in the lightning and the rain and rainbow which follows. Though appearing in many forms, Thunder Beings are often represented as giant birds. The Lenapi people, who inhabited the lower Hudson valley and what is now New Jersey, understood Thunder Beings to resemble huge partridges, and to live in the great gorge of the Pan's celebrated power source, Niagara Falls.

For the Sioux, a person who dreamt of Thunder Beings was a Heyoka, someone with great powers in both war and healing. In 1931, the Heyoka Black Elk described his vision of Sioux rebirth to the writer John Neihardt in terms of a visit with six Thunder Beings (he called them a circle of grandfathers) who lived in a rainbow lodge. His dream ratified by the advent of the Messiah Dance, Black Elk began decorating buckskin shirts with mystic symbols that were soon integrated into the dance, meant, to the consternation of the authorities, to make their wearers immune to bullets.

During Messiah Dance ceremonies people danced for hours and collapsed in ecstatic visions. As destitute as the Sioux by then were, for most whites in Nebraska, the endless dancing and drumming, the nightly bonfires, could only mean a new uprising. A National Guard general reported "great lights and signal fires shone from the bluffs and hilltops a few miles distant from Pine Ridge, and the Bad Lands were ablaze with lights that could be seen for miles."

The panic led to the murder of Sitting Bull during an attempted arrest in December 1890. Slightly less than two weeks later, the Seventh Regiment, Custer's old troop, while attempting to disarm some braves in a camp of 350 Minneconjou Messiah Dancers at Wounded Knee Creek, two-thirds of them women and children, opened up with four automatic Hotchkiss guns.

American Horse, another Congress Sioux, recalled the scene:

> [A] woman with an infant in her arms who was killed as she almost touched a flag of truce . . . The women as they were fleeing with their babies were killed together, shot right through . . . [Children] came out of their places of refuge, and as soon as they came in sight a number of soldiers surrounded them and butchered them there.

A running fight ensued and lasted two days. Black Elk, who heard the shooting from a distance, raced to help, he told Neihardt, wearing his ghost shirt, singing to the great spirits:

> A Thunder-being nation I am I have said.
> A Thunder-being nation I am I have said.
> You shall live. You shall live . . .

> [We] charged down the draw toward the captives. I could feel the bullets hitting me but I was bullet proof. I had to hang on to my horse to keep the bullets from knocking me off. I had the sacred bow with me and all I had to do was to hold the bow toward the soldiers and you should have seen the soldiers run! . . . If I had had a gun I could have killed a lot of them.

The cavalry suffered dozens of casualties, but the Indians were near starving, and the weakest among them began dying in a fearsome blizzard that hit the day after the massacre. Chief Young Man Afraid of His Horses, also at the Buffalo Congress, convinced the holdouts to surrender. Wounded Knee was a defeat in battle and a spiritual calamity, crushing the last vision of Indigenous resistance and rebirth; the old life was gone.

Perhaps thanks to Kicking Bear, the Messiah Dance was revived at the Pan; the *Libretto*'s description of it is notable for the sympathy and respect shown for its origins and performance.

> To aid the coming of the Messiah the Indians were to dance night and day until he appeared . . . The dance was called the Ghost Dance by the white people. It was not a war dance, it was an invocation.

So in a place named Buffalo, one bright with burning lights, the Messiah Dance was performed once more, this time without interference from the whites. How this struck the Indians assembled there is anyone's guess.

On September 1, a week after Buffalo Bill arrived, Cummins debuted "an Indian marvel who defies electricity." A man named Peta would walk "a cable 100 feet in length and stretched 200 feet above the earth." Furthermore, "the cable is charged with 2,000 volts of electricity and when he walks this cable the current passes through his body [on which] are strapped numerous incandescent lights and the moment his feet touch the high cable the incandescents illuminate. As he walks along, sheets of flame shoot from the cable and his body."

We have, alas, no clue who Peta was. While possibly a circus performer dressed as an Indian, chances are he was one of the Iroquois who worked in high steel construction, riveters renowned for their superb balance and relaxed nerves. As for the electricity, current will pass through any ungrounded human with no effect beyond a certain tingling and a cheerful smell of ozone.

In his wonderful 1949 essay *The Mohawks in High Steel*, Joe Mitchell takes up the story of the people he calls the Caughnawagas, Mohawk men who, confined to their Canadian reservation, stoutly refused to do farm work. "[S]ome made moccasins and snow shoes and sold them to jobbers in Montreal," writes Mitchell. "A few who were still good at the old Mohawk dances came down and traveled with circuses. Caughnawagas were among the first circus Indians."

In 1886, Mohawks hired for scut work at a construction site for a rail bridge over the St. Lawrence River began to demonstrate highly unusual skills:

> As the work progressed, it became apparent to all con-cerned that these Indians were very odd in that they did not have any fear of heights. If not watched, they would climb up into the spans and walk around up there as cool and collected as the toughest of [the] riveters [ex-sailors used to working the rigging of tall ships]. [The Indians] were as agile as goats. They would walk a narrow beam high up in the air with nothing below but the river, which is rough and ugly there to look down on, and it wouldn't mean any more to them than walking on the solid ground.

The Mohawks pestered the foremen to show them how to handle a rivet gun, then the highest paid job in construction. In short order, three Iroquois riveting crews were traveling from one building site to another.

If Peta's identity may never be known, of far greater impor-tance is *what* he represented to the assembled Native Americans watching him every night: nothing less than a Thunder Being. The blazing figure shooting lightning high above the midway was a living Indigenous answer to the settlers' immobile Goddess of Light. Beginning three days before the president's arrival, the manifest avatar of the Messiah Dance, a figure promising violent change, sudden death, and a powerful healing, appeared above the Pan each night around nine.

On September 6, after a tour of the Niagara Falls power station, McKinley returned to the Pan. First stop was the Iroquois Mis-sion, a bark-sided frame house with Iroquois artifacts, which had the sanction of the Indian Affairs bureau. It was a good policy alternative to the Indian Congress, and sat on the opposite side of the fairgrounds from it. Local Seneca were assembled in something like an honor guard on each side of the president's path into the building, though the resemblance of this to another, less salutary, Iroquois formation, the gauntlet, was one more detail not noted at the time.

A crush of onlookers surged forward as McKinley walked into the building, breaking the cordon of troops holding them back. Recollecting the event three weeks later, the Mission director said it gave him the feeling that something had gone wrong with the day.

From there, the president's entourage visited the Mexican pavilion, where it was serenaded by the marimba orchestra, before preceding to a 4 pm public reception at the Temple of Music.

Only ten minutes after McKinley's arrival at the Temple, his chief of security, George Cortelyou, ordered the doors shut. His attention had been drawn to a suspicious looking man in the reception line: rough clothes, olive-skinned, with black eyes and mustache, an Italian anarchist from central casting.

A year earlier, Gaetano Bresci, an emigrant anarchist from Paterson, New Jersey, had sailed back to Italy and shot dead King Umberto. Joseph Petrosino, a New York police sergeant, weeks before warned the security chief of an Italian anarchist cell intent on striking in Buffalo. Cortelyou and his men accosted the suspicious Italian, who was, it transpired, a sincere American patriot, only wishing to meet the president.

During the distraction, a handsome, sandy-haired man in a striped three-piece summer suit, Leon Czolgosz, stepped up to the president with an Ivor Johnson revolver hidden in the handkerchief in his right hand. While the Temple organist softly played Schumann's ethereal *Träumerei* ("Dreaming"), he raised the gun and shot twice. The handkerchief burst into flame and dropped to the floor. McKinley fell back holding his chest as Cortelyou caught him. Both men tumbled into a row of potted palms. A six-foot-six African American, James Parker, a waiter from

Atlanta directly behind Czolgosz, knocked him down. McKinley's security detail began a vigorous beating.

"Go easy on him, boys," McKinley is supposed to have said, considered enough to have saved Czolgosz from being stomped to death on the spot. Soldiers with fixed bayonets injured several people in clearing the building.

A witness outside recalled:

> A whisper began to pass from mouth to mouth like an electric current, "The President has been shot!" Low murmurs on the part of the men and quiet sobbing from the women began to slacken the tension. Suddenly the clanging bell of an ambulance was heard . . . All at once some one caught sight of a man being conducted to a carriage, and the cry broke out, "The Assassin!" . . . Cries of "Lynch him!" "Shoot him!" "Kill the brute!" rent the air about me, and made me shudder at the sudden awakening of vindictive and vengeful desire.

Anthony Scinta, my young grandfather, was outside waiting to shake McKinley's hand, "It was pandemonium," he told me sixty-five years later.

Pandemonium was the word used most frequently in the papers the next day, and one which again unconsciously reflected the Exposition's name. The word was employed by the Edison Company, in its catalogue description of its newsreel *The Mob Outside the Temple of Music at the Pan-American Exposition*, released on September 11, 1901.

The movie is nearly without drama; in fact it shows little besides hats and the backs of the heads of men and women massed outside the hall. The camera pans slowly left to right across the crowd, clearly on a platform only slightly off the ground. People push tightly together, their attention directed forward. Several men are seen on a dais in front of the building.

Two sit writing at a table, reporters very likely. The tall helmets of police can be glimpsed as the camera swings right, taking in, as the film ends, the rest of the crowd somewhat lateral to the Temple.

Only two faces can be made out near the camera. A man in a derby and eyeglasses looks over his shoulder into the blank glass eye of the future, and a child in a round straw hat, perhaps two years old, held up by an adult, stares seriously. Alas, no sign of young Anthony. But an intrepid boy might have done his best for a better view, and climbed onto the Edison Company's platform in the effort to do so. And, indeed, we see a boy very near the camera about five seconds before the film ends.

He cranes his neck above the crowd, his face, overexposed—a blank—in about a one-quarter profile, his hair black and wavy. Though anonymous, something about the shape of his head seems familiar, He looks a lot like me at twelve.

The boy puts on a cap. The film ends.

McKinley was taken by electric ambulance to the Exposition's infirmary. Czolgosz went in a fortified horse-carriage to the police station downtown, where a lynch mob soon gathered. The renowned Buffalo surgeon Roswell Park was operating at Niagara Falls that afternoon. McKinley's personal doctor was elsewhere on the crowded, chaotic grounds.

Dr. Matthew Mann, the most able physician immediately available, was a gynecologist with no experience treating gunshot wounds, and had to operate without the benefit of electric lights. Though bulbs encrusted nearly every building on the grounds, none had been installed inside the infirmary. A relay of mirrors channeled daylight into the provisional operating room.

The first bullet had blown a button off the president's vest—and here recall the small button Blue Horse took off his own coat, a gift the president scorned—and was found just under the skin. The second angled through McKinley's enormous belly and was lost inside. After some searching, Mann assumed it had lodged in lumbar muscles where it would do no further harm. Though the x-ray machine was one of the modern marvels exhibited at the Pan, doctors were reluctant to try it on the wounded president.

Worse, Mann used neither antiseptic nor rubber gloves during the operation, then closed his incision without draining the wound. McKinley died eight days later of a raging infection at an impromptu clinic set up at the Milburn mansion. Wounded by Czolgosz, McKinley was killed by his doctors.

It was clear to his medical team after forty-eight hours that the president was a goner, but they said nothing to reporters. Newspapers, which were at the time little more than boosters of the Exposition and the Republican Party, felt obligated to give optimistic reports on McKinley's condition up until the morning he died. (Deadlines forced one paper to carry news of his death behind front-page stories detailing his improved condition.) Vice President Theodore Roosevelt, who had first rushed to Buffalo only to resume his vacation two days later, was called back at the final hour. The news of McKinley's death fell like a blow, all the harder for being widely unexpected.

He lay in state for a day at Buffalo City Hall, 100,000 people filing past. The body returned to Washington on a seven-coach, black-draped funeral train. The Buffalo viewing was notable for the presence of Geronimo and others from the Indian Congress who, according to the papers, also sent a wreath of blue asters and a card of regret. "[A] delegation of sixty-five braves and squaws and papooses . . . dressed in their full Indian regalia filed past the casket, each dropping a white carnation upon it."

The papers also reported Geronimo's eulogy, and though it was interpreted then, and has been since, as a sincere statement of loss, it has a distinct ambiguity that speaks to competing feelings of grief, as well as a sense of certain accounts settled: "The rainbow of hope is out of the sky," it begins.

> Heavy clouds hang about us. Tears wet the ground of the tepees. The pale faces, too, are in sorrow. The great chief of the nation is dead. Farewell! Farewell! Farewell!

The White Men's sorrow matches that of the Indians' now, and one might note a measure of satisfaction behind those repeated *Farewells*.

Two days following the shooting, papers reported the circumstances in which the president's brother, Abner McKinley, was told the news. He was a guest of the Colorado and Southern Railway, on an excursion train in a canyon south of Denver, when word came by special telegraph. The president of the C&S described the moment:

> There was a terrible flash of lightning, followed directly by a crash that shook the granite mountains . . . I called Abner McKinley to one side. Between the crashes of heaven's artillery I read the message. Mr. McKinley put his hand to his head and staggered. With each step almost, there was a terrific crash from above . . . Then came the torrent . . . the most astounding masses of water, great sheets of it. The heavens wept with us. There was a rainbow, the like of which few men have ever seen. It was an arch of crimson and gold that rivaled the noonday sun.

Almost as if Thunder Beings had visited and moved on.

After McKinley died, the Exposition organizers redoubled their efforts towards commercial gaiety, measures that had an increasingly crazy edge. Full-page newspaper ads chronicled the extra amusements planned for Railroad Day in late September: weddings performed in a lion's cage, a swimming race for elephants, a parade of "Rail Road Magnates." There was also Pain's Human Bomb: one Louis Stevens would, at the finale of a daylight fireworks display, ascend in a huge balloon with a "Gigantic Bomb," after the detonation of which he was to drop safely back to earth via parachute.

Though it rained, the Railroad Day crowd was the biggest of the summer. The *Courier* reported that as dark fell

Pandemonium [*that word again*] broke loose . . . Bazoo
bands, horns at the lips of men, women and children
let go with a roar loud enough to be heard on Mars.
Fireworks were sent heavenward in quantities to make
the moon look dim.

But by then the Pan was a magnet for the morbidly curious, and
though sales of items picturing McKinley and the Temple were
brisk, "after the shooting of the president, the country had lost
its taste for the Exposition and as the weather turned colder, the
tourists stopped coming."

The Pan ended up losing investors over $6 million, default-
ing on over $3 million in bonds, the balance being bailed out by
the state. More distressing for civic pride, the closing ceremonies
on Saturday, November 2, were followed by a rampage of gang
vandalism, as hundreds of city toughs demolished as much of
the gaudy, crumbling plaster buildings as they could.

Electric light bulbs were jerked from their posts and
thousands of them were smashed on the ground.
Some of the midway restaurants were crushed into
fragments under the pressure of the mob as if they
were so much pasteboard. Windows were shattered
and doors were kicked down . . . Cleopatra's needle
was torn to the ground.

That night, "Pain's final grade salute" went skyward at 11:45. And
at midnight, in a solemn ceremony in the midst of the gathering
mayhem, the Electric Tower was switched off forever.

By one in the morning,

[P]olice on the grounds could not handle the fierce
mob. [Reinforcements] seemed only to increase the
fury of the violent mob . . . The police used their
batons freely and it was reported that several people

had to be taken to the hospital . . . At an early hour
this morning the police were still chasing the howling
mob around the grounds striking right and left with
their clubs trying to subdue the crowd.

Also on that final day, the Indian Congress had one last
sham battle, this one at the sport stadium, with a company of
the 14th Army Infantry, a recreation of the Battle of Little Big
Horn, the soldiers winning this time. There is an Edison newsreel
of the performance, and in seeing it, one realizes with a small
shock that it is nothing less than the very first Western movie,
an action shoot-'em-up with real Indians.

The camera is fixed at one end of the field, and only pans
slowly back and forth. The film begins with a brief view of the
Indians parading on their ponies past the camera. Once the firing
starts, the soldiers hold the foreground and the Indians, a mass
of riding, running, and shooting figures, charge at them. The
whole field is framed against a backdrop of enormous columns
and arches at the top of the stadium, which add a peculiar Roman
aspect to the scene of men frantically shooting at each other. (An
estimated fifteen thousand blanks were fired during the show.)

Plumes of smoke drift up from both sides so as to create a
screen, which, interestingly, the Indians use to cover their running advances. Mounted Indians can be made out through the
smoke, circling and firing at the troops, and, as a dozen startling
silhouettes ride between the soldiers and the camera, we see the
troop is surrounded. There is an army counterattack, followed
by another Indian advance.

The Indians come closest to the camera in the last minute of
the film, running up out of the hanging smoke in a curious bent-
knee lope, to fire once, and then retreat into the haze. The soldiers
have hunkered down very near, some practically underneath, the
camera. Then, in a bit of action that still brings a chill over a
century later, a very real bayonet is fixed to a rifle near the lens.
The troops mass, then charge. The Indians scamper back across the
field, leaving behind a number of "dead" from both sides.

There's a cut, and the last few seconds of the film are of what must have been the grand farewell: a crowd of Indians in the middle of the field fire their rifles into the air as they walk off.

One paper reported a curious coda. While the fallen Indians and soldiers still lay on the field, "The Red men and the squaws marched to the very center, where they held ceremonies for the dead in which there was much wailing." It is, of course, unclear which dead, those before them or those of the past, were being mourned. However, the rites completed, the dead arose for the farewell volley seen on the Edison newsreel.

News accounts also note that the Indians presented Cummins with "a beautiful diamond stud" at the end of the show, adding that "they will leave at an early hour this morning." It seems likely that the Indians' train pulled out of the Pan's station while police were still chasing rioters across the dark and ruined fairgrounds.

Evidently, Cummins got more than a diamond pin. His 1912 biography notes that

> At the close of the Pan-American Exposition in 1901 he was urged by the different Indian Chiefs to visit them personally during the ensuing winter at their different reservations in the Far West, which invitation he gladly accepted.
>
> While visiting what remained of the once great Sioux nation, he was greatly honored by being adopted by the venerable Chief Red Cloud as his son and was afterwards received by the entire Sioux tribe as a brother, and was elected, with full honors, a Chief and permitted to sit beside his Indian father in Grand Council, an Indian honor never bestowed upon a white man. He was given the name of Chief La-Ko-Ta, which means "Chief of all Indians."

Apparently Cummins' show, now called the Little Buffalo and Wild West, toured Europe and Australia up until the start of the First World War. By then Cummins's name had disappeared from the program, whether from death or retirement is unclear. We might draw from the above that there's History, and then there's history; the official story, and then everything else, a welter of competing accounts with cryptic meanings and no clear explanations, which is probably a fairer, if confusing, representation of life than the one generally found in history books.

For Italians, those ancestors whose own mysterious histories I came to Buffalo to try to untangle, both *story* and *history* are covered in a single word: *storia*. While, strictly speaking, the distinction is clear when used in context, the word is emblematic of an ancient Mediterranean world, when history could *only* be stories; an old world that lasted well into the twentieth century, when it was still possible to listen to Palermo's public storytellers, *i cuntastori*, telling tales of the Normans and the Crusades, of the great hero Orlando.

For the story never really ends. Though the Pan may have been forgotten, it didn't go away. And the mystery surrounding McKinley's murder, that sense of unknown forces behind the killing in the Temple of Music, survived in song. A sort of charge went through American music in its immediate wake. "The hot stuff came in nineteen-two," Jelly Roll Morton told Alan Lomax in a recorded interview thirty-five years later, recalling the first shock of jazz that followed ragtime.

The Pan's exuberant and pleasurable musical innovations— Hawaiian slide guitars, German yodeling, Italian crooning—raced into the country's musical bloodstream, where they joined existing forms, diffused, and evolved. Aware of its size, breadth, and diversity for the first time, it is almost as if the country began to listen to itself in a new way. The same summer, a field anthropologist in Mississippi made note of a startling style of singing and guitar playing he heard among field workers, which came to be called the blues.

As for Native Americans, they did not vanish, as was so confidently expected; in fact, a case can be made that those assembled took what happened in Buffalo as a great sign. Even if you don't accept that Thunder Beings struck down the White Chief, the Messiah Dance and the electrified Indian still stand at the beginning of an Indigenous rebirth.

In 1990, the Native American performance scholar William Powers wrote that "since the turn of the century, Plains music and dance have become symbolic of American Indian resistance to wholesale adoption of Euroamerican culture." He specifically credits Wild West shows. We might now add the 1901 Indian Congress.

Buffalo's was the largest of Cummins's three Congresses (the last was at the 1904 St. Louis Fair), which drew together in one place a greater number of traditional tribal enemies than Cody's shows did, as well as intra-tribal political rivals—the resisters and accommodationists; Christians and those who kept the old religion. After 1901, a new Native American identity emerged from the wreckage of the old, an identity vitally alive today in yearly powwows across the country. The grand entry, which started every Congress performance and Cody show, is now the traditional beginning of every powwow. The War Dance is still danced, only now the songs recall Native warriors in the South Pacific, Vietnam, and Iraq.

Professor Powers credited his love and understanding of Sioux culture to his mentor, the distinguished Indian dancer and teacher, Frank Afraid of Horse. Frank, grandson of the Congress performers Little Wound and Young Man Afraid of His Horses, was thirty in 1901 and might reasonably be assumed to have been in Buffalo with them. (By then the Feds had long stopped keeping track of who was in those shows, and outside of those chiefs listed in the *Libretto*, there's no telling who was there that summer.)

That the twentieth-century revival of Indigenous culture is generally called the Pan Indian movement might be credited to the wit of Fate.

The Exposition buildings were torn down that winter, except for the two built for long-term use, buildings that today house the

Albright-Knox Museum of Art and the Buffalo Historical Society. There was talk of preserving the Electric Tower, but it was too flimsy to last long. (A nearly exact copy, a bank building, went up in downtown Buffalo three years later, very near a remarkable knockoff of the Temple of Music/Ethnology buildings.) The rest of the land was cut into tidy residential lots, leaving behind very little to indicate the Exposition's ground plan.

But the Pan survived; first in the vast, electrified amusement parks at Coney Island, then in every large city, and now Disney World. The Trip to the Moon concession was bought and reassembled the next summer at Coney's Steeplechase Park. In 1903, Luna Park opened there, with brightly colored pavilions webbed-over with some 250,000 electric bulbs and offering many of the same midway attractions as the Pan, including an Eskimo village and a working display of baby incubators.

That next year saw the Coney Island debut of Dreamland, its name taken from the Pan's central midway attraction. The new Dreamland boasted one *million* bulbs, 100,000 of them covering a recreation of the Electric Tower, called now the Beacon Tower.

Leon Czolgosz was executed in the State of New York's electric chair, five days before the Pan closed, following a trial so fast, with lawyers so indifferent to his case, that it amounted to an official kangaroo court. In an era when the lynchings of African Americans were common front-page stories, the authorities probably felt they'd done enough keeping Czolgosz from the mob outside the jail the night of the shooting. No mitigating evidence was introduced on his behalf, a plea of insanity was almost immediately disallowed, and death was the only sentence afforded. It was carried out with such dispatch that it's clear no one wanted him to survive the fair.

Leon was, in fact, erased completely; his body was dropped into a pit in the Auburn prison yard with two gallons of sulfuric acid poured over it. The corpse dissolved within hours and was covered without a marker.

Though his body vanished as completely as the Electric Tower, Czolgosz survived, too, though transformed appropriately enough into musical form. A ballad, sometimes called "Zol-gotz" (his name so rendered for easy singing), or sometimes the "Whitehouse Blues," was widely known. It was performed by the song collector Bascom Lunsford, singing and playing banjo, for the Library of Congress around 1946.

To a melody that jerks and races, Lunsford sings:

> Zol-gotz, mean man
> He shot McKinley with a hand'chif in his hand
> In Buffalo, in Buffalo.

The third verse has a succinct account of what followed:

> The pistol fired and McKinley falls
> And the doctor says, "McKinley, I can't find that ball."
> In Buffalo, in Buffalo.

The penultimate verse goes:

> Seventeen coaches all trimmed in black
> Took McKinley to the graveyard, but never brought
>   him back
> To Buffalo, to Buffalo.

Actually, McKinley's funeral train had seven cars trimmed in black, but *seventeen* fits the measure. (In the last verse, the cars carry Roosevelt to the White House.) In 1926, Charlie Poole, a profane Kentucky wastrel and banjo player who sang in the keening nasal style typical of mountain music, recorded a version of "Whitehouse Blues." In the quarter-century following the assassination, the song had lost all reference to Czolgosz, while adding grotesque humor and a heavy helping of weirdness. The first two verses:

> 'Kinley hollered, 'Kinley squall.
> Doc said, "McKinley, I can't find that ball."
> From Buffalo to Washington.

> Roos-velt in the White House, he's doin' his best.
> 'Kinley in the graveyard, he's takin' his rest.
> He's gone, a long time.

Several other verses, likely pulled from other songs, make the train a larger actor in the story:

> Pain [?] the train, she's just on time.
> She runs a thousand miles from eight o'clock to nine.
> From Buffalo to Washington.

> Yonder comes the train, she's comin' down the line.
> Blowin' every station Mr. M'Kinley's a dyin'
> It's hard times, 't's hard times.

Parts of "Zolgotz" and "Whitehouse Blues" were combined by A. P. Carter to make "The Cannonball," a quick-tempoed ode to moving on, which the Carter Family recorded in Memphis in 1930. It was sung in a rare solo turn by Carter himself in his odd, trembly voice, above driving guitar lines set down by his sister-in-law Maybelle:

> You can wash my jumper, starch my over-hawls
> Catch the train they call the Cannonball
> From Buffalo to Washington.

> Yonder comes the train, comin' down the track
> Carried me away but it ain't gonna carry me back
> My honey babe, my blue-eyed babe.

McKinley's funeral train, less one car, ended up in another song the Carters recorded that same day, "Worried Man Blues."

> The train that I ride sixteen coaches long.
> The train that I ride sixteen coaches long.
> The girl I love's on that train and gone.

If *that* sounds familiar, it's because in 1954, at Sam Philips's Sun Studio in Memphis, a young African-American piano player, Herman "Junior" Parker, and his band, the Blue Flames, recorded "Mystery Train," a suave R&B number Parker wrote, which borrowed more than slightly from A. P. Carter.

Above a jazzy electric guitar regularly plucking minor notes to mimic the motion of a train, Parker croons in a voice about as far from A. P. Carter's as you can get:

> Train I riiiide, sixteen coaches long.
> Train I riiiide, sixteen coaches long.
> That long black train took my baby and gone.

The drummer brushes the hightop snare and bumps to give the sound of cars lurching forward, the feeling is of a sense of long distances traveled, while Parker's long exhaled *Shhhhhh* leaves the impression of a very hip choo-choo indeed.

Two years after *that*, a young, extravagantly handsome Memphis truck driver, already a rising star, half sang, half wailed a guitar-and-bass country jump number which lacked any notion of urban cool:

> Train I ri-i-i-i-ide sixteen coaches long.
> Well that long black train got my baby and gone.
> . . .
> Train, train, comin' 'round 'round the bend.
> Well it took my baby, but it never will again . . .

Elvis's "Mystery Train" was done with a twangy beat eventually known as rockabilly. Though Scotty Moore's quick-tempo guitar lines reached back to Maybelle Carter's playing on "Cannonball Blues," Elvis's voice, by turns gliding and hiccupy, soaring audaciously from bass to alto and back, seemed to come from no place anyone knew before.

Elvis whoops like a train whistle, then laughs at something as the song fades. McKinley's fateful transit through the Temple of Music, forgotten for so long, was a *real* mystery at last.

Hey-Hey

No question, something new was at large in America in 1901—a sense of greater mysteries floating above prevailing ideas of science and progress. The same summer Buffalo held dueling visions of technology and magic, William James presented his Edinburgh lectures that became *The Varieties of Religious Experience,* which argued in favor of what James called a "pluralistic universe," one in which the Christian God might compete on equal terms with other supernatural beings. Also that summer, James's Harvard colleague, the anthropologist Charles Peabody, while excavating a pre-Columbian Indian mound in the Mississippi Delta at Coahoma, became, he said, distracted by strange music. Professor Peabody is not remembered now for any artifacts he uncovered, but for what he discovered in the air, what he called the "extraordinary" songs of the black men working for him.

Two years later, in "Notes on Negro Music," published in the *Journal of American Folklore,* Peabody said the men's singing was unlike anything he'd heard before, something he described as "autochthonous music [of which] it is hard to give an exact account":

> The music of the Negroes . . . may be put under three heads: The songs sung by our men when at work digging . . . unaccompanied; the songs of the same men at quarters or on the march, with guitar accompaniment; and the songs, unaccompanied, of the indigenous Negroes.

(By "indigenous" he meant the men hired in Coahoma rather than those brought from Clarksdale, ten miles away.) Peabody noted the popularity of hymns and that the guitar playing "was mostly ragtime with the instrument seldom venturing beyond the inversions of the three chords of a few major and minor keys."

Of great interest to later folklorists was Peabody's remark that, in the song of one mule driver in particular, he heard "strains of apparently genuine African music. . . . Long phrases that were without apparent measured rhythm, singularly hard to copy in notes."

One evening Peabody heard a woman singing a lullaby "weird in interval and strange in rhythm; peculiarly beautiful," and compared it to something like contemporary Greek singing, albeit "better done." There was another singer,

> a very old Negro employed on the plantation of Mr. John Stovall of Stovall, Mississippi . . . His voice as he sang had a timbre resembling a bagpipe played pianissimo or a jews harp played legato, and to some indistinguishable words he hummed a rhythm of no regularity and notes of apparently not more than three or more [sic] in number at intervals within a semi-tone. The effect again was monotonous but weird, not far from Japanese.

When researchers in the 1960s began an academic search for the roots of blues music, Peabody's account was considered crucial evidence of time and place. Stovall and the neighboring Dockery plantation were already recognized to be the home ground for a generation of musicians born between 1880 and 1910 who made records that embody what has been regarded by many later listeners as the essential blues: a black man's conjuring of hard times with a voice and a guitar.

However, Peabody had qualified his observations in "Notes" with a word that music writers tend to ignore. He wrote "apparently" when citing "genuine African origin." Going forward, the assumption has been that the music *could only* be African. Left unconsidered also is exactly how much African music Peabody was familiar with. More definitely, he had compared what he heard to Japanese music, which, considering the nineteenth-century fad for oriental arts in elite Victorian Boston, was probably something he had at least a passing familiarity with, if only by way of *The Mikado*. More likely Peabody imputed African origin to what he heard strictly on the basis of the skin color of the singers.

The other renowned early account of the blues was written by W. C. Handy in his 1941 autobiography, ambitiously titled *The Father of the Blues*. In 1903 he was a coronet and guitar player leading a small Delta dance orchestra when one night, stuck in the train station at Tutwiler, Mississippi, about thirty miles south of Coahoma and fifteen miles outside Clarksdale,

> A lean, loose-jointed Negro had commenced plunking a guitar beside me while I slept. His clothes were rags; his feet peeped out of his shoes. His face had on it some of the sadness of the ages. As he played, he pressed a knife on the strings of the guitar in a manner popularized by Hawaiian guitarists who used steel bars. The effect was unforgettable. His song, too, struck me instantly.
>
> Goin' where the Southern cross' the Dog.
>
> The singer repeated the line three times, accompanying himself on the guitar with the weirdest music I had ever heard.

Handy and Peabody are usually paired in books like this one as clear evidence of a vivid music unique to the Mississippi Delta. Handy called it "a kind of earth-born music." *Earth-born* is exactly synonymous with *autochthonous*, which is a synonym for *indigenous*. Somewhat undercutting his claim to be the music's father, and the theory of others that it originated in the Delta, Handy also said that it was "familiar throughout the southland."

Peabody's trenchdiggers and Handy's depot guitarist are essential figures in a folklore describing how music rooted in African modalities and created by Mississippi sharecroppers was captured in the recordings of Delta performers, that it was part of the great black migration to the north, especially to Chicago, where it took on an electric, sexy, big-city throb that captured the imaginations of young white people as nothing quite had before. Next stop on the narrative is, inevitably, how it gave birth to rock 'n' roll.

That broad outline is fundamentally correct. But like most broad outlines, it hides a lot. For example, after decades of looking, *no one* has *ever* discovered *any* musical forms in Africa that can be considered to be the clear and unambiguous roots of the blues.

The writer Francis Davis puts it succinctly in *The History of the Blues*: "[T]o hear the blues as a west African import creates its own share of confusion. In the absence of recorded evidence, we can't even trace the blues back to slavery, much less Africa." Blues historians, erring on the side of caution, date the birth of the form to the late nineteenth century, in the wake of reconstruction. As Davis notes, "Even [W.C.] Handy . . . goes on to allow that his 'fondness for that sort of thing' began a decade or so earlier."

If the music was, as Handy said, "familiar throughout the southland," then its origin may well be much earlier than the late nineteenth century, to a time when the Delta was still the haunt of Indian, panther, and bear. Historically, the ubiquity of the music has been credited to itinerant musicians in the minstrel and medicine shows that toured the rural south, playing to black and white audiences, from the 1840s until the Great Depression. Increasing rail connections in the same period, where track miles more than doubled in the South between 1880 and 1890, are also considered an influence.

But we must guard against mistaking catalyst for cause. While increased communication between once-isolated communities undoubtedly helped musical styles evolve, it does not explain why Handy felt the music was at once so familiar and so weird.

By 1925, as Elijah Wald relates in his fine book *Escaping the Delta*, the blues was already a national pop music fad, having begun a few years earlier as a haunting song style of certain female vocal entertainers, mainly, but not exclusively, black: big stars like Mamie Smith, Ma Rainey, Alberta Hunter, Sophie Tucker, and Bessie Smith. If Scott Fitzgerald can be taken as an authority, the blues captured a national mood of sadness and drift among the nation's youth in the wake of World War I. The success of blues records encouraged companies to seek out similar material from a variety of artists.

With the advent of the electronic microphone in 1925, the old harsh, nasal style of singing, useful at a time when singers had to be *heard* in noisy places, gave way for subtler vocal effects, including quietly sung phrases, spoken asides, and falsetto vocals. In his book *Deep Blues*, the writer Robert Palmer notes specifically that falsetto singing is an African effect. Bantu vocalizing, he wrote, "includes whooping, or sudden jumping into falsetto range, which seems to derive from the pygmies who were the area's original inhabitants."

In raising the idea of an indigenous geographic influence on musical style, Palmer never considers what connection Peabody's ditchdiggers, with whom he begins *Deep Blues,* may have had with the *original inhabitants* of Coahoma County. Neither does he mention that falsetto singing is also a feature of Native American music, where it represents the voices of spirits.

One senses something in Palmer's writing that the author can't quite name. Consider his description of Muddy Waters, born McKinley Morganfield, on the occasion of Waters's first recording session, in a shack in Stovall in 1940, for the song collector Alan Lomax: "Muddy was a vigorous twenty-six-year-old," Palmer writes, "with high cheekbones and cool hooded eyes, features that lent him a certain Oriental inscrutability."

The question of North America's original, or indigenous, inhabitants hardly ever comes up in popular histories of

American music, the assumption being that the land inhabited by the European arrivals, and their slaves, had been mainly clear of earlier people and empty of song. Africa and the British Isles were seen as the only possible sources of the music that evolved from that place and time. The *possibility* that the musical traditions of indigenous peoples might be central to American harmony has never been articulated, much less considered at length.

This is pretty remarkable, not only because so many of the musicians—black, white, and brown—had pronounced Native American roots, but by the given historical details of the settlement of the North American continent. Professor Peabody's reactions to the workmen's songs—"monotonous" and "weird," he said—is pretty much how Europeans described American Indian music. That Peabody may have been closer to the mark when he said the music sounded Asian is, for many, counterintuitive.

Between 1600 and 1840, three cultures—Native American, African, and European—each with a highly evolved choral tradition, came to encounter one another, in war and peace, by choice and under duress, in the old and new settlements of the vast American interior east of the Mississippi. To assume that only *one* of these cultures predominated in how the music evolved, or that another had no influence *whatsoever*, flies not only against logic but also in the face of any practical knowledge about how musicians work.

Consider also how connected to the specific landscape the Indigenous tradition would have been. If any musical style prevailed, it was probably the one that reflected the *strangeness* of the new land to those who had only recently, either by force or choice, arrived there; one that also reflected the despair, the *blues*, of those who saw the old way of life die.

Our accepted history says the blues is of African origin, and that any blue notes heard on early country music records, and there are a lot of high and lonesome twangs, got there by way of black musicians that the white musicians heard.

But something about that accepted history doesn't add up. After almost half a century of extensive research and, beginning in the 1960s, a wave of associated books, blues antecedents in Africa remain undocumented. Though certain traditions of musicianship, along with the banjo, can be traced there, nobody's proved that the regular rhythms, tonic intervals, vocal techniques, and the individual let-me-tell-you-how-things-are-with-me at the heart of blues music are originally African. Contemporary writers, such as Bruce Cook, Francis Davis, Elijah Wald, and Marybeth Hamilton, have maintained for over a decade that the origin of the blues is empirically unknowable, that the idea that the blues is even a distinct musical form is a nostalgic social fiction created by white songcatchers and record collectors.

Hundreds of blues songs were recorded in the 1920s and '30s by black and white rural musicians from one end of the South to the other, the tip of an aural history that stretches back into the acoustic past, the music of churches, dance halls, political campaigns, neighborhood socials, minstrels, and medicine shows.

And given the ubiquity of the music across the South, and the flexibility of its form, we might consider if, rather than being transmitted from blacks to whites, the blues had been gained commonly by both; and that what we now call blues and country music are divergent branches of a single root, one indigenous to North America.

The blues—the popular twentieth-century song form—came first from the *blues*, a way of feeling in music. The flattened notes and vocal swoops, those high and lonesome sounds, sung by some as a hoot and by others like a yodel, were heard in Texas and Oklahoma, Virginia and Tennessee. Those sounds varied, of course, from region to region, depending on what different people wanted to hear, but not so much as to be unrecognizable.

There was, indeed, something like a shock of recognition when phonograph records finally let people at one end of the South hear music from the other. Black people in Arkansas enjoyed country stars like Jimmie Rodgers and Uncle Dave Macon. One mountain musician, Roscoe Holcomb, years later recalled first hearing a blues record by Blind Lemon Jefferson, a black man from Texas, and feeling something inside himself set free.

In 1928, some Creek musicians from Oklahoma, Big Chief Henry's Indian String Band, recorded a novelty record called "Indian Tom Tom," a sprightly, two-and-a-half-minute number with a bouncy Native American chant backed by a swinging fiddle and guitar. What's so interesting about the song is not the melding of two putatively unrelated styles, but how *easily* the older form fits into the newer one.

So there might be something wrong with our history. The hidden story of American music is spread, like dinosaur bones in the Gobi, in plain sight across a landscape of old 78s. And if those bones have not been noticed, it's because people decided they shouldn't be.

For 250 years, when the far west was still east of the Mississippi, three cultures clashed and combined in the great American interior. It might not be a coincidence that what is now considered the cradle of country music—east Tennessee, western Virginia and North Carolina, northern sections of Georgia and Alabama—covers exactly that land held by the Cherokee Nation at the end of the American Revolution.

History, of course, says that the Cherokee were forced out, rounded up by the Army and transported to the Oklahoma territory, a district set aside by the federal government in the early 1830s as a final homeland of the Native American nations of the East and Midwest. The South was cleared of its indigenous inhabitants in one decade. The Cherokee transit, in 1839, was the last and also one of the harshest, called now The Trail of Tears.

But history, it turns out, misses a lot; southerners were mostly interested in bottom land for cotton planting. Those Cherokee living far up mountain hollers in Virginia and North Carolina, some two thousand of them by one estimate, stayed where they were, either passing as white or protected by such white neighbors and kin they had.

Note too that the legendary Mississippi Delta is in fact a misnomer, being the broad alluvial plain of the Yazoo River, which joins the Mississippi between the bluffs of Memphis and Vicks-burg two hundred miles downstream. Nearly all of the Yazoo delta was swamp until the 1880s. By then, the cotton land in the rest of the old Confederacy was exhausted from over-farming and infested with boll weevils. A syndicate of plantation owners began to drain and clear the Yazoo swamp with gangs of black workers. The work gradually revealed an immense level plain of black, wildly fertile soil that yielded astonishing harvests of cotton.

Much of the land remained wild into the twentieth century. "Even now," reads a 1907 account, "deer, bears, panthers, wolves, and deadly snakes are not infrequent." It was, in fact, the last untouched land east of the Mississippi.

> The forests which still cover a large area are composed of a variety of trees—sycamore, ash, elm, hackberry, hickory, and more distinctively, the cypress, tupelo gum, the red and black gums, and the holly. The oaks, of which there are many species, are decorated with clusters of mistletoe; grapevines hang in myriad ropes and tangles; woodbines and other creepers clamber to the tops of the tallest trees, and palmettos give a semi-tropical aspect to the woods.

High-water berms formed by regular flooding created natural levees, which the first inhabitants built upon. These high grounds were flood refuges, home sites, and burial places for successive waves of Native people, and were home to the Natchez, Choctaw, and others at the European arrival in the early sixteenth century. The Spanish did not bother the Indians much, but around 1730 the French cleared out the Natchez, with Choctaw help, who themselves were removed to Indian Territory slightly more than a hundred years later.

But *removal* mainly stands for the invisibility the young American republic granted the Indians. The Mississippi WPA guide states that the Tunica people, who earlier lived along the Mississippi, "emigrated to Louisiana [in 1817] where they intermarried with both the French and the Negro," implying that that somehow they stopped being Native Americans. The WPA guide also says that three thousand Choctaws, in spite of the 1830 treaty, "refused to leave Mississippi [and] still till the soil of their ancestors." The number of Choctaws who stayed is by some estimates thought to have been as high as seven thousand, living in the deeper reaches of the Yazoo delta, too hard to reach on land too wet to plow. The Creeks, a people composed of the shattered clans of other tribes, were sent west from Alabama in 1836, though several hundred of them managed to stay right where they were.

Only slightly better known is that the southern Native nations were slave-owning societies, one more European custom adopted by affluent members of the so-called five civilized tribes. Consequently, hundreds of slaves were transported to Oklahoma as property. To recall a time when cruelty like this was given the cover of law is, in no small way, to criticize everything that followed upon. Better then that people forgot.

Indigenous people have never based tribal membership along racial lines. Though a child of a Native mother was automatically a member of the tribe, membership was also conferred by adoption, a practice that became more and more common as native populations collapsed after exposure to European diseases. Consequently a person may look Indian and lack tribal status, while others who resemble mainstream Americans are tribal members. It cannot be emphasized enough that culture defines kinship.

It is more interesting that, however McKinley Morganfield appeared to the song collector Alan Lomax (and Lomax was fond of reputing Chinese admixture among Delta blacks), Morganfield told Lomax his name was Muddy Water (adding the plural s when he got to Chicago)—a name, he explained later, his grandmother gave him for how much he liked playing in puddles when he was a boy.

Muddy's near Mississippi neighbor, and chief professional rival in Chicago, Chester Arthur Burnett, was called Wolf by his grandfather, a Choctaw named John Jones, Wolf said, for the animal which still prowled the Delta when Chester was a boy. (He added *Howlin'* when he turned pro.) These two names, drawn from early encounters with the natural world and kept by those men through life as formative signs of power and accomplishment, are, of course, Indigenous emblems and eventually came to be more real than their Christian names, now known to only devoted fans.

In his introduction to a 2000 edition of collected blues histories from the 1960s, Paul Oliver, the dean of blues historians, concedes that "as the twentieth century has drawn to a close, there has been an increasing awareness of the most intractable problem in the history of the blues: how it began."

He was likely thinking about Bruce Cook's admirably contrarian 1995 book, *Listen to the Blues*, written as a particular rebuttal to the theory, held by Oliver, that the blues held specific elements (*retentions* is the word used) of the music of Mali and the Senegambia. "And while there is no disputing that the blues is essentially Negro music," Cook writes, "we can certainly question the implication that it was cut from whole cloth (or at least that the cloth was quite so black in color)." Cook had put to rest any myth of absolute and unilateral African transmission, quoting musicologist Richard A. Waterman:

> There are no African retentions, as such, in the blues. But undoubtedly influence was great in determining the form the blues was to take. Just how we can go on specifying the extent of this influence is a question still open to debate.

Cook also includes the expert testimony of Buddy Guy, who, after a trip to Africa, said he didn't hear any relation between African music and the blues.

> [D]on't start me to lyin', because I don't. Not of what I've heard yet. No, I mean, I met some people there and they told me that this is where it all came from,

you know, and I haven't found anything yet . . . The
blues is a different thing, man. I mean, ain't no sense
of me lyin', 'cause you know better. The blues is, you
know, a feelin'. You got to feel it to play it.

In his 1981 travel memoir, *The Roots of the Blues*, the musician Samuel Charters, who studied the early form of the music in
his 1959 book *The Country Blues* (indeed, the title soon defined a
genre), describes a trip along the Gambia River to Banjul, Mali,
searching for that link. Charters went to Senegal to study the
griots, singers of tribal biography and history. Itinerant musicians
who accompany themselves on the kora, a harp-like, 21-string
instrument, griots were felt to be early exemplars of bluesmen
like Charlie Patton, Henry Thomas, and Robert Johnson. The
problem with that theory, for blues history anyway, was that
Charters found nothing in the griot repertory, or their role in
society, with any American parallels.

Griot songs were mainly long litanies in praise of, and
commissioned by, local chiefs, offering extensive ancestral detail.
The private world of personal sorrow and resolve at the center
of the blues—told in simple, repetitive verses, regular rhythm,
and a standard three chords—was unknown in the west African
tradition.

By the end of his trip, Charters

understood, finally, that in the blues I hadn't found a
music that was part of the old African life and culture . . . The blues represented something else. It was
essentially a new kind of song begun with the new life
in the American South.

Earlier, Charters had seen something at a festival that looked
familiar.

In one of the groups I could see more than seventy
boys dancing around [a] spirit figure . . . [which]

stumbled along in confusion, his spindly body hung with a felted, festooned costume so heavy it weighed him down.

This recalled, he says, a Mardi Gras morning in New Orleans twenty-five years earlier, where he'd seen "an older boy in a wildly colorful costume . . . white dyed feathers hanging from the arms and legs, and crowning all of it, a magnificent Indian headdress, its beaded headband slipping down over his painted face."

For Charters, the Mardi Gras Indian's costume was "an exuberant exaggeration of something that may have been worn for one of Buffalo Bill's Wild West Shows." But Choctaws once participated in the Catholic carnival as enthusiastically as that remote city's Latin and African inhabitants, long before Andrew Jackson got to town, much less Bill Cody.

Slave-owning allies of the French who lived along the Mississippi far north of the city, Choctaws were more welcome in the revelry than blacks: "In the early years of Mardi Gras, blacks were banned from the main parades and 'masking Indian,' as it's called, was a ruse for inclusion." Apparently, racial boundaries in that colonial city were as ambiguous as upriver property lines.

The New Orleans Indians whom Charters witnessed that Mardi Gras morning sang songs, he recalled, with "incomprehensible words or phrases," such as,

Here we're runnin' in the Indian land
Hey, hey To Weh Bakaweh.

Perhaps because his African voyage had borne such scant fruit, Charters was drawn to a conclusion that appears to be based more on wishing than observation: "I understood for the first time that the phrases I thought were incomprehensible like 'To Weh Bakaweh . . .' must be African."

That the words may well have been picked up while "runnin' in the Indian land" and that *Weh Bakaweh* sounds more like patois for the archaic *Way back a-ways* possibly never dawned on him. Instead, Charters decides that *Bakaweh* must be "from one of the languages along this coast. [But] I was never able to locate it."

It is not my intention to pick on Sam Charters, a fine and knowledgeable writer who has done more for the recognition and appreciation of idiomatic American music than most anyone. However, to overlook the possible Indigenous American origins of what was so vividly presented before his eyes and ears that Mardi Gras morning indicates something like a fundamental dislocation, a culture-wide bias which no old 78s, by themselves, could possibly triangulate away.

Inside that Mardi Gras chant is an exclamation used with such ubiquity in American popular song that it's almost invisible, two words that appear over and again, from Jimmie Rodgers's "Blue Yodel #10" to Henry Thomas's "Cottonfield Blues." Betty Lou DeMorrow uses them to great effect in a smutty little ditty from 1933 called "Feels So Good"; Bobby Darin gave them a hip, Vegas snap in "Mack the Knife"; they're the refrain of Oklahoma-born Woody Guthrie's "New York Town," and they kick-off the second verse of the first original song Bob Dylan ever released: "Hey-hey, Woody Guthrie, I wrote you a song."

In his Thunder Being vision, which he described to John Neihardt, the Sioux medicine man Black Elk saw a "black hail cloud, still standing yonder watching, filled with voices crying 'Hey-hey! Hey-hey!' They were cheering and rejoicing that my work was being done. And all the people now were happy and rejoicing, sending voices back, 'hey-hey, hey-hey.'"

It was a common exclamation of the Plains peoples, intended to call the attention of the spirits, either in joy or regret. Black Elk also told Neihardt that they were the last words of Crazy Horse after he was bayonetted by an Army private at Fort Robertson, Nebraska, in 1877.

Hey-hey.

My, my.

In examining the particular nature of Delta-style blues, early researchers soon focused on one man, Charlie Patton, whose recordings and performances inspired a generation of musicians (chief among them Howlin' Wolf and Roebuck "Pops" Staples) before his 1934 death.

Patton, the top Delta performer for almost 20 years, spent his adult life traveling. A farmer's son who lived among farming people, by all accounts Patton disdained manual labor; he depended on various women for support, and had several wives. Friends said he generally considered himself better than others, *especially* darker-skinned African Americans, and was prone to back up his prejudices with drunken brawling.

Despite his temper, Patton was mainly recalled with an affection bordering on reverence. "He was a really great man," Staples recalled. Howlin' Wolf said he followed Patton whenever he could, begging him for lessons. The local record company scout, Henry Spier, a white who brought Patton to Paramount Records, thought Charlie was the best performer he ever saw.

Patton's contemporaries made vivid, often haunting records: "Sleepy" John Estes, Skip James, and "Mississippi" John Hurt, for example. Son House—a younger man who performed with Patton—had a strident vocal delivery and played steel guitar with a stark power that the more fastidious Patton never delivered on record. It is House who is now considered, for all the midnight dread his music calls up, the first distinctly Delta-style blues musician.

But as a picture of Patton emerged in interviews with surviving musicians, fans, and record company executives, and as more was learned about his role as mentor and teacher, he was judged the central figure of an astonishing musical movement, a tradition that stretches from Handy's Tutwiler station guitarist to Robert Johnson, Muddy Waters, Howlin' Wolf, and Buddy Guy.

"Different [players] from different places would come and try to learn from Uncle Charlie," his niece remembered, "and they would hang on to him, trying to learn how to play like he could play . . . When they couldn't learn, Uncle Charlie dropped them and catch on to the best ones." Wolf idolized Patton, going to hear him wherever he could, trying to copy how he played. One night at a juke joint, "Patton heard the young man plinking away outside. He marched out, grabbed [Wolf] and said, 'Come on up here and play with me son!' "

"The Indian boy learns the legendary history of his nation coincidentally with its songs," observed one early study, "and the vocally gifted youngsters are carefully taught by the old men and women to the end that no song of the tribe be forgotten." Patton was determined to transmit *something*, and though Wolf was a foot-and-a-half taller and probably outweighed him by at least a hundred pounds, Patton felt no compunction about soundly cuffing his giant student upside his head if he thought the kid wasn't concentrating.

The fad for CD box sets has made Patton's singing and playing more accessible now than it's ever been. Digital technology has cleared away as much record noise as possible, and interest in his music has grown in the last few years. It is something of a miracle that Patton's recordings survive at all. His record masters were sold for scrap after Paramount Records went bankrupt. Some records exist only in single copies, and those so worn as to present the ears, in spite of the pronounced noise reduction afforded by modern digital technology, with a hissing curtain of decay.

Though Paramount was the top blues label, it was the subsidiary of a Wisconsin furniture manufacturer. Its inferior shellac disks wore out quickly, creating a vexing scrim of white noise between the music and modern listeners. This blizzard of sound now adds even greater urgency to Patton's music. There was always something insistent in the sound of his voice, a measure of his will that demanded to be heard. And Patton's music has survived with a weight and power that his first listeners could never have known.

The very recent discovery of a full portrait photo of him, a publicity shot made for Paramount, only adds a haunted corporeal aspect to his return to audible life. It is the only known, indisputable photograph of Patton in existence, most likely taken in Milwaukee in 1929, discovered in the family archives of a former Paramount employee only in 2001. Before then, Patton's one likeness was a grainy headshot cropped from that full portrait and used in ads for his records.

The full likeness is a revelation, showing a slight, swarthy man wearing a suit coat too big for him, a collar shirt, and a rakish bow tie. He lounges alertly in a high backed chair with a guitar on his lap. He holds it with the fingers of his left hand splayed across the neck in a way that will perplex any guitarist. Famous for his clowning (Son House's word) while performing, Patton is either giving a hint to his open-tuning playing style or shamelessly goofing. Every inch a dandy, he crosses his legs casually, one knee resting above the other in baggy, cuffed trousers. His shoes are polished and he is wearing spats.

But stranger than Patton's extravagant footwear, or the way he holds his guitar, is that part of the photo that is the most familiar, his face.

He was at least thirty-nine when the picture was taken, but looks barely out of his teens. Though dark, Patton is clearly of some European descent. Most of his Delta contemporaries called him an Indian. His hair, parted on the left and pasted down, is straight and fine and appears to have amber highlights. The expression on his face is as enigmatic as his possible origins. He neither smiles nor scowls, just looks past the camera, avoiding its stare and so ours. There is a visible seriousness to his pose, something alert and deliberate, a holdover from the portrait photographs of the previous century, which even by 1930 had not entirely gone out of style.

It is Patton's ears, which stick out like the moth-wing folds of his bow tie, that demand the most attention. Bing Crosby had the same ears; so did country musicians like A. P. Carter, Dock Boggs, Charlie Poole, and, later, Hank Williams. W. C. Handy wrote in his autobiography that, according to his "Grandma Thumuthis," his own jug ears "indicated a talent for music." Whether or not big ears signified a greater capacity to hear and transmit music in the preindustrial past, they appear as an apt and pervasive ornament on many rural musicians.

Patton's music has a frantic extravagance; his deep voice divides again and again into a variety of growling vocal effects, spoken, sung, and sometimes groaned. His guitar playing, like the way he's holding the guitar in that picture, confounds contemporary analysis—strange pitches and loping tempos. Crowned the King of the Delta Blues fifty years after he died, Patton inspired younger players with his skill as an entertainer and by the rambling, irresponsible, dandified figure he cut. And while other musicians worked to pick up a few of his style points in dressing, and a lick here and there, no one copied the way Patton played. *That* was impossible.

It is generally agreed that Patton was singing and playing guitar in public by 1910, both alone and with other musicians, mostly fiddlers and guitarists. Hearsay has it that he learned how to play from Earl Harris, an older man of considerable mystery, a drifter who never made records, considered by some to be the first identifiable blues performer. (Some suspect Harris was the guitarist Handy heard at Tutwiler.)

Whenever Patton began his education, he was clearly a seasoned pro when he made his first records in 1929. Though he mainly recorded blues songs, people recalled that Patton played and sang a variety of tunes: two-steps, rags, waltzes, and Tin Pan Alley standards. A passage from Howlin' Wolf's biography gives a great sense of the man's appeal:

> Patton was the best guitarist in the Delta . . . snapping and bending strings with his fingers or making them sob and moan with a slide, he attacked the neck of his instrument like a hound dog shaking a stick. An astounding showman, he beat his guitar like a drum, played it between his legs or behind his head, rode it like a pony, and threw it up in the air and spun it, all the while maintaining a driving dance beat in 4/4 time with the accent on the 2 and 4—a metric novelty that he popularized and may have invented.

All of the above appear on two sides from his first session: "Down the Dirt Road Blues" and "Pony Blues." On "Dirt Road," Patton effects an eerie jangling by rapidly plucking the high strings while stomping his feet in a galloping beat. The effect sounds more like a drum and rattle than anything from a guitar. The song itself is as much chanted as sung, an anthem of embarkation, though it takes some effort to understand what he's saying:

I'm goin' away-y-y-y-y-y to a land unknown. [?]
I'm goin' away-y-y-y-y-y to a land unknown.
I'm worried now but I won't be worried long.

My rider has something, she tryin' to keep it hid.
My rider has something, she tryin' to keep it hid.
Lord, I got somthin' to find that dawther [?] with.

I feel like choppin' chips flyin' everywhere.
I feel like choppin' chips flyin' everywhere.
I been to the Nation, mmm Lord but I couldn't stay
    there.

Instead of "chips flyin' everywhere" one could be excused for thinking Patton is singing "chil'ren I've everywhere," which was apparently the case. Many words in Patton's recordings were clarified by his surviving friends in interviews years later; Son House admitted there were some phrases he never did understand.

The "Nation" where Charlie could not stay was the popular term for Oklahoma Indian territory, which disappeared when Oklahoma became a state in 1907. "The Nation" appears in lyrics to a number of songs recorded in the twenties and thirties.

In his "Shanty Blues," "Texas" Henry Thomas sings:

I'm going to the Nation,
I ain't gonna make no trouble.
Show me a woman anybody can trust.
Cause me to weep, cause me to moan,
Cause me to leave my home.

While Andrew Baxter, a black Cherokee fiddle player from Georgia, sings in "Bamalong Blues":

Been to the Nation and I just got back.
Been to the Nation and I just got back.
Been to the Nation and I just got back.
Didn't get no money, but I brought the sack.

No one today is sure exactly what "Bamalong" means, though some guess it is a variant of "Babylon," which makes little linguistic sense when Baxter sings in the first verse, "I ain't gonna be in the second Bamalong." If, though, he is singing about a second 'Bama, a home for people forced from the *first* Alabama, then that report of comings and goings from the Nation holds up. "I ain't gonna be in the second 'Bama long" is not too removed from "I been to the Nation, Lord I couldn't stay there."

The ubiquity of verses regarding comings and goings from Oklahoma Indian Territory speaks to a common, if not exactly broad, experience among southern blacks. Indeed, in the wake of the Civil War many blacks left the Old South for Oklahoma. Many Oklahoma blacks, the descendants of slaves first transported with their masters in the 1830s, went back to the old Confederacy, only to return, sometimes years later, to seek tribal membership or residence on the reservations. The bids of many of these returnees were denied by tribal authorities (hundreds of cases documented by the Dawes Commission are still on file in Washington); consequently, "Didn't get no money, but I brought the sack" was once something like news.

There is a sense of admonishment buried in the songs too. The third verse of Baxter's "Bamalong Blues" goes:

You didn't want me, don't you dog me 'round.
You didn't want me, don't you dog me 'round.
I didn't come here to be nobody's dog.

While Henry Thomas sings a very old verse:

You caused me to weep,
You caused me to moan,
You caused me to leave my home.

In 1835, some twenty-three thousand Creek Indians, along with about nine hundred of their slaves, were taken from Georgia to Oklahoma. A witness to their forced march later wrote that

> an old woman carrying a small bundle of her belong-
> ings . . .began a *sad song* which was later taken up by
> the others . . . "I have no more land. I am driven away
> from home, driven up the red waters, let us all go, let
> us die together." (emphasis mine)

It is no exaggeration to say that, by 1890, song lyrics about "weeping," "moaning," and "leaving home" probably resonated far more to the survivors of the ethnic cleansing of a half-century earlier, a song sung in code to white America, than any heartsick lovers, black or white, mooning around the Victrola. The blues are songs of resilience, not resignation, of course. But if we just change "die" to "live" in that Creek woman's song, we would sure enough find a world of blues.

In their cranky biography of Patton, Steven Calt and Gayle Wardlow take specific issue with the notion that Charlie was Native American: "If either parent was of Indian descent, theirs was a distinction shared by less than two percent of Mississippi's colored population [in 1880]." But in the wake of Reconstruction, as the South sank into a swamp of racial paranoia, the designation "colored" came to mean only "nonwhite." At the same time, the census characterized people with even one-sixteenth African parentage as "Negro"—the so-called One Drop Rule. Consequently, an Indian with one black great-grandparent could easily become a Negro, while a white man with a single Indian great-grandparent suffered no parallel shift in official status.

Broadly speaking, Indians with some European parentage remained classified as "Indian," those with close African relations were inevitably judged "Negro." By such niceties in nomenclature were a people allowed to vanish, an opportunity that, considering the brutal weight of history, many might have accepted with no small relief. This way, too, Indians who might still claim a status as an independent and sovereign people were mainly eliminated, while blacks, who had no rights in the first place, replaced them in nearly equal numbers.

Which is one way 250 years of history gets erased in about 20.

The sad truth remains that there's no way of knowing for certain what Native American music sounded like at the European advent. Contemporary accounts, mainly of missionaries, only emphasize its strangeness, a combination of drums and wailing. "Several times have I assembled the urchins to join in sacred song," notes a character in Fenimore Cooper's *The Last of the Mohicans* (1826), a ragged frontier choirmaster describing his efforts to teach hymns to Mingo children, "and as often have they responded to my efforts with whoopings and howlings that have chilled my soul."

"The so-called settlement of America," writes historian Francis Jennings, "was a *resettlement*, a reoccupation of a land made waste by diseases and demoralization introduced by the newcomers." The survivors of once-formidable tribes, most of which collapsed in a generation, might join traditional rivals or create, as with the Mississippi Creeks, the Lumbee in North Carolina and the Florida Seminoles, a new nation from the remains of several others.

Though the tribes along the Mississippi suffered a population collapse as severe as that of the coastal New England nations, it occurred out of the sight of Europeans. The tribes of the vast interior forests along the eastern and western sides of the Appalachians, from northern Georgia into northern New York, though suffering great losses, avoided the worst effects of the epidemics. They held on to the steep, densely wooded terrain that made them a force very much to be reckoned with in the first three centuries of European settlement.

Iroquois was the French name of people who called themselves "Hodenosaunee." They ran the European fur trade from the Hudson River to the western extreme of Lake Superior, and from the St. Lawrence into parts of Virginia, where they regularly warred against their distant Cherokee cousins. The Iroquois mainly advanced Britain's interests over France, but were cagey enough to play each against the other.

The Cherokee's lands included what is now West Virginia, most of Tennessee, the Virginia mountains, and the hills of northern Georgia and Alabama. So long as there remained international competition for commercial license of the American interior, those two main tribes, and their allies, held final advantage on the ground.

The French and Indian War, for years called Washington's War in honor of the rash Virginia militia lieutenant who started it by attacking the French Fort Duquesne, gave Canada to the English, ending European rivalry in North America. Where once "military alliances kept settlers off Indian lands west of a line a hundred miles or so inland from the St. Lawrence River to the Gulf of Mexico," Indian wars thereafter, observes Anthony F.C. Wallace, "were fought primarily about land."

The English mainly attempted a just administration of Indian concerns, in effect using the natural boundary of the Appalachian/Blue Ridge chain to separate seaboard colonies from Indian territory. The Iroquois and Cherokee were broadly sympathetic to the British cause during the Revolution. Western settlers had shown little respect for the Crown's agreements with Indigenous nations in the first place, and were pleased to take the fight to them when they had the chance. Indeed, for two years, while the British mostly held the seaboard, the Colonial Army waged total war against England's Native allies in Ohio and western New York.

As usual, Indians scored some impressive early wins, but were no match for the manpower, persistence, and total-war tactics of the American army. They eventually suffered devastating defeats, especially the Seneca in western New York, who underwent a series of massacres and the wholesale destruction of towns and cropland. The martial capacity of the Iroquois was crushed.

Iroquois country was afterwards divided by treaties with the American government and sold off, the Mohawk and Seneca retaining isolated reservations in Canada and in the northern and western regions of New York State. These remained largely intact, if destitute, holdings into the twentieth century. Even though the Cherokee had suffered fewer losses in the war just concluded, and came out of it with a fairly secure legal and social standing, within sixty years their land was taken and most lived in Oklahoma.

Between 1790 and 1830, the Cherokee made an astounding cultural expansion that brought them on par with white society. A written phonic alphabet was created, encouraging a fad for reading and writing. A bilingual newspaper soon followed. Crops were diversified, weaving and forging introduced, along with the holding of livestock. Wealthy Cherokee, mainly drawn from the families of mixed Native and European backgrounds, began a plantation system of agriculture and held slaves. Though interested in cultural accommodation, the Cherokee also insisted on sovereign nation status and, after a final territorial concession in 1794, refused to cede any more land to the United States.

The War of 1812 drew aggrieved tribes—the Delaware and Shawnee in Ohio; Creeks, Chickasaws, and Choctaw in Alabama and Mississippi; and the Seminole, in what was still Spanish Florida—to take up arms against the United States. The result, of course, was no better than earlier conflicts. Though Cherokee fighters had joined Andrew Jackson's campaign against the Creeks in Alabama and the British in New Orleans, the postwar mood among southern whites was not to admit any difference between *good* Indians and bad.

As early as 1810, conservative Cherokee accepted the government's offer of land in Arkansas. By 1817, eastern Cherokee had a government with a bicameral legislature, judiciary, and executive branch. A new constitution, modeled on the United States,' was ratified in 1827, declaring the Cherokee nation "sovereign and independent." For the State of Georgia, this was unacceptable: "Left to themselves the Cherokees would become a prosperous, independent commonwealth, and they would never sell their land (indeed, by Cherokee law, the further sale of land to the United States was a crime)." In December 1828, following

Jackson's election, the state legislature assumed jurisdiction over the Cherokee homeland.

In 1827, Martin Van Buren toured Georgia and the Carolinas looking to marry the desires of planters to the needs of New York merchants. The outcome of this was the creation of the Democratic Party and the election of Andrew Jackson president. Though Jackson had won his most important military victories with Native help, he roundly despised the resident southern tribes. Southerners wanted Indians out of Georgia, Alabama, and Mississippi, and Jackson was pleased to oblige.

Indian relocation became official federal policy with the Indian Removal Act of 1830, which, justified in measured humanitarian terms, passed after close votes in Congress, and in opposition to a ruling by the Supreme Court, never enforced, which struck down Georgia's 1828 law.

By 1839 Indian removal was largely accomplished, completed during Van Buren's administration. Jackson retired to his plantation near Nashville, where his sons-in-law got rich on insider sales of Cherokee land, and where he was certainly able to witness, if he so chose, the wretched procession of Cherokee as they filed past the town that winter.

Census figures recorded that the Cherokee brought with them around two thousand slaves; the Creeks traveled with nine hundred; the Chickasaw had 1,156. Just as interesting is the number of Indians who managed to stay in harsh landscapes where no authority dared follow. Besides the Choctaw and Chickasaw who vanished into the remote reaches of the Yazoo swamp, approximately one thousand Cherokee moved into the hills of North Carolina. An unknown, though large, number of Creeks and runaway slaves joined the polyglot Seminole.

During the Civil War, the southern Indian nations in the Territory mainly cast their lot with the Confederacy, further antagonizing the federal government. The war over, and plains tribes offering the latest, and last, armed resistance to white settlement, any widespread public sympathy for Native Americans had vanished. An army that had only recently laid waste to large sections of the South was sent west to focus its rage on Native people there. Over the next thirty years, plains Indians were herded like cattle and slaughtered like buffalo.

A treaty in 1866 finally abolished slavery in the Oklahoma Territory and dictated enrollment of freedmen into their former owners' tribes. These reparations were far more than anything required of white slave owners. Perhaps as a consequence, relations since between the two groups has been freighted with ill will. The Chickasaws, who had a reputation for treating slaves harshly, offered their freedmen nothing.

After 1900, as the government prepared the final assumption of Indian land into the Union, the Dawes commission was set up to establish land rights for freedmen in the new state of Oklahoma ahead of the wide privatization of tribal land. Testimony, sworn and corroborated, was taken for several years regarding former ownership, parentage, and established residence at Emancipation for thousands of people. By 1900, over twenty thousand blacks were given some form of tribal recognition, while at least as many were refused. And so the verse "I been to the Nation, mmmm, Lord I couldn't stay there" was once news.

It wasn't until after the plains tribes had been confined, during the era of Wild West shows, that anything like a comprehensive survey of Native American music was made. Even then, it was limited to those people west of the Mississippi in which the old ways were still in living memory.

A groundbreaking study appeared in 1893, a monograph from the Peabody Museum, *A Study of Omaha Indian Music*, written by the ethnologist Alice Fletcher. Soon after beginning fieldwork with the Omaha a decade before, Fletcher became seriously ill and spent several months, she said, recuperating in the field, "ministered to in part by Indian friends . . . [who] would often at my request sing for me." In hearing the Indians, what had begun as a frustrating case study suddenly took on a new life. Fletcher recalled, "They sang softly because I was weak and there was no drum, and then it was that the distraction of noise and the confusion of theory were dispelled, and the sweetness, the beauty and meaning of these songs were revealed to me." Her paper describes broad characteristics she found in Indian music and, with the help of two assistants, one Native American, the other a classically trained musician, provided piano transcriptions, admitted approximations, of Indian songs.

The scores' tempi, meant to stand for drumming, vary wildly, though 2/4 and 4/4 rhythms predominate. There was no melody to speak of, or it was rather utterly flexible to the needs of the singer and lyric, chants usually of one or two phrases repeated over and over. There was no set key; rather, each singer used whatever felt comfortable to them. Though the remarkable variety and uses of songs, Fletcher reported, could change among tribes, styles were widely transmitted: "Indian songs I have discovered travel far, and those of one tribe are soon at home in another."

Vocal techniques included tremolo effects and falsetto and bass singing. Descriptive mimicry, of voices and rhythms, also played a significant role. The songs used a pentatonic (five note) scale, a de facto blues form, and abrupt modal jumps, to tonic fifth and seventh (so called blue) notes, were employed frequently in the transcriptions made by Fletcher's assistants.

Indian songs, Fletcher noted, were often specific testimonies of the singers themselves, using words that were often "taken apart or modified so as to make them more melodious. [Many songs] are furnished wholly with syllables which are not parts or even fragments of words but sounds that lend themselves easily to singing."

That the above also describes something a lot like yodeling, or moaning, should not be overlooked. Indeed the vocal techniques of such Delta performers as Howlin' Wolf, Charlie Patton, Ishmon Bracey, and Robert Johnson are all characterized by techniques Fletcher observed among Omaha singers. Another blues player, a street preacher from Texas, Blind Willie Johnson, recorded only religious numbers and was noted for his open-tuned slide guitar playing and growling singing voice. (Johnson's growl especially resembles the throat-singing still extant in remote parts of Asia.) His wordless, moaning, three-minute slide guitar meditation on the Crucifixion, "Dark is the Night," is transfixing, one of the essential expressions of the American soul.

"Music is no mere diversion from the Indian point of view," the musicologist Frederick R. Burton wrote in 1909.

> It is not separated from ordinary experience by being classed as an art, but is a feature of daily homely use and necessity. The Indian has a song for everything— his gods, his friends, and his enemies, the animals he hunts, the maiden he woos, the forest that sighs around him.

Though redolent of running-maiden romanticism, and ignoring the role of female vocalists, Burton grasped music's essential presence for Native people. When W. C. Handy describes how he came to comprehend music in childhood, his language is nearly the same:

> As a child I had not heard the Pipe of Pan, but pastoral melody was nevertheless a very real thing to me. Whenever I heard the song of a bird . . . I could visualize the notes in the scale . . . I knew the gait of horses by the rhythm of their hooves. As I grew older I added the saxophonic wailing of the moo-cows and the clarinets of the moody whippoorwills . . . *This was the primitive prelude to the mature melodies recognized as the blues.* (emphasis mine)

Elsewhere, Handy recalls how fond he was of hunting with a bow and arrow and notes how skilled Grandma Thumuthis, she who said his ears were so special, was at herbal remedies. The ability to heal with native plants was everywhere at that time considered an

Indian art: a knowledge technology that grew from centuries of observation, passed on, perhaps as legacy, by Indigenous people to their new relations.

Rural churches may well have been where musical styles met and combined. Missionaries established extensive social connections to Native Americans, and traditions of musical worship might remain in a region even after the local Indian society there was abolished. Indeed, church music may have been the main way assimilated people allowed themselves to feel the power of the old life.

Shape-note singing, favored by Baptists who considered musical instruments the Devil's playthings, was also widely popular among the southern tribes. Knowing this, one cannot now listen to examples of this haunting choral music without hearing certain harmonic dissonances that resemble nothing quite so much as full-throated Native American psalmody.

East of the Mississippi, writes the global musicologist Bruno Nettl, "The most distinctive feature is the development of responsorial singing—shouts thrown back and forth between leader and chorus." Here, of course, is another putative African trait, one observed in early black churches, and attributed also to English Protestant services. Whatever its provenance, call-and-reply singing was evident among all three groups of the eastern frontier early enough in their common history so as to make it finally impossible to judge who exactly got it from whom.

Though Indigenous people employed bows and arrows for hunting (warfare, in the main, was a hand-to-hand business), those east of the Mississippi had no stringed musical instruments. Their music was mainly vocal, with drum and rattle accompaniment. Some tribes had reed flutes, which made the voice, drum, and fife common instruments to the Native, European, and African American frontier cultures.

It cannot be asserted beyond question that the traits Fletcher and others documented among the western tribes were shared earlier by nations east of the Mississippi. But a broad west to east migration of the Iroquois and Cherokee has been shown conclusively to have taken place before European arrival, while the cultivation of maize spread from the Aztecs to the Algonquins of the northeast very early. It does not stretch credulity to suppose that several of the musical tropes Fletcher observed among the Omaha people were common to most Native North American societies.

A 1936 study of Cheyenne and Arapaho music, in describing the Owl Dance, gives some idea of the permeability of influences: "Men and women dance as partners [not normally done] . . . When a man at the drum calls 'Cut your corners sharp!' the dancers go into a zigzag and when he calls 'Jelly roll!' they swing around."

(And, really, is anything more universal than that sweet jelly roll?)

Perhaps the best available examples of nineteenth-century black song styles are on the twenty-three recordings made in Chicago in 1927 and 1929 by "Texas" Henry Thomas, a railroad vagabond born in 1874. Besides "Cottonfield Blues," discussed above, Thomas recorded only three other outright blues songs. The balance is a selection of square-dance numbers, ragtime songs, and vaudeville material that was already well out of style by the mid-1920s.

One would be hard pressed, however, to find a more charming idiomatic American music. Thomas has a rich, melodic voice and a trilling guitar technique. He uses a capo far down the neck for many songs—effectively shortening the strings to create a high, bell-like tone which he emphasized by rapid strumming. Thomas's songs are fast-tempoed and infectious, with mainly very simple arrangements, most no more than two distinct chords that avoid monotony by way of skipping dance beats and cheerful vocals.

While later-developed blues songs repeat the first line once before adding a concluding phrase, Thomas, as did Patton, sings the same line three times. His "Texas Worried Blues" is a collection of such:

I got the worried blues, God I'm feelin' bad.
I got the worried blues, God I'm feelin' bad.
I got the worried blues, God I'm feelin' bad.

You can box me up and send me to my Ma.
You can box me up and send me to my Ma.
You can box me up and send me to my Ma.

If my Ma don't want me send me to my Pa.
If my Ma don't want me send me to my Pa.
If my Ma don't want me send me to my Pa.

I'm gonna build me a heaven of my own.
I'm gonna build me a heaven of my own.
I'm gonna build me a heaven of my own.

I'm gonna give all the goodtime women a home.
I'm gonna give all the goodtime women a home.
I'm gonna give all the goodtime women a home.

Repeated phrases are, of course, a hallmark of Indian songs, and Thomas's heavy use of reed flutes, called quills, are not only charming anachronisms but indicate another Native influence. Thomas used quills to imitate a train whistle in "Railroadin' Some," which is little more than a singing call of towns and lines he'd passed along (punctuated by his cheerful calling, "I'm on my waaaay . . .") set to a skipping guitar line.

In citing the use of mimicry in Omaha singing, Fletcher noted that

A man, when accepting the gift of a horse, will render his song of thanks as if he were singing it while riding the animal; his notes will be broken and jarred in pitch, as if by the galloping of the horse. Or, as in the Mekasee songs, the warrior will so manage his voice as to convey the picture of the wolf trotting or loping over the prairie.

A stunning illustration of exactly the sort of mimicry Fletcher documented can be heard in Charlie Patton's signature song, "Pony Blues," in which he varies the beat and vocal inflection in several passages to give the feeling of a trotting horse:

> Got a bran' new-ooo-ooo-ooo Shetlan', man, already
>   trained.
> Bran' – new – Shet – lan' – bay – bee – al – ready
>   – traaaaain. . . .
> Gonna get in the saa-dle, ti-en-up on your reins.

Other examples of mimicry can be heard in the various "Fox and Hound" songs recorded across the south, musical and vocal recreations of the sounds of fox and coon hunts. Thomas has a frantic, stylized number called "The Fox and the Hounds," which mixes wildly blown quill calls with vocal yips and barks as well as stray phrases from other songs like "Liza Jane." (One can safely say that no other song quite like it was ever recorded.) The harmonica player De Ford Bailey, one of the first Grand Ole Opry stars (and one of its few black performers), was famous for his "Fox Chase," as well as performances in which he imitated the clatter and whistles of trains.

Indeed, the train whistle, turned so easily into a seventh-note wail of loneliness amid vast spaces, a lament in and of itself, appears transformed again into the blue falsetto yodels of Jimmie Rodgers, Robert Johnson, Tommy Johnson, Emmett Miller, Hank Williams, and, on "Mystery Train," by the young Elvis. Howlin' Wolf employed it to a chilling degree on "Smokestack Lightnin'," a train song he recorded for Chess Records in Chicago in 1956.

An anthem of fear, rage, and loneliness, "Smokestack Lightnin' " begins with a nine-note refrain picked out on electric guitar. A drum joins in on a loping 2/4 shuffle. The melody, barely more than a blues scale, sounds like something at once very old and just born, like something looted from a tomb. There is a muted echo in the air, a menacing presence; notes from a piano appear half-heard; the guitar and drums sound like they are in a jail cell. Only Wolf's vocal and harmonica come through with anything like clarity, and they are terrifying. He begins in full cry, a yell designed to make the listener jump.

> AHHH-OH, smokestack lightnin' shinin' jes like
>   gold.
> Ahhhh, don't ya hear me cryin'?
> Wooo-oooo a-woo-ooo a-woo-ooo-ooo
>
> Ohhh . . . tell me, baby, wha's da matter here?
> Ah don'tcha hear me cryin'
> Wooo-oooo, wooo-oooo, woo-oooo

The *a-woo-ooos* can be a beast howling or the whistle of a train passing through without slowing down, on its way God knows where. The final verse is a nightmare telegram of a vicious act and a surreal departure.

> Ah oh—who bit yo' baby sister?
> I been gone—little bitty boy—derby on
> Wooo-oooo, wooo-oooo, woo-oooo

Wolf's biographers connect the terror in "Smokestack Lightnin'" to the nearly sadistic cruelty inflicted on the young Wolf by his stepfather. Beaten and worked like a slave on the man's farm, Wolf ran away when he was thirteen, hopping a freight train to Dockery to look for his biological father. It was there he met Charlie Patton, and where his father bought him his first guitar.

But as terrible as the vision of "Smokestack Lightnin'" is, the song also conjures up the ferocious pride of someone who has walked through hell and can tell you about it. That bull roar is something heard on Charlie Patton's records too. But Patton affected his growl, one of many voices he used on record, while Wolf's natural speaking voice was very rough and, at six feet three and three hundred pounds, he had the build to match the sound.

Wolf adapted "Smokestack Lightnin'" from Patton's record "Moon Going Down," on which Patton sings lines he lifted from "Stop and Listen," a song by the Mississippi Sheiks:

> Lord the smokestack is black
> And the bell it shine like, bell it shine like
> Bell it shine like gold.

The Sheiks were a string band from Bolton, Mississippi, made up of members of the Chatmon family, renowned musicians with a broad repertory who played frequently for white society dances and made and sold a lot of records. It was the Chatmons who recommended Charlie to Paramount's Henry Spier in 1929.

The melody of "Smokestack Lightnin'" was also lifted from "Stop and Listen" (the title comes from warning signs posted at gateless rural rail crossings), a slow blues drag about the death of a lover that also relied on a mournful imitation of a train whistle.

> Ever' day have been, baby,
> Long ol' lonesome day
> Now don't ya hear me talkin', pretty Mama?
> Ever' day have been
> Long ol' lonesome day.
> Cryin' seem like to-ooo-ooo-ooo . . . huh
> It's a-ooo-ooo-ooo
> Same old way-ee.

Another arresting example of musical mimicry was record-ed in 1927. Andrew Baxter, a black Cherokee from northwest Georgia, and his nephew Jim (some accounts call them father and son) were brought to Charlotte, North Carolina, by a white band, The Georgia Yellowhammers, to back them on a record session. The Yellowhammers apparently held the Baxters in no small awe:

> The half Cherokee Andrew Baxter was an old time
> fiddler . . . According to local tradition he was a pro-

ficient musician at age nine. Gus Chitwood says that [Andrew] and his son James, a guitarist, often played with and for Bill Chitwood [founder of the Yellowhammers and father of songwriter Jimmie Chitwood] and other whites. "They could play breakdowns; they could play blues; they could play church music; they could play anything."

There's a photo of the Baxters taken at a fish fry in 1945 where they were the entertainment. They sit holding their instruments in the shade of a tree, dressed nattily in summer suits, collars, and knotted ties. Andrew, though quite dark, has the characteristic features of many Native Americans: high cheek bones, a round face, and calm, almond-shaped eyes.

The Baxters recorded nine songs in total—three in 1927, the rest in '29—all of them laden with a wistful beauty gained from Andrew's fiddle playing and some very inventive guitar bass runs by James. They were the first to record "K.C. Moan," a riverboat/railroad song "familiar throughout the southland." But their masterpiece from their first session, "The Moore Girl," is so original, so old and so new, that it might be the most astonishing display of innate musicianship on record until Charlie Parker's "Cherokee" came along twenty years later.

"The Moore Girl" is less a song than an extended musical mimicry of several trains as they pass in the hours after midnight. Its verses come nowhere near rhyming, and most of the words are spoken, not sung, by Andrew. But whatever else "The Moore Girl" may be, it is unquestionably a work of virtuoso fiddle and guitar playing by two musicians who have clearly worked together for quite some time.

It begins in a bouncy 4/4 time, the fiddle circling the same four notes over and over, part of a square-dance reel, as the guitar bounces in bluesy bass counterpoint in harmony but no particular order—as rambling as the fiddle is monotonous. After a quick eight bars of this, Andrew announces

> This is the Moore Girl. This train runs tomorrow
> morning at three o'clock. It is supposed to blow at
> every station . . .

"Moore Girl" was what some country people called "The Mogul,"
an Atlanta express train, and no sooner does Andrew speak the
name then Jim's guitar takes off in spiraling chromatic runs up
and down C and G scales.

The fiddle keeps to its tight circular melody until Andrew
announces that "It blows something like this" and commences
to mimic the sound of the train's whistle, a C7th cry lasting four
bars as the guitar lopes in a regular pattern underneath, itself
approximating the sound of wheels on track.

Once the Moore Girl blows by, the Baxters return to the
main melody, Andrew cutting a tight reel pattern while Jim rang-
es about anywhere he wants. "Next train runs at four o'clock.
It blows like this," Andrew says before fiddling another whistle,
slightly different than the first. "Next train runs at five o'clock. It
blows like this—passenger train"—this one has a slow, drawn out
call; you can nearly feel the engineer giving the cord three long
pulls and one short. Then Andrew switches tracks:

> I went to church after that—was a pretty nice service.
> Then one of the sisters got happy [??] and began to
> moan something like this.

Now the fiddle reflects how that sister sounded, which was,
not surprisingly, a lot like a train going by. "Her words was
this," Andrew says and begins to sing, the fiddle following each
inflection:

> Ha-a-a-ve mer-cy, Lo-o-o-rd
> Ha-a-a-ve mer-cy, Lo-o-o-rd
> Ha-a-a-ve mer-cy, Lo-o-o-rd
> On my poor old soul.

And with a quick four-note flourish, "The Moore Girl" ends as quickly as it started.

While certainly a gimmick now, and a corny one at that, mimicking trains may have been the first reply Native people made to the presence of the enormous machines as they made their way through the country. As their old lands became divided by tracks, it is possible that some Indians gained some mordant amusement, a measure of which might be heard on "The Moore Girl," from mimicking the sounds of the strange metal beast.

There is a striking historical correlation, too, between the submission of Indian nations from 1840 to 1890 and the appearance of railroads. Rail lines could not be built until the territory could be freed of Native claims and any further trouble. For fifty years in most of America, the advent of the railroad was visible proof that the Indian was gone.

But something else happened as the old order gave way to the new, something in the realm of coincidence that raises the possibly of an organic nature to accident. The driving rhythms of a train over rail ties, those steady 2/4 and 4/4 beats that ended up in the blues and rock 'n' roll, were exactly those used in Indian songs and dances. Even if the people who heard the land's music were cleared away, it seems an essential rhythm still drifted up from the ground.

A 1943 study of black life in colonial South Carolina described

> slender boats . . . [which] were the central means of transportation . . . for two generations . . . They were hollowed from a single cypress log by Negroes or Indians, who were then employed . . . to pole, row, or paddle them through the labyrinth of low-land waterways.

It is worth noting that Indians in South Carolina were once employed on scarcely better terms than Africans. By the 1720s, after war against the Tuscaroras and Yamassees, planters collected around fifteen hundred Indian slaves. Indeed, Indians were enslaved in great numbers in the 1700s before widespread cotton cultivation made the wholesale transportation of forced labor from Africa desirable.

For the English, the main problem with Indian slaves was that when they ran away, they had places to run *to* and were thereafter extraordinarily difficult to retrieve. When Africans, abstracted from homes across the ocean, ran off, they had no particular place to go. Some got caught, some came back on their own, but many certainly found new homes in the interior.

With the growing traffic in human beings from Africa in the 1800s, "[t]he final extinction of Indian slavery was in part due to the absorbing of the Indians by the more numerous Negroes." Of course, frontier permeability ran in all directions:

> In 1854 Father William, a priest of the Catholic Church, describes [the Pamunky in Virginia] in these significant words, "Few of them, however deserve the name of Indians, so mingled are they with other nations by intermarriage. Some are partly African, others partly European, or, rather I should say Virginian."

In 1843, white citizens in King William County petitioned the Virginia legislature to remove the land rights of the Pamunky because they had, apparently, become blacks. The petition was denied.

North Carolina has the perfect geography for fugitives: obscure coastal inlets leading to rivers, which eventually reach the mountains. A colonial governor of Virginia stipulated that North Carolina "always was and is the sinke of America, the Refuge of our Renegadoes."

A North Carolina Lumbee historian charts the migration this way:

> Europeans and Africans who could not or did not want to participate in South Carolina's and Virginia's

booming plantation economies found a place [for] escape . . . Slaves escaping for the port towns of Wilmington or New Bern and even from the Cooper River and low country plantations of South Carolina may have also found a home among the Lumbee River "Tribes" of Indians, escaped Africans and Indian slaves, Highland Scots and other "renegade" elements of colonial society converged on southeastern North Carolina.

The early-twentieth-century black historian James H. Johnson cited examples of exactly this mix of humanity in colonial records from New York's Long Island to Mississippi, a reality summed up by the contemporary historian William Loren Katz: "It had become clear to any who cared to look [by the early 1800s] that native Americans east of the Mississippi had become a bi-racial people (with a sprinkling of white blood)."

Though the American experience leading to the Civil War has been long under examination, it is only recently that the specific subject of the social survival of fugitive and marginalized people—so-called tri-racial isolates—during that period has preoccupied historians and genealogists. Even so, the broad artistic results of that mixing, in stories and music, have never been considered until very recently.

Fiddle players of any color were welcome everywhere in the antebellum south. Slave musicians were rented or loaned to neighboring plantations for dances. Some owners allowed slaves to keep what they earned playing music. Needless to say, these itinerant musicians had a tremendous social mobility and, toting their means of support with them, made for very successful escapees. Historical accounts of early American black music are replete with early classified ads offering rewards for fugitive musicians.

1743—Cambridge. A Negro Man belonging to James Oliver of Boston doth absent himself sometimes from his master: SAID NEGRO PLAYS WELL UPON A FLUTE, AND NOT SO WELL UPON A VIOLIN

1745—RAN-away from Capt. Joseph Hale of New-
bury, a *Negro* man named *Cato* . . . TOOK WITH A
VIOLIN AND CAN PLAY WELL THEREON

1748—Ran away from his Master Eleazer Tyng,
Esq. . . . A Negro Man Servant Call'd Robbin, almost
of the complexion of an Indian . . . talks good English, can read and write, and plays on The Fiddle

1791—RUN AWAY—a Negro man named Robert, 23
years old, about five feet, ten inches high, speaks good
English, is a fiddler and took his fiddle with him.

1734—Runaway, the 26th of June last, from Samuel
Leonard of Perth Amboy in New Jersey, a thick short
fellow having but one eye. His name is Wan. He is
half Negro and half Indian; he had on when he went
away a blue coat. He plays the fiddle, and speaks good
English and his country Indian.

As far back as 1819, in a tract meant to correct doctrinal
error in Methodist congregations, one John Watson observed,
"In the *blacks'* quarter [of Philadelphia], the colored people get
together and sing for hours together . . . in the merry chorus-
manner of the southern harvest field, or husking frolic method,
of the slave blacks; and also very greatly like the Indian dances."

One hundred and fifty years earlier, Morgan Godwyn,
another minister, after a brief sojourn in Virginia, "returned to
England, horrified by the abject state of the Negroes and Indians."
Godwyn claimed to have witnessed idolatry among the blacks,
"for that they use their Dances as a means to procure Rain."

The historian Dena Epstein notes the first purchase of American Indian artifacts by the British Museum in 1753: "Among the
objects from America was . . . 'An Indian drum made of a hol-
lowed tree carv'd the top being braced with pegs and thongs with
the bottom hollow from Virginia.'" A twentieth-century curator

cataloging the drum notes: "Although described as Indian, this drum was more probably made by Negroes and may even have been brought from Africa. The drum is typical of the Ashanti of Ghana." It is unlikely to have dawned on the British curator that the drum may have indeed been a genuine Indian artifact, as he or she likely has no idea what *genuine Indian* means, provided it has any meaning at all.

By 1934, the Great Depression had cut record sales by eighty percent from 1920s levels. The recording careers of most artists simply ended. Location sessions became too expensive to justify, and those rural musicians who still had a relatively wide following, like Patton, Jimmie Rodgers, and the Carter Family, had to travel to studios in Chicago or New York to record.

Dying of congenital heart failure compounded by his chain smoking, Patton went to New York with Bertha Lee Jones, his last wife, a woman half his age, for what would be his final session. Made for the American Recording Company, it yielded an amazing fifteen sides in two days, a punishing schedule clearly meant to extract as much material as possible from an artist with his back to the wall. Patton re-recorded several earlier hits, sides which demonstrate both his reduced skills and fierce will.

"There are also songs," writes Bruno Nettl, "said to be taught by the guardian spirit, which the recipient is to sing only when he is near death." Whatever the reason, in his last trip to a recording studio, Patton left behind what can only be considered his death song: "Oh Death."

It is the most abject performance he ever put on record. His voice is a raspy growl, showing the effects of his heavy smoking as well as a throat slashing the year before—some say administered by Bertha Lee during a quarrel. Patton won't, or can't, finish a single line of the song, relying on Bertha Lee and his slide guitar to begin or end phrases. As on all his recordings, the guitar playing on "Oh Death" is mesmerizing, with a walking bass line that is as regular as a tolling bell in counterpoint to slide phrases on the high strings which shadow his words. The song is a three-minute visit to a dying man who neither accepts nor denies the imminence of death, something rendered as a nearly physical presence:

> Won't you move my pillows and turn my bed
>   around?
> Lord I know my time ain't long.
> Oh Death, oh Death, you stole my mother and
>   gone.
> Lord I know, Lord I know my time ain't long.

As the song comes to a close Patton sings a refrain in something close to a gasp:

> Oh hush, oh hush, there's someone calling me.

And for the first time, Bertha does not repeat the line exactly:

> There's someone callin' *you*

she sings.

The mystic voice calling is perhaps the most extreme presence in the cosmos of the blues; something that puts the singer in the sights of fate, the world, even heaven itself; placing him at the crossroads where fate can't be denied. Standing at the center of the four quarters in his great vision, Black Elk said he heard a voice:

> [The bird] said: "Listen! A voice is calling you!" Then I looked up at the clouds, and two men were coming there, headfirst like arrows slanting down; and as they came, they sang a sacred song and the thunder was like drumming. I will sing it for you. The song and the drumming were like this:
>
> Behold, a sacred voice is calling you;
> All over the sky a sacred voice is calling.

On "Oh Death," Bertha sings the last line,

> Lord I know, Lord I know

a line Patton finishes with a low, final

> My time ain't long.

He died six weeks later in Cleveland, Mississippi, shortly after giving the twenty-three-year-old Howlin' Wolf a final guitar lesson. Bertha Lee recalled Patton smoked furiously through five packs of cigarettes during the session before letting up. "Charlie worried that boy for hours," she remembered thirty years later.

The Shadows of
Certain Sounds

If some have sensed, however remotely, a Native American presence in the roots of the blues, its place in country music has been
overlooked completely. The tremolo and twang—that sound,
after all, of an arrow leaving a bow—the sere vocals, the yelps
and calls, which sets American mountain music apart from the
Celtic example heard, say, in Nova Scotia, may be the shadows
of certain sounds abiding in the land at the European arrival.
As stated, the broad oval encompassing eastern Tennessee, West
and western Virginia, Kentucky, the mountains of North Carolina, north Georgia, and east Alabama—the land of the Cherokee
nation at the end of the Revolutionary War—is the cradle of
country music.

Consider the putative "father of country music," Jimmie
Rodgers, a white blues singer sometimes called the Blue Yodeler.
The tubercular ex-railroad brakeman was the first singer to cut a
solo record backing himself on guitar. In a scant six years of fame,
before dying from tuberculosis, Rodgers recorded some ninety
songs that gathered together every strand of popular American
music—mountain ballads, love songs, Hawaiian pop, big city jazz,
and blues—and presented them with an affable southern charm.
Jimmie was everyone's friend: at once a rascal, true-blue lover,
affectionate son, and loyal pal.

His success was unprecedented, selling millions of records,
mostly in the South, at a time when a 78 cost a day's pay for
most of his fans. Rodgers sang with a sly sincerity underscored

by the fact that for the extent of his professional career, he knew (and ignored) that he was dying.

His playing and singing were uniquely his own—a relaxed, apparently simple musicianship that favored feeling over technique. Rodgers's gift was to offer the democratic notion that anyone could do what he did. His voice, which he cleared with lemon juice and drugstore whiskey before performing, was open and friendly sounding. Nearly all his songs were punctuated at least once by his characteristic yodeling refrain, equal parts Swiss warble, rebel yell, and blues falsetto, an aspect of Rodgers's spirit that remains something of a mystery to this day. No one can say for certain where it came from, or exactly what it meant.

Though Rodgers's six years of fame are as well-documented as any pop star's, his first twenty-five are nearly opaque. Born in central Mississippi to a railroading father and sickly mother, from whom he likely contracted his tuberculosis, he had little schooling and no steady home after age six, when his mother died. Into his teens, Rodgers earned money by running errands out of pool halls and barber shops. When fully grown, his father got him a job as a railroad brakeman, and he worked for ten years on lines between Atlanta, Mobile, and New Orleans, occasionally branching into Texas.

All through his railroad years, Rodgers was apparently entranced by show business, mainly the minstrel and medicine tent shows that traveled the South, setting up anywhere some money might be coaxed from the locals. It is not altogether clear whether he felt an innate drive to perform or if he regarded singing and playing as just a more pleasant way to make money while rambling around.

Whatever the case, by twenty-eight, Rodgers was too sick to continue rail work. Brakemen at the time needed to hop from car to car, manually setting the brakes on each one to slow a train, dangerous and grueling work that must have offered great satisfaction when done well. Rodgers turned to music as a last resort to support a wife and child. While his chops never much impressed most of the professional musicians hired to play on his records, Rodgers was a sensitive and dedicated performer who, once he became a star, worked ceaselessly to entertain and could charm packed houses without visible effort.

Short and slim, he was the epitome of the pool hall sport, even when poor, dressing impeccably in jacket, tie, and straw boater. Once in the money, he favored long cars and white ten-gallon hats. In publicity photos (and few pictures exist of him before then), he displays the gaunt, pallid features of the mortally ill. (He used morphine, prescription whiskey, and, according to Maybelle Carter, marijuana to deaden what must have been excruciating chest pain.) His face was long and handsome, with dark eyes (the left one drifted), a pointed chin, and large hooked nose, which may have appeared bigger in pictures for the thinness of his face.

It would have resembled a death mask without Rodgers's nearly constant smile, which is bright and ineffably sad: a scrim of endurance, cheerful and heedless, certainly appealing to many of his fans, for whom life was no great bargain either. Rodgers presented a portrait of the blues in his very features.

He spent two years scuffling around the depot towns of the rural South, singing and playing at fairs, club meetings, and conventions with an assortment of musicians, before getting a chance to record two songs for the Victor company in 1927, at a now famous audition in Bristol, Tennessee. It led to a stardom that now seems as unlikely as it is enduring.

Though *unlikely* is perhaps unfair. Rodgers had an uncommon artistry. He and Louis Armstrong, a contemporary, were the first performers to define—if not create—the expressive emotional possibilities of American pop music. If Armstrong's genius lay in finding new idioms for vocal and solo instrument performance, Rodgers's gift—for there is no other word to describe the ease and confidence with which he sang and played guitar while dying of a wasting disease—was to incorporate old and new styles into a brash music that suited no one more than himself.

Because of poor health, Rodgers never toured any farther north than Washington, DC, nor west of Arizona. Most of his records were made at makeshift studios in Texas and Tennessee and at the Victor recording plants in Camden, New Jersey, and New York City. A notable session in Los Angeles, where he had gone to recuperate, yielded "Blue Yodel #9," on which Armstrong himself played. True to the professionalism of both men, it is a fine single, though not as extraordinary as it might have been.

Nevertheless, Jimmie Rodgers was a *blues* singer who made blues records. This point tends to bother people who consider the blues to be an idiomatic and exclusive black form, one appropriated by white performers looking to cash in with white audiences. However, black musicians like Armstrong, Blind Lemon Jefferson, and Ma Rainey were already very popular with white record buyers, and Rodgers's records were widely enjoyed by southern blacks. When college kids in the sixties resurrected the careers of the Delta guitarists Mississippi John Hurt and Skip James, the only numbers the old bluesmen wanted to play together were Jimmie Rodgers songs. Howlin' Wolf told an interviewer at the time, "I was inspired by the records of Jimmie Rodgers . . . because he would sing some parts in a head voice, like the Swiss yodelers." He told another interviewer, "I couldn't do no yodelin', so I turned to howlin'. And it's done me just fine."

After the record sales categories of *blues* and *hillbilly* were defined in the twenties (the more respectable term *country* came into wide use in the fifties), American rural music began evolving along divergent lines. Only then could issues of authenticity arise. Purists could argue fine points, but how the blues of Lemon Jefferson or Bessie Smith should be more authentic than that of Jimmie Rodgers has never been exactly explained.

There are many differences between Jimmie's blues and those of black performers, of course, and one may certainly prefer one style, one sound, over another. But to say that the blues sung by a white man dying of a wasting disease is less a true measure of a troubled mind than blues sung by a blind black man is hard to defend.

The notion of "authenticity" is largely meant to advance ideas of form over feeling, something to create a field for study.

Feeling can be had by anyone, but who can judge authenticity besides experts? A song changes each time someone learns how to play it, becomes better or not. Authenticity is a dodge, a tool, a matter for further study. No one cared about authenticity in American music before records came along.

Bristol, Tennessee, where Jimmie made his first records, is a town so literally on the state line that the Virginia border runs down Main Street. In August 1927, the recording director of the Victor Company, Ralph Peer, set up a field studio on the second floor of an empty store there to record local musicians. By then, Peer had been in the business for thirty years, starting as a twelve-year-old stock boy at Columbia's Kansas City warehouse. He was chief of recording for the Okeh company before moving on to Victor in 1925.

For thirty years after Edison's invention, phonograph machines were esoteric luxuries, and records mainly reflected the cautious taste of the well-to-do: opera singers and classical musicians, society dance music and show tunes, marches, polkas, and sentimental ballads were what sold. Somewhat lower on the taste scale were ethnic comedy skits and songs featuring stereotypes of commonly ridiculed minorities of the day: Yiddish peddlers, Irish laborers, German shopkeepers, and, of course, lazy, stupid (though sly) minstrel Negroes.

Though phonographs and records became more affordable starting in 1918, in 1924, thanks to radio and the death of Caruso—who alone accounted for about one-quarter of all records sold—sales had dropped fifty percent from their peak three years before. Victor hired Peer to reverse that trend. His instinct was to discard the bourgeois taste of the records that weren't selling and to record music that people were actually listening to on radio—local artists playing for small communities in what was still a very diverse, unhomogenous national culture.

At Okeh in 1923, Peer discovered his first rural phenomenon, a Georgia fiddler named John Carson, after an Atlanta record dealer begged Peer to record him. Carson cut two sides,

"Little Old Log Cabin" and "The Old Hen Cackled and the Rooster's Going to Crow," in an empty Atlanta warehouse, using the old acoustic technology that required the musician to sing and play into the mouth of a big horn that transferred the sound via a needle that cut into a spinning wax master disk. During his session, Carson stood too far from the horn and the fidelity was, Peer recalled, "pluperfect awful."

Peer had five hundred disks shipped to Atlanta with blank labels so as not to jeopardize Okeh's reputation. However poorly the records sounded, the dealer sold them as fast as they could be taken out of the box. He demanded fifteen thousand more. After sales passed the half-million mark, Peer ordered Carson to New York to re-record the two songs and add several more. "Log Cabin" backed by "Hen" eventually sold a million copies. Peer soon found another country star, Ernest Stoneman, from Iron Ridge, Virginia, who had a hit the next year with "The Wreck of the Old Ninety-Seven," a railroad tragedy ballad. In 1925, Vernon Dhalhart, a pop tenor, had a hit with the same song for Victor, which prompted that company to offer Peer a job.

In accepting Victor's offer, Peer stipulated that his salary was to be a dollar a year. In recompense, he retained publishing rights to all new material produced by artists he discovered. From this unheard-of arrangement, the modern music business was born.

Victor traditionally paid performers fifty dollars a side, a good month's wages for most Americans, plus a percentage of one to two cents for every disk sold. Disks cost approximately thirty cents to manufacture and retailed for as much as seventy five cents. As publisher, Peer's cut was also about two cents per disk, plus a percentage of sheet music sales, plus a percentage of any cover versions of the songs. In those far-simpler times, Peer was also agent and de facto business manager for most of his talent, dispensing advances as needed against royalties.

In order to market records more effectively, Peer divided the vast southern rural market into white *hillbilly* and black *race* categories. Lacking any personal racial animus, Peer tended to look down upon his poor and unsophisticated rural musicians, regardless of skin color, in a paternal, big city way. While no one ever accused Peer of double-dealing exactly, he always kept a farmer's caginess about how well his publishing business did, and he died at home in Beverly Hills, in 1960, a very wealthy man.

Peer had initially gone to Bristol to record more sides from Stoneman. Disappointed with the results, and so as not to waste money, he told a newspaper reporter that the Victor company was in town for a talent search, paying fifty dollars for every song accepted. The response was immediate and huge. In the next week, Peer auditioned dozens of musicians from the surrounding countryside, and recorded some twenty acts. The Carter Family cut five songs; two days later, Rodgers recorded two. Peer knew immediately that with the Carters he'd found something rare and fine; with Jimmie he wasn't so sure.

Rodgers's first song, a lullaby dating from the Civil War, did not impress Peer, and he asked for something original. Rodgers obliged with "The Soldier's Sweetheart," a song he'd "composed" several years before.

The first thing one notices in "Sweetheart" is how well Rodgers's voice sounds, bright and clear. He sings slowly, exhaling the lines in a style befitting a mournful ballad (the soldier dies in Europe), while strumming and picking his guitar. It sold well enough for Peer (who years later recalled Rodgers as something of a talented charity case) to set up another session five months later when Jimmie was in New York. Rodgers telegraphed Peer to say he'd be passing through but in fact was nearly destitute and had borrowed money to go to the city, confident that Peer would make more records. That session yielded the first "blue yodel," "T for Texas," which sold a million copies in one year.

"Blue Yodel #1," as it came to be known, is a no-frills twelve-bar blues. At three-and-a-half minutes, it could have ended after the first verse or gone on as long as the singer thought of words. Over the next six years, Rodgers recorded thirteen blue yodels of such uniformity that they can be considered sections of one long song.

Rodgers sang and played "T for Texas" solo, thumbing a regular walking bass line while brushing the high strings of each chord with his fingers. Like all blues, the song does not tell a story as much as become part of one—the story of the person singing it to you, someone you immediately want to know better.

> T for Texas, T for Tennessee.
> T for Texas, T for Tennessee.
> T for Thelma
> That gal who made a wreck out of me-eeeee.

That *me* keens up sharply, without warning, and is capped with a falling yodel that speaks more of Appalachia than the Alps.

> If you don't want me, Mama, you sure don't have to
>   stall. (Lawd, lawd)
> If you don't want me, Mama, you sure don't have to
>   stall.
> 'Cause I can get more women
> Than a passenger train can haul.

> I'm gonna buy me a pistol just as long as I'm tall.
> (Lawd, lawd)
> I'm gonna buy me a pistol just as long as I'm tall.
> I'm gonna shoot poor Thelma
> Just to see her jump and fa-aall

Another vocal upsweep finishes "fall" and launches another yodel.

> I'm going where the water tastes like cherry wine.
> (Sing 'em, boy, sing 'em)
> Lord, I'm going where the water tastes like cherry wine.
> 'Cause the Georgia water tastes like turpentine.

> I'm gonna buy me a shotgun with a great long shiny
>   bal. [barrel]
> Gonna buy me a shotgun with a great long shiny bal.
> I'm gonna shoot that rounder
> That stole away my ga-ha-ha-al.

Rather drink muddy water and sleep in a hollow log.
Rather drink muddy water and sleep in a hollow log.
Than to be in Atlanta
Treated like a dirty daw-haw-haw-awg.

Bragging, carefree, full of violent plans and resentments, the words are drawn from the great river of blues lyrics, simple declarative phrases that gain the weight of meaning only as the singer chooses, modifies, and sets them in place to create an individual portrait: loveless blues, illness, fights, drinking, drifting, all emblematic of real struggle that ends in that rest afforded by a death usually more welcome than not.

Rodgers's guitar playing relied on running bass lines that transition from one simple chord to the next with a loping ease. This regular to-and-fro thumping, an audible heartbeat, is a unique characteristic of American country playing, something not heard in Scots-Irish fiddle reels or the polyrhythms of the transported African people, and one more characteristic common to Native American music.

Standard tuning of the low E and A strings allows a sound as regular as footsteps to be made with the simplest fretting and thumb-picking. What isn't easy about a walking bass is its shape—the ease and inventiveness good players employ moving from one chord to another. Depending on their skill with these so-called bass runs, guitarists like Rodgers with otherwise mediocre technical skills can engage listeners with beguiling expressions of wit and feeling. No other instrument offers such expressive possibilities to musicians who are less than virtuosos.

A year before the Bristol audition, Rodgers was entertaining at a Rotarian convention in Asheville, North Carolina. A local player recalled:

A boy came in there by the name of Jimmie Rodgers, a yodeler. The boy that played with him looked like he was a Cherokee Indian—his name was Ernest Helton—I believe from Glen Rock Station, North

> Carolina. They'd sit around and practice, this boy played guitar for Jimmie, things like "Right Down Through to Birmingham," those nice runs. They went over good, and everybody commented on the easy way Jimmie could yodel.

Rodgers's biographers, Mike Paris and Chris Comber, observe that "those nice runs" would seem to suggest that "[Helton] was playing the same [bass] runs that Jimmie later made so much a part of his own guitar style." Others believe Rodgers got the yodel from Helton, too.

Helton and his brothers had a string band, which cut a few disks in 1924 and '25 and performed on an Asheville radio station, specializing in what was even then called "oldtime" music: banjo tunes with flat, nasal singing. There is no recorded evidence of Helton's runs on banjo, though those heard on the Baxters' recordings probably don't differ much from what the Heltons played.

The Italian word *scale* means *stairway*, and anyone who has spent any time in southern Italian towns knows that walking mainly involves trudging upstairs or down. Scales may indeed be music's first metaphysical concordance: the ascents and descents of early sacred choral music mirroring the supposed progress of the soul through life and emblematic of the overland journeys Christian pilgrims made to holy shrines.

Keyboard and fretted instruments, which divide lengths of string into regular, visible portions, are especially suited to the easy articulation of scales. The guitar, with more frets than the fiddle, which has none, and a greater octave range than the banjo, offered mountain musicians a new and simple way of expressing something very essential about their daily lives. What one hears in the scales of mountain music is indeed the landscape out of which the music came, the up-and-down courses of the mountain trails themselves. And expressions like "walking bass line" or "those nice guitar runs" attest to finding one's way through some territory on foot.

The scales Rodgers might have picked up from Helton were not his only gimmicks. Like Andrew Baxter, Jimmie had an arresting way of imitating a train—a wheezing, two-toned "Hoooo-hooo-ooooo," clearly enabled by his ruined bronchial tubes—that does not sound like anything produced by a human voice. Rodgers used it most memorably to kick off one of his biggest hits, "Waiting for a Train," a classic ode to drifting.

Another Rodgers gimmick, one also used by Charlie Patton, was spoken phrases to comment on the sung verses. Usually bragging, sometimes deprecating, these comments were always jaunty and wry. It should come as no surprise that he employed "Hey-hey" quite a bit, on Blue Yodels #3, #4, and #10, as well as "The Brakeman's Blues" and "Memphis Blues."

Rodgers's "Hey-hey" was a special treat, capable of expressing both mild regret and satisfied bragging, at once cheerful and broken down. For Rodgers, "Hey-hey" is shorthand for a secret, good news or bad, without tipping off exactly which it may be.

Peer's other great discovery of the Bristol sessions, Alvin Pleasant (A. P.) Carter, along with his wife, Sara, and her cousin Maybelle (who was also A. P.'s sister-in-law), had spent the better part of a day to drive the thirty miles to Bristol from their home in Maces Springs, Virginia. The songs they recorded were immediate hits.

Maces Springs was on Clinch Mountain, an extended rift line which runs through Virginia into Tennessee. A. P. sold fruit trees to farmers in the obscure hollows on both sides of the ridge, and first heard Sara Dougherty singing in a farmhouse as he walked by. Obsessed with music, A. P. went to see who she was, and a year or so later convinced Sara to marry him. The duo mostly played church socials and quickly became known for their vocal harmonies. Maybelle Addington, a shy guitar player a few years younger than her cousin Sara, eventually joined them. With Sara on autoharp and A. P. occasionally on fiddle, which he mostly carried as a prop, the Carters became full-on local entertainers, with a wide repertory of hymns and mountain ballads.

Maybelle was twenty-three, petite and soft spoken, with doe eyes and wavy brown hair, a technical virtuoso who played with a pellucid simplicity that becomes hard only when you try to copy it. Her innovation was to thumb-pick intricate bass melodies while strumming her fingers across the high strings to add harmonic chords and fills, a technique far more sophisticated than anything Rodgers accomplished. However hard to duplicate, Maybelle's sound was an invitation to follow, and it is no exaggeration to say that all country guitar playing since evolved from it.

Sara was tall, with long, jet-black hair and deep, dark eyes that reflected the seriousness she put into her rich contralto voice. A taciturn woman, she had few interests outside of her three children and singing (and she was not all that interested in singing); her marriage to A. P. appears to have been unhappy nearly from the start.

If Sara was mysterious, A. P. was plain odd. Over six feet tall, more than slightly resembling a young Abe Lincoln, he had a distinct physical tremor, the result, said his mother—who was part Cherokee and from a long line of fiddle players—from lightning striking a tree she was standing nearby when pregnant with A. P. The tremor also manifested in Carter's strange, warbly tenor voice.

He could go for hours without saying a word, then speak as if only to himself. His younger brother Ezra, who married Maybelle in 1926 (their daughter June married Johnny Cash), was the outgoing one, obsessed with trains, fast cars, gadgets— the future. A. P., on the other hand, was entranced by the past. He could get up and without a word leave home for days, walking or, once the record money came in, driving among remote mountain settlements to visit the sick, gossip, buy old sawmills (which he collected on his property), and hunt down lyrics and melodies he could record.

He was not picky. Romantic pop songs on nineteenth-century sheet music meant as much to him as aires and verses that ran back to sixteenth-century Britain. And he was pleased to visit black families as well as white. Thirty years later, one black mountain musician, Esley Riddle, recalled meeting A.P., who immediately invited him to his home in Maces Springs, where Riddle stayed for a week. He was soon accompanying Carter on his music hunts: "He'd just go in [to people's homes] and tell them, 'Hello, I was told by someone that you got a song, kind of an old song. Would you mind letting me hear it?' And they would go get it and sing it for him." A.P. and Sara's daughter Jeanette remembered, "He always was in the deepest study. And he'd walk like that up and down the railroad tracks, always with his hands behind his back, in deep study. He was a-searchin'."

Of the five songs the Carters recorded for Peer in Bristol, only the very first one was not released at the time. "Bury Me Under the Weeping Willow" is a droning lament of lost love, which Peer was perhaps understandably reluctant to put out. The other songs are fine, sentimental ballads revolving around family and religion; "Willow," however, is about faithless love, remorse, and death:

Oh, bury me under the weeping willow,
Yes, under the weeping willow tree.
So he may know where I am sleeping,
And perhaps he will weep for me.

The vocal harmonies have a wildness, a tuneless, slightly off-key wail which the other Bristol recordings don't. Their voices rise and fall in unison and are centered around A.P.'s very pronounced tremolo, a style that remarkably parallels one heard in Delta musicians like Booker T. "Bukka" White, and ragtime singers like Gus Cannon and Henry Thomas.

"There is no uniform key for a song," Alice Fletcher wrote of Omaha music. "[I]t can be started on any note suitable to the singer's voice." One hears something very much like this in "Willow": each voice seems in its own key. The first song the Carters recorded feels centuries older than the rest of their Bristol session.

After their Victor contract expired in 1934, the Carters followed Peer to Decca and made a remarkable series of records
over the next two years that showcased everything they'd learned
in seven years of performing. Maybelle's guitar playing gained
lightness and fluency. Her singing with Sara became just as
assured, adding a further depth and warmth to their harmonies. On "Black Jack David," cut in New York in 1935, the two
women sing the whole song together, Maybelle taking the high
parts with a beguiling sweetness. A. P.'s voice is there, too, in a
ghostly, barely heard undertone.

The song begins with Maybelle picking out a skipping melody, something as sprightly as the Carters ever recorded together,
before the ladies begin to sing:

> Black Jack Davy came ridin' through the woods
> And he sang so loud and gaily,
> Made the hills around him ring
> And he charmed the heart of a lady,
> And he charmed the heart of a lady.

After a bright guitar solo:

> "How old are you my pretty little miss?
> How old are you my honey?"
> She answered him with a silly smile,
> "I'll be sixteen next Sunday [sundee, they sing]
> I'll be sixteen next Sunday."

> "Come go with me my pretty little miss,
> Come go with me my honey.
> I'll take you across the deep blue sea
> Where you never shall want for money,
> Where you never shall want for money."

> She pulled off her high-heeled shoes
> They were made of Spanish leather.

She put on those low-heeled shoes
And they both rode off together,
And they both rode off together.

The final verse is reserved for something like remorse, or at the very least a sense of rough new circumstances. The girl also seems older than sixteen; indeed, it does not seem like the same girl at all:

Last night I lay in a warm feather bed
Beside my husband and baby.
And tonight I'll lay on the cold, cold ground
By the side of Black Jack David
By the side of Black Jack David.

Black Jack David is one of the oldest songs the Carters recorded. In Francis Child's extensive 1898 study of British folk songs, it is listed as number 200, "The Gypsy Laddie."

The song was also known as "Johnny Faa," the traditional name Scots gave to every gypsy chief. Scotland expelled gypsies in 1540 and again in 1609. The penalty for return was death, and documents detail several executions of Johnny Faa: in 1611, 1616, and 1624. The latter occasion came after Johnny Faa persuaded Lady Jane Hamilton, a former lover, to leave her husband, the Earl of Cassilis. The lovers were quickly tracked down, eight gypsies hanged, and Lady Jane sent to a tower her husband had built for her, reportedly decorated with carved stone heads of the eight gypsies.

The earliest version of the Johnny Faa ballad has the gypsies arriving at the Earl's estate,

And, oh, but they sang bonny.
They sang sae sweet and sae complete
The doon cam oor fair lady.

A symbolic exchange of garments follows.

> "Sae take frae me this gay mantle
> and bring tae me a pladdie.
> For if kith and kin and a handsworn
> I'll follow the Gypsy Laddy."

After which, she runs off with the band, declaring,

> "Yestreen I lay in a weel made bed
> And my guid lord beside me.
> This night I'll lie in a tenant's barn
> Whatever may betide me."

Other British variants of the song have the lady removing fine gloves to take her lover's hand. The low-heeled shoes and David riding through the woods first appear in America. Other American variations have David coming over the hills or running through the woods. Note there were no forests in Scotland, its woodlands clear-cut by the end of the 1600s. In the mid-1700s, enclosure laws forced peasant Scots from common lands, a measure justified by their rulers as a means of reforestation, an injustice that sent many of them to the Virginia mountains.

And there Johnny Faa was transformed in a way that does not now fully meet the eye. Basically, he became an Indian.

When Native Americans captured white settlers they wished to keep, usually grown children, they took their shoes and gave them moccasins, a practical and symbolic means of initiating them into a life that required traveling long distances on foot. This is exactly the exchange made in "Black Jack Davy," the little miss changing her high-heeled shoes for low-heeled ones, before she rides away.

John Tanner, kidnapped in Kentucky in 1789, age eleven, recalled, "The shoes I had on when at home they took off, as they seemed to think I could run better without them." The remarkable autobiography of Mary Jemison recounts her 1758 kidnapping by Shawnee/French raiders from her father's farm several miles from

Philadelphia when she was about thirteen. Her parents, siblings, and neighbors were marched into the wilderness as "an Indian went behind us with a whip, with which he frequently lashed the children to make them keep up." Pursuit was inevitable and the raiding party moved as quickly as possible. The next evening after supper, "an Indian took off my shoes and stockings and put a pair of moccasins on my feet, which my mother observed." From this her mother understood that Mary would be spared the fate of the rest of them, and told her so, saying that Mary would be safer with the Indians than if she ran into the woods alone. A younger boy was also given moccasins and the two of them were taken from the group to sleep.

> The next morning, the Indians led us off as fast as we could travel, and one of them went behind and with a long staff, picked up all the grass and weeds that we trailed down by going over them . . . each weed so nicely placed that no one would have suspected that we had passed that way.

("I'm a tail dragger," Howlin' Wolf would sing two hundred years later. "I wipe out my tracks.")

The others were gone and Mary would recognize her mother's red hair on a scalp she saw drying the next day. The Shawnee gave Mary to a Seneca family in what is now western Ohio as compensation for a brother killed in the war. Several weeks later, Mary was adopted by the Seneca sisters.

> [They] immediately set up a most dismal howling, crying bitterly and wringing their hands . . . one of their number began, in a voice somewhat between speaking and singing to recite some words. In the course of that ceremony, from mourning they became serene . . . I was made welcome amongst them as a sister . . . and was called Dickewamis [meaning] a pretty girl, a handsome girl or a pleasant good thing.

She lived as a Seneca, mainly in western New York, in relative contentment for more than sixty years, refusing several opportunities to return to settler society. (The polite voice in which her story is told is clearly that of the schoolmaster who took down Mary's words, and is presumably meant to express the idea that a lifetime spent among Indians could not erase her essential Whiteness.) Twice widowed and the mother of several children, Mary's story is notable for her sympathy and resolute endurance. As such, she was one of the lucky ones at the time.

> [D]own across the Middle West, and into the deep south, there existed a rural and small-town white population that had borne the brunt of the Indian wars, from the beginning of the French and Indian War in 1755 to the end of the Creek War in 1814 . . . thousands of white families had lost members, in battle or in raids on farms and frontier settlements.

It is altogether remarkable that the great body of American folksong—songs that most historians will say were made specifically for the telling of news—lacks any ballads which explicitly deal with Indian massacres and kidnappings. There are musical accounts of escaped murderers, killings of innocents, train wrecks, mine disasters, and ship sinkings. We have songs about assassinations and gunfighters, Civil War battles and lonely graveyards. But nothing regarding the main horror of almost two centuries of conflict from New England into Louisiana.

It is a strange omission, an absence that says more than any existing ballads might. (Peer recorded one possible exception, in 1928, one of the strangest American records ever made, "Indian War Whoop," by Hoyt Ming and His Pep Steppers, a square dance band from Tupelo, Mississippi—three minutes of fiddling, foot stomping, hand clapping, and a keening, wordless falsetto.)

Perhaps the whole subject was too frightening to the mainly British Protestant transplants, who, from the time of the earliest settlement, most feared losing their identity as Christians and

Englishmen in the New World, of being transformed by the wilderness into savages themselves. To be murdered in the forest, or, worse, to have their women and children carried away by devils, was too terrifying to contemplate, even in song.

Better to imagine a terrified woman begging mercy from a wicked rounder than a pagan savage. Itself a lurid, popular image, the kneeling woman pleading for mercy first appeared in a widely reproduced 1804 painting by John Vanderlyn, *The Death of Jane McRea*, based on the brutal 1777 killing of a woman by Indians near Saratoga, New York. (Both the incident and painting inspired James Fenimore Cooper to write *The Last of the Mohicans*.)

The fear of kidnapping and massacre was better mitigated in the shape of either a heartless rambler who murders unsuspecting girls from jealousy, to avoid marriage, or just for fun, or by way of charming, ambiguous interlopers like Black Jack David. For Indian life also had an undeniable appeal, and names like Black Jack were given by settlers to familiar Indians. (Mary Jemison mentions one Captain Little Billy.)

The murder ballad, a folksong variety carried from Britain, was a hardy and popular form in early mountain music and has proved a favorite to this day. "The Knoxville Girl" and "The Banks of the Ohio" are perhaps the most famous examples; others include "Henry Lee" and Dock Boggs's frightening "Pretty Polly."

In the introduction to his *Lost Highway: The True Story of Country Music*, Colin Escott considers Boggs, whose 1927 recordings, he writes, "opened a window on a closed-off world." Escott does not say exactly what that world was, besides remote and strange, one far removed in temperament from its British antecedents:

> Dock Boggs' part of Virginia had been settled for 150 years by the time he was born in 1898 . . . The names in the cemetery were almost exclusively English, Irish, and Scots, but those interred were not the sons and daughters of Albion. Not anymore. Some-

thing happened in the darkness and isolation of Appalachia—something that transformed the songs from
the old country, just as it transformed the migrants.

Escott observes that the music from the British Isles, and he
could have added the Celtic regions of France, survived in Nova
Scotia and Newfoundland almost intact. However, in Appalachia
it was warped and hardened by the American experience. He
leaves readers to consider what exactly that experience may have
been. "Such music," Escott concludes, "could only be produced
by a life of unimaginable harshness."

That harshness was, of course, nearly two centuries of
clashes and strife, as Indigenous people of the Appalachians
met, warred with, and were eventually routed and transported
by the new settlers. No one made music more emblematic of
this inland turmoil than Boggs, a white, banjo-playing Virginia
coal miner who recorded eight songs in New York City in 1928,
then disappeared into the hills: eight performances that are, in
the words of Greil Marcus, "[s]o strangely demanding as to lead
a listener to measure what he or she knew of the American
voice, . . . a small body of work so dissonant that like black
gravity it can seem to suck into itself whatever music might be
brought to bear upon it."

Boggs's signature songs "Country Blues," "Sugar Baby," and
"Pretty Polly" can still terrify listeners with their apparently bot-
tomless menace, indeed a "black gravity" that obscures as much
as it reveals or, rather, reveals certain things in a way as to keep
them mostly obscure. For though every recorded musical performance becomes an artifact, and though that artifact, like all
artifacts, accumulates mystery over time, there is something at
the heart of Boggs's singing, in the words and music, that points
to certain origins that may or may not be germane to Moran
Lee "Dock" Boggs himself, but were very much at work in the
conflicting Appalachian forces that formed him.

"Pretty Polly," "Sugar Baby," and "Country Blues" are to
this day paralyzing documents, radiating a fierce charge in their

sound that many critics have struggled to define. First is the unavoidable fact of Boggs's voice, sneering and scabrous, a brutal apotheosis of that nasal delivery used so artfully by Rodgers. There's nothing fun about Boggs's singing. It is melody without music, a sneering modal chanting that neither considers nor cares about any European tradition.

Then there's his banjo playing: bumping chromatic steps, fingerpicked on single strings in direct contravention to the prevalent clawhammer style, which, as its name implies, involves short downward strums across the strings. And Boggs picked out blue notes, those flat fifths and sevenths, for reasons which no one can quite explain. Marcus, who has written thorough appraisals of Boggs, considers "Country Blues" in terms of early influences:

> As a small boy he followed a guitar player called Go Lightning, who lived in the black settlement of Dorchester, above Norton; Boggs would beg him to play John Henry. From a black string band he watched as part of a Dorchester crowd and from Jim White, a black banjo player with blue eyes, he got the idea of playing the banjo like a blues guitar.

Marcus does not attempt to determine the influence behind Boggs's singing voice, mentioning only some female vocalists Boggs said he listened to on the radio. But he writes beautifully of its nature:

> It is an imp that disorganizes all that is held together by rhythm and melody; it confuses performance with visitation, spinning words away from their lines, mere vowels into huge syllables their words do not recognize and can barely hold . . . Their unwieldy new phonemes drag the listener out of whatever life she might have flattered herself to have inhabited and into the air.

Marcus notes the circular design of the tune Boggs picks on the banjo, a small vortex that has almost nothing to do with the melody he sings, which is really not a melody at all, but a tuneless chant up and down a single drawn-out chord. The words are not sung so much as beaten from a drum.

"Country Blues" is a common enough song in the rounder's lament tradition, where the singer asks his audience to consider their lives in elegiac ways. It begins,

> Come all you goodtime pee-eee-ple
> While I've got money to spend.
> Tomorrow might be Monday [Boggs pronounces
>   Monday as money]
> And I'll never have a dollar nor a friend.

The next three verses deal with fickle friends, unfaithful women, and warnings to others to mend their ways. By the fifth verse the singer makes it clear he's in jail; the next one describes his frame of mind:

> All around the jail house is hainted, good people.
> Forty dollars won't pay my fine.
> Corn whiskey has surrounded my body, poor boy.
> Pretty women is a troublin' my mind.

Then comes the lament:

> If I'd a listened to my Mama, good people,
> I wouldn't'a been here today.
> But a' drinkin' and a' shootin' and a' gamblin'
> At home I can not stay.

The singer is dying:

> Go dig a hole in the meadow good people.
> Go dig a hole in the ground.

Come around all you good people
And watch this poor rounder go down.

He does not expect to be laid to rest in Christian earth, either, only buried in a meadow. The last verse is either a taunt or warning directed at the woman who wronged him:

When I am dead and buried,
My pale face turned to the sun.
You can come around and mourn, little woman,
And think of the way you have done.

The image of the fickle lover mourning at the lonely grave of the one he or she wronged is common in mountain music, most beautifully expressed in both the Carters' "Bury Me Under the Weeping Willow," and their 1930 recording "Will You Miss Me When I'm Gone?"

There is, however, something stranger than a lonely grave in the last verse of "Country Blues" the shadow of someone, a clue: "My pale face turned to the sun." The earliest citation Websters gives for *paleface* is from 1822: "American for a Caucasian."

After nearly three minutes of modal chanting entirely congruent with Native American vocal tradition, a chant that is also a death song, the narrator insists "I ain't an Indian." But "turned to the sun" certainly implies a funerary tradition outside Christian burial, one that may not involve the complete covering of the body. Nearly all Indigenous burial customs involved some egress for the spirit to leave, and sometimes revisit, the grave. The Iroquois, for example, buried their dead leaving a slight opening in the grave, "through which [the departed spirit] might reenter its former tenant." Taking the singer at his word about his pale face, we are then left with the possible story of a half-breed comfortable in neither European nor Indian spheres.

There is nothing in Boggs's autobiographical recollections, made after folk researchers found him retired from coal mining in the early sixties, that ties him to Indian ancestry. Recall, though, that his banjo teacher, Go Lightning, came from a settlement further up the mountain from Boggs's own, from the sounds of it as hard to reach as any place in the Appalachians. Even the name Go Lightning, something drawn from the immanent world, seems to point toward a Native past and culture.

By the twentieth century, Boggs's droning singing style might have become detached from any specific memory and simply abided as local custom. Boggs's "Country Blues," knowingly or not, was a bitter archaic threnody of gambling (an especially cherished Cherokee pastime), drinking (also widespread), and violence (ditto) by a man adrift between two worlds—a central figure, of course, of the American frontier.

The writer Malinda Maynor, in describing the music of the Lumbee Indians of North Carolina, gives a good description of Boggs's own: "You cannot dance to it, but it can be fast; there is not much ornamentation. . . . [The singing has] an open-throated nasal quality [with] a different sense of pitch from standard western music."

Alice Fletcher, writing five years before Boggs was born, approaches the same native subject with language not unlike Marcus's. "[T]o meet the demands of the rhythm of the music, the words . . .are frequently taken apart and melodious syllables interpreted, giving the newly formed word a measure it did not possess in ordinary speech; accents too are changed to meet the exigencies of rhythm."

In this light, Marcus's appraisal of Boggs's vocal technique, "[a]n imp that disorganizes all that is held together by rhythm and melody," gains new meaning. The word *imp*, defined as a consort of the devil, was generally applied to American Indians in the seventeenth century, a figure who could literally "drag the [settler] out of whatever life she might have flattered herself to have inhabited."

Perhaps it is we listeners who have now been dragged out of a life we thought we knew and away from a music we assumed we understood, leaving in front of us, as they stood before the first sailors who landed here, before every African who got away early, standing as they have been standing for more than five hundred years, whether we see them or not, whether we hear them or not—and certainly whether we like it or not—are the Indigenous people of our enormous land.

In considering the Native American roots of American roots music, one can make too much of blood inheritance. Andrew Baxter, A. P. Carter, and Howlin' Wolf are known to have had native forebears. Others, like Charlie Patton and Robert Johnson, have family backgrounds inferred from comments made by contemporaries. (Johnson has been written about extensively and well elsewhere, which is why he is not broadly considered here. His protégé, Robert Lockwood, suggested Johnson was part Indian: "Never had a beard, never shaved. That's an Indian trait.")

A suspicion lingers around others, like the Chatmons, W. C. Handy, and Jimmie Rodgers. The names Carter, Chatman, Patton, Rogers (Jimmie's father added the 'd'), and Bozeman (Jimmie's mother's maiden name) are all featured on US government lists of southern Indian families transported to Oklahoma. There are, indeed, very many more contemporary musicians—Bo Diddley, Jimi Hendrix, Charlie Feathers, Robbie Robertson, and Link Wray—whose Native antecedents are well known.

For most musicians, though, Native ancestry is impossible to tell and pointless to speculate over. Whether Dock Boggs sang in such a distinctly Native style because of deep and obscure inner sources, or whether he simply reamplified a mode of performing that was familiar to him, does not alter the nature of his work or the landscape it presents us with. Many of its early listeners considered the blues to be the devil's music, and for too long in America Indigenous people were called devils too.

If Native harmony is indeed the essential source of the blues and country music, then it is in the DNA of American life, abiding in the nation's soul, indelible at its heart.

By 1933, Jimmie Rodgers was in mounting debt and gravely ill. Though popular as ever, thanks to the Depression his record sales were a fraction of what they'd been a few years earlier, and his poor health made touring nearly impossible. Certainly aware his time was short, Rodgers contracted with Peer to record twenty-five songs in New York that May. Too sick to endure the rigors of train travel, he left Galveston on a ship with a nurse. A cot was set up for him at the Victor studio on East Twenty-Fourth St. (The same one where, twenty-three years later, Elvis recorded "Hound Dog" and "Don't Be Cruel"), but even with frequent rest, Rodgers could complete only twelve tracks in eight days.

The last session was like his first, mainly Jimmie and his guitar. Remarkably, it is impossible to tell just how sick-unto-death he was. There is, though, a distinct feeling of resignation hovering over the music, a bittersweet counterpoint to the cheerful optimism Rodgers usually tried to project, something taught by the guardian spirit, which the recipient is to sing only when he is to die.

You can hear it in the first song, "Blue Yodel #12."

> Since my Mama's gone I got that achin' heart
> disease.
> Since my Mama's gone I got that achin' heart
> disease.
> It works just like a cancer,
> It's going to kill me by degrees.
> (Yodel-ay-he, oh-lay-hee, oh-lay-hee . . .)

In the next song he sings:

> While shadows of loneliness linger,
> I'm dreaming with tears in my eyes.

He followed "Dreaming with Tears in My Eyes" with "The Old Cowhand's Last Ride," another lonely grave song. But it is the following number, "I'm Free (From the Chain Gang Now)" that is Rodgers's purest expression of letting go (and was one of the last songs Johnny Cash chose to record in the weeks before he died.) It is a sentimental tale of a man wrongly jailed, but Rodgers's voice exudes the quiet happiness of someone about to be released from more burdens than he can name:

> I got rid of the shackles that bound me,
> And the guards who were always around me.
> Like a bird in the tree, I found my liberty,
> And I'm free from the chain gang now.

The session over, Jimmie spent what he probably knew was his last day on earth touring Coney Island's rundown amusement parks with his nurse. Early the next morning, the entertainer now considered responsible for the sale of more guitars than anyone else died in his Manhattan hotel room a few blocks north of Times Square.

Blue Devils

After a long season amidst the persistent mysteries of American music, what remained for me to account for was why its Indigenous roots were so cryptic in the first place. Put bluntly: why hadn't anyone mentioned it before? Official history is finally a pedagogic concern; by habits in education are people trained to look for evidence in some places and not others. If the true history of American music is fugitive, there was probably a reason why it had been driven away. What's astonishing is how easy that reason was to find.

In 1941, Melville Herskovits, a professor of anthropology at Northwestern University, published a book that changed the academic and wider culture's view of African Americans forever. *The Myth of the Negro Past*, the fruit of nearly twenty years of field research, took specific aim at the variety of tendentious beliefs in use since slave days to deny black people status as American citizens and human beings.

Herskovits had received his doctorate at Columbia under Franz Boas, who came from Germany in 1887, mainly to study the Native culture of the Pacific Northwest. Hired by Chicago's Columbia Exposition to set up a Pacific aboriginal village with living exemplars, Boas was enraged when his serious anthropological display ended up on the midway. However, the artifacts Boas collected became central to Chicago's new Field Museum, where he worked before going to Columbia University in 1899. He created the country's first PhD program in anthropology there six years later.

Before Boas's arrival, American anthropology focused on Indigenous people exclusively. Anthropology's broad assumptions were that all societies developed along the same distinct stages, that written language defined "advanced" and "primitive" peoples, and that the only focus of anthropology was the study of primitive societies.

At Columbia, Boas insisted that the notion of an inevitable path of social evolution was based on an essential misreading of Darwinian theory. Men are not descended from apes, he said; rather, both men and apes are fully developed beings who share a common ancestor. Likewise, each of the world's cultures has evolved equally, developing in relation to the unique forces and needs each faced in particular places at particular times. The notions of primitive and advanced societies, and that primitive ones could be expected in time to catch up with the European example, was an utter fallacy. Equally fallacious, Boas said, was the notion that anthropology's sole focus should be nonliterate societies; the assumption being that without writing, and so a written history, nonliterate societies had no history, and that they therefore existed in a childlike social state that, logically, required the adult supervision of Europeans, a supervision that mainly consisted of, in alphabetical order, anthropological study, Christianity, and colonialism.

In fact, Boas proposed, anthropology was a means by which all societies could and should be studied, and understood thereby. Furthermore, this understanding should not be based merely on the hierarchical categorization of artifacts, a method exemplified perfectly at the Ethnology Building at the Buffalo fair, but in long-term empirical inquiry into each social environment. Extensive fieldwork was necessary to examine language, physical forms, social customs, and archeological evidence.

Under the force of Boas's ideas, anthropologists fanned out across the world, Alice Fletcher to study Omaha music, Charles Peabody to excavate mound-builder sites in the Delta, and, later, Margaret Mead to Polynesia and Melville Herskovits to the West Indies and South America. By broadening the vistas of thorough anthropological study to include active social customs, Boas also more or less created modern musicology, a study of evanescent performance artifacts that coincided, perhaps not coincidentally, with rapid developments in the technology of sound recording.

Working with his wife, Herskovits amassed hundreds of hours of field recordings of folksongs, hymns, and religious ceremonies from Haiti, Jamaica, Trinidad, Brazil, and Surinam. That aural collection, along with decades of observations regarding food, tools, musical instruments, textiles, and social hierarchies at both ends of the Middle Passage, allowed Herskovits to show very clearly how African slaves carried their cultures mainly intact to their lives in bondage, and that those connections to Africa thrived into the twentieth century. After stints at Columbia and Howard universities, Herskovits founded the nation's first department of African studies at Northwestern in 1948.

The central myth he dispelled was that the culture slaves carried with them from Africa was soon erased by exposure to a "superior" European culture. Attendant myths surrounding this central fallacy included the "happy darkie," an individual untroubled by a history of coercion and bondage; that people sent from Africa had been the stupidest and most tractable of the population there, with no broad cultural or social ties to their homelands; that they could only mimic in primitive ways the white race's means of expression, in dress, speech, music, and dance—in short, that American blacks were moral, spiritual, and cultural children, utterly dependent on white social guidance and rule.

With *The Myth of the Negro Past*, Herskovits almost single-handedly created the field of African American studies by conclusively showing that people transported from Africa in fact came from specific places, what is now Togo, Ivory Coast, Benin, Nigeria, and Ghana, and from specific tribes, notably the Yoruba, Fon, Wolof, Mande, and Mina; that many were transported specifically for their skills in agriculture and crafts; and that they kept with them a profound culture that was reflected everywhere in African American society, one that had in fact worked its way into the wider culture of the United States—in language, religious practice, cuisine, and, of course, the performing arts. Also that, far from happy with their status as chattel, Africans had offered a constant level of insubordination and threat of insurrection, a danger that was met by increasingly organized vigilante measures taken by an increasingly paranoid slave-holding society.

But for certain Americans one problem with Herskovits's work, one bordering on the political, remained. So-called African retentions were far more obvious and widespread among people in Brazil and the West Indies than in the United States. Even accepting that Herskovits's broad propositions were proven, there were qualitative differences between the cultural expressions of Africans sent to South America and North America that had to be accounted for.

Herskovits proposed that the main cause was the atomization of slavery in England's continental colonies; that there were many more small-hold slave-owners here than in Jamaica, Cuba, and Brazil, where huge plantations were the norm. Consequently, North American slaves lived together in much smaller communities, and in closer contact with whites.

Lacking a large-group dynamic, and subject to greater social mixing, Africans in North America consequently underwent a pronounced cultural assimilation. While at Howard, Herskovits published a survey stating that over 25 percent of black Americans identified some Indian ancestry. Though this study was subsequently challenged for its reliance on anecdotal evidence, no one questions that the percentage of mixed African/Indigenous ancestry is fairly high.

However differences between black cultures in North and South America were accounted for, the fact remained that unambiguously Afrocentric traditions did not exist in such numbers in the United States as elsewhere in the hemisphere. Consequently, *The Myth of the Negro Past* could not by itself sweep away racist assumptions as thoroughly as they deserved to be.

Lurking in the weeds too, and what makes Herskovits's book rather dated now, is the mutability of culture. While identification of group traits is desirable in pursuit of knowledge, its practice can also lead to new conundrums. Reduced to cases, at what point might an individual stop being Indian and start being African, or European? Or that European become an African, an Indian? What exactly determines such things?

Of course, the luxury of considering these questions at length was absent in an era when one group of Americans was denied the most basic civil rights, while another had been hounded to the brink of cultural extinction. Herskovits believed that education could effect political change and he intended *The Myth of the Negro Past* to demolish notions of innate biological determinism. Issues of mixed blood only confused things.

Acknowledging Negro-Indian contact, he wrote:

> That in most of the New World, as well as in the United States, this contact was continuous from the early days of Negro slavery has not been well recognized as might be. Students of the American Indian have speculated on the amount of Negro influence to be discerned in the present day tribal customs of certain Indian groups who either possessed Negro slaves they later absorbed, or offered haven to escaped Negroes, giving them places as members of the tribe. But the possibility of Indian influence on Negro behavior either directly or at second hand through the taking over of Indian customs already accepted by the whites, has not figured in terms of the possibilities that have been envisioned by analyzing the forces which impinged on the Negro in his new habitat.
>
> It is apparent that in merely raising these questions, the need for reexamination of the problem is indicated.

But Herskovits here refers to race mixing pretty abstractly ("absorbed"?), while the academic reexamination of the subject which he thought was necessary in 1941 did not begin for over half a century.

An early outcome of Boas's Columbia anthropology program was a pronounced shift in academic perspective. Native Americans were no longer the central focus of field study. This might have been partly due to the dwindling number of "traditional" Indian societies following the shattering of existing nations as sovereign states when Oklahoma was granted statehood in 1907. Or it could simply be that the study of Indigenous people had become passé at last—a nineteenth-century remnant. Charles Peabody, in Mississippi in 1901, is a perfect example of the paradigm shift; there to uncover Native American artifacts, his attention is drawn to the black field workers he has hired, and the expressions of what he takes to be African aires.

Coinciding with this shift in academic focus was an exponential increase in the black middle class and its system, albeit segregated, of higher education. Through the 1920s and '30s, black composers and performers created a magnetic interest among white artists and intellectuals on both sides of the Atlantic in, what was termed broadly at the time, Negritude.

So the times influenced Herskovits as much as he influenced his time. Intrigued as he may have been by the confluence of Native American and African culture in the United States, by the 1930s—and especially following publication of *The Myth of the Negro Past*—in academia and the popular mind, the American Indian was Out and the African American was In.

If Herskovits's call for a further study of Indigenous/African cultural mixing was mainly ignored, another of his proposals had been underway for some time at the Library of Congress. "Far greater attention must be given," he wrote, "to nonreligious folk music of United States Negroes than has hitherto been accorded songs of this kind . . . But the actual melodies and rhythms of work songs, of songs of recrimination and ridicule, of prison songs, are needed to supplement the rather extensive collections of spirituals available for study." He was referring elliptically to the work that Alan Lomax, a young man he'd known since at least 1937, had been doing with the Archive of American Folk Song at the Library of Congress.

In 1932, Alan's father, John Lomax, moved from Texas to Washington, DC, for research in the archive. Two years later, he was a consultant and curator of the collection, with a mission to expand its holdings of field recordings—a job he had largely created for himself. By then, he was sixty-seven, a former college professor and banker. He first collected cowboy songs as a boy in Texas, publishing two volumes of them by 1919. After leaving academe for the business world, Lomax was still a widely respected figure in American folklore studies when the bank employing him failed in 1931, the same year his wife died.

Lomax came to DC with his four children, treating the Library of Congress post, mainly funded through grants he arranged, as a family project. All his children worked with him, most notably Alan. He was an outgoing eighteen-year-old in 1933 when he and his father made a song-collecting trip across the West and South in a Lincoln with a custom-built, battery powered, five-hundred-pound recording machine, which cut sound onto aluminum disks, in the trunk.

To find examples of "pure" folk music, the elder Lomax had long canvassed prisons for men kept isolated for years, on the theory that the songs they knew could not have been influenced by radio or records. That summer he hit paydirt in Louisiana: a prisoner serving a sentence for attempted murder at the Angola prison farm, one Huddie Ledbetter, called Leadbelly, sang songs and played guitar with a uncommon power.

The predominant story, which Leadbelly apparently believed and Lomax never contradicted, was that Lomax persuaded the Louisiana governor, a hammy, corrupt good ol' boy named O. K. Allen, to pardon Ledbetter on the strength of his singing. (Prison records show no special arrangement was made for his release, which came shortly after Lomax's visit.) Nevertheless, a grateful Ledbetter sought out Lomax and became his driver on further song expeditions. In turn, Lomax became Ledbetter's guardian and business manager (claiming three-quarters of all concert fees and exclusive copyright to the songs), thus maintaining a paternal control over his career. In the publicity that followed—Leadbelly became something of a sensation—the elder Lomax cultivated a portrait of benevolent master to a grateful boy-man. He booked Leadbelly into concert halls, where he sometimes performed in prison stripes or overalls (like Patton, Ledbetter had avoided farm work, and wore suits offstage).

The songster soon chafed under such control. He disliked revisiting penitentiaries, where Lomax had him play for the often exhausted and sullen prisoners, hoping to encourage other musicians to step forward. Back east, Lomax decided that Harlem living (where Ledbetter befriended Cab Calloway) with the money earned from performances would quickly ruin his protégé. He sent Ledbetter and his wife Martha to live in a farmhouse in Wilton, Connecticut.

"That Leadbelly grew increasingly truculent," writes historian Marybeth Hamilton,

> could have surprised no one but Lomax himself . . . In March [1935], the two toured colleges across New England and upstate New York, and from the outset Leadbelly flatly refused to be chaperoned. In Rochester he headed for the city's black district and disappeared for twenty-four hours; in Buffalo he turned down a room at the 'colored' YMCA in favor of what an appalled Lomax described as 'a low down dirty back room . . . down an alley on Williams Street.'

It was in, of all places, Buffalo, at the university library, where Ledbetter, resplendent in a green-and-yellow checked suit, finally confronted Lomax, demanding the money he earned on the tour and gesturing towards a pocket where he kept his blade. Lomax was frightened and humiliated; two weeks later, Ledbetter and his wife were back in Louisiana.

The experience exhausted Lomax and, nearing seventy, he increasingly turned work over to Alan. Fundamentally very conservative, John Lomax was also unhappy with the policies and programs of Roosevelt's New Deal. Alan, on the other hand, was broadly sympathetic to ideas of social and economic justice, and explicitly promoted such in his work for the Library. Once retired to Texas, John worried that his son was mixing with Communists.

In 1937, at twenty-two, Alan replaced his father as the Archive's assistant curator, and went on to create a miraculous sonic portrait of the era. Besides ethnic choruses, rural work chants, and children's playground songs, Alan "filled the archive's shelves with material that John Lomax would never have countenanced, from proletarian folk songs by Woody Guthrie to militant union tunes by Aunt Molly Jackson to an eight-hour interview with Jelly Roll Morton, an attempt to document the 'folk roots' of jazz, a music that his father detested."

What's more, Alan remained close to Leadbelly, who had successfully sued John for his concert proceeds, and helped the performer when he returned East to resume his career. In 1939, after Leadbelly was jailed in New York for stabbing a man during a fight, Lomax quit doctoral studies at Columbia to organize a legal defense fund. By 1941, after Leadbelly's release, Alan guided his career, arranging radio and nightclub bookings at the start of what was to become the New York City folk music scene.

And it was in 1941, coinciding with the publication of *The Myth of the Negro Past*, that Lomax, assisted by two African American researchers from Fisk University, John Work and Lewis Jones, undertook a two-year study of Coahoma County, Mississippi, the site of Peabody's musical discovery forty years earlier.

There Lomax met and recorded Muddy Waters and Son House (unaware that House had made records for Paramount with Charlie Patton a decade earlier); these were seminal recordings of great power that nevertheless spoke more to the American present than an African past.

Branded a "Red" in 1950, Lomax took his open-ended recording project to Europe, working with the BBC to document vanishing folksong traditions in England, Spain, and Italy, and stayed away for ten years. Lomax believed that the power of folk music, broadly heard, would improve the world; his achievements in service to that idea, and to the cause of human expression, are many, priceless, and profound.

That said, Alan was egotistical and demanding, fiercely protective of his mission, which he considered nothing less than the guardianship of the true spirit of American folk music. On one memorable occasion, at the Newport Folk Festival in 1964, Lomax assaulted Albert Grossman, the slick manager of several folk music acts (and no small S.O.B. himself) after becoming enraged by a performance of the electrified Paul Butterfield Blues Band. (Bob Dylan, another Grossman client, would perform with Butterfield's band there the following day, an event that rang down the curtain forever on Lomax's folk music orthodoxy.)

Recent scholars accuse Lomax of minimizing, in fact suppressing, the contributions of Jones and Work to the Coahoma project, and his memoir, *The Land Where the Blues Began*, often leaves the impression that he single-handedly wielded recording equipment to uproot Jim Crow where he could.

Rightfully, Lomax considered himself a crusader, and the autobiography frames a broad quest to level the racial barrier, to connect with authentic, marginalized people. In his telling, however, one eventually suspects the project was fueled less by the humbling attitudes of sympathy and gratitude than a mix of academic self-righteousness and white guilt.

Lomax worked in violent places during cruel times, and if he is guilty of a certain prejudice it was opposed to something far worse. For Lomax the field researcher, "steeped in the politics of the Popular Front . . . with an impassioned commitment to racial justice," the blues needed to be from somewhere specific. *The Land Where the Blues Began* codified his predominant myth that the music was formed from "the melancholy dissatisfaction that weighed upon the hearts of the black people of the Mississippi Delta."

And seeing no further than skin deep, he placed the roots of the blues firmly in what he felt was imported African soil. To make the case, however, Lomax mixed definitive statements with generalities in an argumentative bait-and-switch.

He believed that the harsh levee camps and prison farms would produce, as usual in the black tradition, a musical response: "It came in the sudden emergence of the lonesome holler, and later the blues, notable among all human works of art for their profound despair." Never mind that the blues trades in more than just profound despair. As Elijah Wald has pointed out, the men who developed the Delta blues were, for their time and place, widely traveled musicians who despised manual labor and earned pretty good money entertaining people. And, as witnessed during the Creeks's removal from Georgia, psalmody against cruel circumstances is a fundamental human act.

Without a thought to the pronounced Afro/Indigenous culture that existed in what became northern Mississippi for the better part of three centuries, Lomax offers zero evidence of a sudden emergence of field hollers (which locals mainly called corn songs) there. Indeed, the whoops and modal shifts of the hollers on many of his field recordings sound closer to Plains Indian singing than anything yet recorded in Africa.

Elijah Wald describes one such holler recorded at Parchman prison farm in 1947, sung by an inmate called Tangle Eye:

[I]t is a blues only by the loose definition that applies that word to any sad Delta song. It has no blues structure, or indeed any structure at all. Tangle Eye starts off with a long, wordless, vibrato-laden moan, a hmm-mmmmmmmm that rises a moment, then sinks and trails off in a wisp of melisma . . . Then he begins to sing words: "Well I wonder will I ever get back home, *hey, hey-ey-ey* . . ." For the next three minutes, he blends stanzas of lonesome nostalgia . . . with word-less moans and cries, sometimes floating in mellow falsetto, sometimes rumbling like underground lava. (emphasis mine)

Wald points out that Lomax

recorded Delta-style hollers in other regions, especial-ly in the Texas river country, but believed he could always trace a Delta source. Other folklorists, such as David Evans, believe that Lomax was too narrow on this point [and] that similar hollers have been record-ed from cattle herders in Colombia and Venezuela.

Lomax cites "very similar songs . . . among the Wolof and Watu-si for example," but adds, "[i]t seems, in fact, that this song type, which we might call the high, lonesome complaint, is one under-current of music in the whole of civilized Eurasia . . . from the Far East to Ireland."

So the blues trail is really very broad indeed. Never consider-ing the migration across the Bering land bridge, Lomax remained "confident that the original of the levee holler will one day be found among the pastoralists of Northwest Africa" (as if such a thing could be dug up like a fossil). "Senegalese slaves were prized for their skill with animals, and I suppose that some Wolof, brought to Mississippi, successfully tried out this animal-handling song on his work team, and the melody caught on." To be candid here: the more one considers this statement in light of the context of Native America, the more absurd it sounds.

Like Charters and Oliver, Lomax beat African bushes without quite finding what he was looking for. Once though he possibly got closer to the answer than he realized: producing in the seventies "a TV program about the origins of the Delta blues, I needed a levee-camp scene. . . . Not long afterward . . . I was draining a jar with a raffish crowd of levee-camp veterans."

(Lomax's readers by this point should be resigned to his reflexive blend of fellowship and condescension.) He sets up an interview with four old-timers, among them a man named Joe Savage and another named "Bill Gordon—burly, smiling, but serious, a pork-pie hat shading a copper skin and high cheekbones that spoke of Native American ancestry—his role was to tell it straight and unadorned." Clearly Lomax, like Professor Peabody in 1901, had no idea exactly what it was he heard.

In the promotion of Leadbelly in the forties, we find articulated for the first time a durable American myth: the itinerant Negro bluesman proclaiming basic human truths, which white America would do well to attend. The marketing of the rural black experience, as both a source of music and harsh critique of the status quo, began here.

The myth, of course, does not lack merit. All sincere artists strive to connect inner visions to the wider world. And an American century replete with racist laws, world wars, and rampant domestic paranoia required no small correction. But while promoting the blues performer as a burdened Atlas, suffering Prometheus, and wandering Odysseus, the myth, though a useful prop for politics, helped hide a truer world.

Electric microphones and recording devices were powerful new tools for anthropologists to study nonliterate societies. But it fell to an ex-anthropology major from the University of Washington, Harry Smith, to use the commercial products of the technology for his own mystic survey of the United States. The field recordings Smith collected came with labels, and he found them in warehouses and people's homes, where they'd been sitting for at least twenty years.

Smith's mother was a schoolteacher on a Lummi reservation in Washington State, and by the time he was fifteen, he had made dozens of field recordings (now lost) of Lummi and Sumish ceremonies. He matriculated at the University of Washington to study anthropology, but dropped out in 1944, when he was twenty-one. He moved to Berkeley to make mystical, hand-painted films, smoke marijuana, and collect old 78 rpm records, which by the late forties—if they'd survived wartime scrap drives—were selling for pennies.

In 1952, Smith released *The Anthology of American Folk Music*, a box of six LPs on Folkways Records. It was a collage of recordings—presented, Smith said, in a specific order—made between 1925, when electric microphones replaced acoustic cones, and 1935, when the commercial recording industry all but collapsed. Called the ultimate bootleg (as rights to the music had not expired, and not been granted), the *Anthology* prompted a rediscovery of idiomatic American rural music, of Dock Boggs, the Carters, Charlie Patton, Henry Thomas, and Charlie Poole, by a generation of young people alienated from prevailing ideas of American order and history.

By directing attention to an era and landscape most Americans were happy to forget (it debuted the first year of Eisenhower's administration), the *Anthology* was a beacon of the fugitive and strange as bright as *On the Road*, written two years earlier and published two years later. Its songs conjured the Civil War and Reconstruction, even the wild Jacksonian frontier, and catalogued the forgotten and barely known aspects of—in Greil Marcus's indelible phrase—"the old, weird America," a violent, haunted land that radiated equal waves of beauty and menace. On it is Boggs's "Sugar Baby" and "Country Blues" and Hoyt Ming's "Indian War Whoop." It reveled in everything that fifties America was dedicated to forgetting.

Marcus, in writing extensively about Smith's project, observes that the *Anthology*'s appeal lay in its

> insistence on an occult, Gothic America of terror and deliverance inside the official America of anxiety and success.
>
> By the early 1960s the *Anthology* had become a kind of lingua franca, or a password for the likes of Roger McGuinn, later of the Byrds, or Jerry Garcia,

founder of the Grateful Dead, for folk musicians like Rick Von Schmidt and John Fahey, for poet Allen Ginsberg [and, Marcus' main subject, Bob Dylan], it was the secret text of a secret country.

The *Anthology* appeared to a lot of young American musicians like an inheritance from an uncle they never knew existed; it kick-started the folk and blues scenes, an appreciation of American roots music that has only grown since. Though the *Anthology* was a collection of what had once been at least regionally popular records (Poole and the Carter Family were included, Jimmie Rodgers was not), most of the musicians had been forgotten and dead for years. Astonishingly, some—like Hurt, Cannon, the Carters, and Boggs—were still alive, pleased for the renewed attention and delighted to reminisce and perform.

In considering Smith's achievement. keep in mind that he was an obscurantist of the first water, a trafficker in recondite symbolic meanings and free associations. His parents were Theosophists and Smith ended his days as Shaman-in-Residence at the Naropa Institute in Boulder, where his rambling lectures, which one can listen to online, were apparently intended to frustrate more than enlighten.

The *Anthology* was packaged as three two-disk volumes, "Ballads," "Social Music," and "Songs," associated with the primal elements fire, water, and air, with record jackets decorated respectively in red, blue, and green alchemical symbols. A fourth volume (earth) was assembled (and included the Carters' "Black Jack David") but not issued until after Smith died.

The *Anthology* resists definitive interpretation, which of course is the whole point. If it is, as Marcus would have it, a secret text of a secret country, then Smith may have indeed meant it to point specifically, albeit occultly, to the Indigenous origins of American music. As it is, the *Anthology* challenged widespread cultural biases against country music, which, in 1952, was considered a lucrative embarrassment, the product of talented simpletons, unworthy of any status in mainstream culture.

If mountain music was then regarded at all, it was as a curiosity, a remnant of Stuart England somehow preserved in the hills of Tennessee and Kentucky and performed by professional entertainers like Bradley Kincaid, John Jacob Niles, and Burl Ives. Commercial country music emphasized showbiz—singing cowboys or rubes in overalls with fiddles and banjos. Its great artists rarely, if ever, performed outside the South and West.

Even as black Americans overthrew the Jim Crow stereotypes of minstrelsy, a no less pernicious prejudice against rural whites remained in place. A July 1965 *Journal of American Folklore* article noted that "The humorous costume in which the hillbilly has been disguised for nearly half a century has obscured his significance to both the general public and the student of culture."

By the 1950s, middle-class blacks prided themselves on the classical music training of their children, on generations born after 1900 which would advance the cause of social equality. Anything smacking of the cotton field, juke joint, or bordello, as Richard Wright and Ralph Ellison made clear in their writings, was an embarrassment, one more way white America could keep respectable, hardworking citizens on the lowest rungs of society.

Smith's *Anthology* tore away the costume of the hillbilly as much as jazz music, and its fiercely intelligent avatars, banished the "Minstrel Darkie." In their wake, one may wonder if the absurd costumes of both white and black might have been worn by some to hide cultural identities that were wholly neither. How many Americans, rather than reveal themselves to greater persecution and scorn as mixed or Native people, had first found something like shelter in the vestments of Zeke and Sambo?

While the Lomaxes were amassing their field recordings, the Works Progress Administration was collecting hundreds of interviews with people then in their 80s and 90s, and several over 100, born into slavery. From Texas to the Carolinas, field researchers posed questions to elderly ex-slaves, typed out their answers, and sent them to Washington.

The collected stories, as a whole, are a portrait of the world represented by Smith's *Anthology*, and a window to the roots of the blues. They recall the outrages and indignities of slavery (the specific details of several memoirs can still induce a faint nausea) while telling exhilarating tales of craft and endurance.

The antebellum society they describe appears nearly as mobile, and far more violent, than our own, with the main difference between that time and ours being a routine willingness among people then to abide by the consequences of their actions, a condition that perhaps defines frontier life. That moral beacon has gone out; our days are mainly cautious and dull.

But once upon a time, surprises abounded.

"I want to tell you about my uncle Tom." The speaker is Cora Gillam of Little Rock, Arkansas. "He was half-Indian. But the Negro part didn't show hardly any. There was something about uncle Tom that made both white and black be afraid of him . . . That Indian in uncle Tom made him not scared of anybody." Tom's master allowed him to learn to read, Cora said, and Tom ran into trouble in Helena, Arkansas, for reading news of the Yankee Army to other slaves. Jailed and promised a hanging, Cora tells how Tom thrashed the first men who came to take him from his cell. "He almost tore that jailhouse down, lady. Yes he did." Rescued from the mob by his master, Tom made it to the Union lines and joined the army, 54th Regiment, US volunteers (colored), stationed in Little Rock.

Tom's mother, Cora is keen to say,

> was full blood Cherokee. She came from North Carolina. In early days my mother and her brothers and sisters were stolen from their home in North Carolina and taken to Mississippi and sold for slaves. You know the Indians could follow trails better than other kind of folks, and she tracked her children down and stayed in the south.

Chaney Mack, 74, of Gulfport, Mississippi, testified to another parentage. "My father wuz a full-blooded African. He wuz about eighteen years old when dey brought him over. He came from near Liberia." Paid to load a ship with a friend, before dey know it de boat has pulled off from de landing and dey is way out in de water and kaint he'p demselves. So dey jest brought 'em on over to Georgy and sold 'em . . . He wuz put on a block and Mr. Holland buyed him. Dat wuz in Dalton, Georgy.

My mother wuz a pureblood Indian. She wuz born near dat "Lookout Mountain" up in Tennessee, on a river, in a log hut. Dey lived in houses and her father wuz de Indian chief. His name wuz "Red Bird." Dey belong to de Choctaw tribe. De white people wuz trying to drive dem out and . . . all my mother's folks wuz killed but her. De white folks took her and give her to Dr. Jernigan.

I can see her now wid her long straight hair in two plaits hanging down her back, black as a crow . . . Dey call her "Big Sarah," and nobody fooled wid her. She walk straight and hold her head high. All of de other niggers wuz afraid of her. She usta whistle "Fisher's Horn Pipe." Dat wuz an Indian song dey sung when dey wuz mad. I never could "ketch" it . . .

De songs my mother used to sing wuz "Over Jordan River, I'm Bound to Cross" and "Swing Low Sweet Chariot" [a song composed by Wallis Willis, an ex-Choctaw slave]. When she sing us to sleep she'd sing: "Bye ye Baby Buntin'—Daddy's gone a'huntin'—To git a little rabbit skin, To Wrop de Baby Buntin' in."

She usta say "Come on—papoo" and den she'd put us in a basket and tote us on her shoulder.

Chaney's memoir has the same notions of pure blood that obsessed whites. Aside from racial categories, the notion of full blood was a connection to a past removed from the changes and confusion of the present American experience. The WPA guide to Mississippi mentions those full-blooded Choctaws farming their ancestors' land almost as if they were removed from time and therefore immaterial for contemporary consideration.

And if the slave memoirs betray an innate fondness for stereotyping, we need to consider the biases of the WPA interviewers, too. For example, there is no great need in Chaney's account to render *was* as *wuz*. Most Americans pronounce *was* as *wuz* anyway. Spelling it so is simply a code indicating that the speaker is illiterate. This rendering of patois is meant to represent authenticity, a signifying notion that informs most reports by the educated on the words and music of unlettered, unsophisticated people.

The accounts of ex-slaves in Oklahoma give us the fullest descriptions of life in an alternate American society. Nearly every slave memoir from the former Indian territory either cites Indian parentage or offers vivid glimpses of life in a Native American world. "There was nobody around the place but Indians and Negroes," said Chaney Richardson, 90, of Fort Gibson, Oklahoma. "I was a full-grown girl before I ever saw a white man."

Henry Clay, age 100 and living in Fort Gibson, Oklahoma, recalled:

> I never did get along good with those Creek slaves out here and I always stayed around with the white folks. In fact, I was afraid of these Creeks and always got off the road when I see Creek negroes coming along. They would have red strings tied to their hats or something wild looking.

In Tulsa, Lucinda Davis, 89, remembered:

> I belong to a full-blood Creek Indian and I didn't know nothin' but Creek talk long after de Civil War. My mistress was part white and knowed English talk . . . I heard it sometime, but it sound like whole lot of wild shoat in de cedar brake scared at something when I do hear it . . . I belong to old Tuskaya-hiniha. He was a big man in de Upper Creek . . . I don't know if old Master had a white name.

The vast majority of the former slaves remembered benign—even kindly—treatment at the hands of their owners. But cruelly treated slaves likely did not live into their eighties. And, too, no one likes dwelling on things best forgotten. Sarah Wilson spoke briefly of her mother's owner in Tennessee:

> He was a white man that married a Cherokee woman, and he was a devil on this earth. I don't want to talk about him none. White folks was mean to us like the devil, and so I jest let them pass.

Ninety-seven-year-old Carrie Davis of Oklahoma City recalled an excruciating scene with something like a happy ending.

> When I was 20 years old, my mother was put on the block with my two brothers. Mr. Hughes, the slave seller, said he had a nigger winch and two bulls to go. My brother Henry shot him and he never got over it. My brother left and they never found him . . . He looked white.

Ms. Davis did not explain if Henry was one of the brothers at auction, where exactly Hughes was gunned down, or if the shooting stopped the sale. She did add: "My mother's father was Dr. Crush, part Indian and Irish. No Negro looking people at all in my family."

We might also consider that under daily circumstances of hard toil and violence, to be merely decently fed, clothed, and housed qualified as kindly treatment worthy of gratitude and loyalty. Mary Grayson, of Tulsa, recalled the man who purchased her mother at age twelve:

> The Creek man that bought her was a kind sort of man, mammy said, and wouldn't let [her former owner] punish her [for running away]. He took her away and was kind to her, but he decided she was too young

to breed and he sold her to another Creek who had several slaves already, and he brought her out to the Territory.

Ms. Grayson details two more attempts to breed her young mother—including two more sales—"until my mammy got married to Mose's slave boy Jacob . . . and went ahead and had ten children for Mr. Mose."

Compared to greater outrages of the period, this appalling treatment did not quite register as cruelty. "We slaves didn't have a hard time at all before the War," Grayson says.

I have had people who were slaves of white folks back in the old states tell me that their masters were cruel to them sometimes, but all the Negroes I knew who belonged to Creeks always had plenty of clothes and lots to eat and we all lived in good log cabins we built.

Creeks apparently allowed their slaves far more autonomy than other tribes, which may account for Henry Clay's fear when seeing them on the open road. "[T]he Chickasaw people didn't treat their slaves like the Creeks did," Grayson recalls. "They was more strict, like the people in Texas and other places."

Music figures in the narratives of several slaves, recollections of playing, learning how to play (one man recounted how he was sent by his master from Georgia to North Carolina for fiddle lessons), or hearing it at dances or in church. "I can make an old fiddle talk," Henry Clay bragged. "So I done pretty good playing for the white dances for a long time after the War, and they sure had some good ones. Everything from a waltz to a Schottische I played."

Vivid memories surrounded the dances the southern tribes held to celebrate the Green Corn Festival, the yearly ceremony to honor the goddess who died to be reborn as maize. Lucinda Davis left an account of the corn festival of the Creeks, which she called a "busk," and the different dances, or "bangas":

De chicken dance is de "Tolosabanga," and de "Isti-
fanibanga" is de one whar dey make lak dey is skel-
etons and raw heads comin to git you.

De "Hadjobanga" is de crazy dance, and dat is
a funny one. Dey all dance crazy and make up funny
songs to go wid de dance . . .

But de worse one was de drunk dance. Dey
jest dance ever which-away, de men and de women
together, and dey wrassle and hang and carry on awful!
De good people don't dance dat one. Everybody sings
about going to somebody else's house and sleeping wid
dem, and shout "We is all drunk and we don't know
what we doing and we ain't doing wrong 'cause we is
all drunk" and things like dat.

(In remembering the African dances her father taught her,
Chaney Mack said, "Dey dance by derselves or swing each other
'round. Dey didn't know nothing 'bout dese 'huggin' dances.")

This carrying on, of hugging and swinging dances, sounds
remarkably like descriptions of typical Saturday nights in the Delta jukes. Sam Chatmon, of the Mississippi Sheiks, who claimed
Charlie Patton was his half brother, told an interviewer that he
never heard the word blues applied to music until he was an
adult: "No, in them days I didn't know nothin' but square dancing and foxtrot and waltz, two-step." Henry Townsend, a blues
singer born in Mississippi in 1909, recalled, "Well, they used to
have several names for them [blues] songs, used to call them,
let's see, a corn song, they used to call them reels."

"Jigs and reels," Elijah Wald notes, were "terms that were
routinely used for any dance that struck respectable people as
wild or unrestrained, whether Irish or African." And further,
"[m]ost experts agree that between a third and a half of the
standard Southern fiddle repertoire is drawn from the black tradition . . . [T]his tradition was very much alive during the blues
era." One is here left to consider what exactly made up that black
tradition.

Given our evolving understanding of the extensive relations between Native and African peoples in frontier America, it can be stated with some confidence that there are no clear lines of cultural influence. Instead of a river from one bright, if distant, source, we have a web, combined strands connected in ways obvious and obscure, a matrix or, seen horizontally, a delta of causes, a thicket of meanings.

And it was indeed in the dense swamps and isolated hollows, those fugitive refuges, where that music was articulated. And that sharing of Indigenous harmony that leapt from voice to fiddle, banjo, and guitar was the mark of an underlying kinship that allowed a recognition over great distances.

Mountain musicians heard something familiar in black blues records. In the 1960s, Kentucky banjo and guitar player Roscoe Holcomb recalled listening to a Blind Lemon Jefferson record for the first time: "Up 'til then, the blues was only inside me. Blind Lemon was the first to 'let out' the blues."

A lot of the connections I've made here might be taken for coincidence; most are circumstantial. But who's to say if coincidence cannot offer valid concordances? To ignore a confluence of incident is to be indifferent to the possibilities of who we might be, and under the circumstances, whom we might become.

Is it a coincidence that Charlie Parker loved country music? (For the stories, he said.) Or that he was first called Indian in Oklahoma by his colleagues in Jay McShann's Territory Band? (Parker stood very still when he played.) A coincidence that Parker redefined the possible in jazz music with a wild solo on the 1944 recording called "Cherokee"?

For in considering how music may have reflected the life of the early American frontier, think of how critical the mere act of listening must have been; not only for hunting and warfare, but as the psyche's immanent grasp of the natural world, the only thing, besides dreams, there was to study.

It is a commonplace to consider how the complete immersion into the facets of nature provide very subtle shadings to the languages of Indigenous people; the many Inuit names, for example, for snow, or the dozen-odd Cheyenne words for their ponies' hair. Modern society has made it to the far other shore, where there are one or two words for toothpaste, or breakfast cereal, and our stores are filled with dozens of types of each. Brand names have replaced the details of the natural world, and we moderns are left, between birth and death, mainly disconnected from the oceanic majority of existence.

Before leaving, let us take up one more fugitive history, one of a word.

Blues first appeared in print to mean feelings of melancholy and unease in 1807, when Washington Irving used it in one of his satirical essays of New York social life collected in the *Salmagundi Papers*: "[E]verybody knows how provoking it is to be cut short in a fit of the blues, by an impertinent question about what is really the matter, when a man can't tell himself." Before then, bouts of melancholy were known variously as an attack or a fit of blue devils, or just a blue devil. The phrase *blue devil* first appeared in the early 1600s, coinciding with the dramatic increase in the New World production of blue indigo dye.

A legume initially cultivated, as its name suggests, in India, indigo was valued since Roman times. Its extracted dye was an exceptional rarity in the Middle Ages, one of the most expensive commodities on earth, transported by Arab traders by caravan from India in the form of sparkling blue bricks. The bricks were dissolved in water to render a rich, indelible stain.

The desire to cut Arab middlemen out of the spice and indigo trade encouraged the Spanish and Portuguese to look for a sea passage to India, Columbus's project in 1492. Finding America, in a fit of wishful thinking he called the people here Indians.

As luck would have it, the Spaniards did find indigo in their new world. Indigo varieties range from Africa across central Asia and into the western hemisphere, patterning the migration of the people with which it came so cruelly to share a name.

Blue is a royal color in Africa and Europe, associated on both continents with the female gods. The Virgin Mary is always pictured in the blue mantle of the Queen of Heaven, while in West Africa, blue is the visible attribute of Erzulie, the goddess of beauty and love. Among Hindus, blue is the color of Krishna, Lord of the Cosmos, and holy men in his service stain their bodies with indigo dye. Mayans dyed human sacrifices blue. The Cherokee and Iroquois colored their hair with indigo and used it as a medicinal plant.

Europeans also considered indigo a drug, and its use was banned in England in the century before 1660. But after the Spanish initiated industrial-scale indigo production in the West Indies, and after taking Jamaica from Spain in 1654, Britain was pleased to join the indigo trade.

Large-scale indigo production, a three-month process from first harvest to final product, was the main work of the Indians enslaved by the first Spanish colonizers. Making even small amounts of dye is a stinking, labor-intensive task. Plantation-scale production was appalling.

> Indigo leaves exuded a strong, unpleasant odor that caused headaches and nausea to those not accustomed to the smell. [N]ative workers who harvested and handled indigo plants were liable to suffer from sexual impotence, accompanied by a temporary semi-lameness of the lower limbs.

Harvested plants, about six feet tall, needed to be pressed underwater until fermented. The resulting mash smelled like rotten meat and drew clouds of flies. It was churned for hours by workers wading in large vats, to oxygenate the solution and cause raw blue particles to precipitate from the rotted plants and settle.

The vats drained into streams, where the waste killed fish and repulsed livestock, and the indigo mud was dug out and refined further by washing and boiling in a series of smaller tubs.

The final extract was then cut into cakes and dried for shipment to market. One hundred pounds of plants were needed to produce four ounces of pure dye, which was nearly precious as gold.

Long-term exposure to the chemicals released as vapor during industrial indigo production caused bronchial lesions resembling tuberculosis. Chemical analysis of indigo waste water has since shown it to be mutagenic, meaning that it tends to increase the frequency of genetic mutation, possibly causing cancer.

Reports indicate that Indians working indigo plantations died, on average, within five years. Sick, ulcerous, impotent, gasping for breath, and stained blue, if these poor souls were not the blue devils of seventeenth-century slang, they were nonetheless wraiths in a hell that would have given Dante pause.

As Indians died off in the Spanish indigo factories, there was an urgent need for replacement workers. And so the transatlantic slave trade commenced in earnest. Africans were considered hardier workers, as Anne Mattson notes: "Because it was thought that the Indians were particularly susceptible to the diseases that bred around the fermentation vats, plantation owners claimed they did most of the field work [i.e., harvesting indigo plants], while black slaves extracted the dye. In reality, the division of labor was probably not so strict." It is probably not coincidental that the Yoruba and Mandinga peoples, societies renowned for their indigo-dyed textiles, made up a large percentage of those souls transported to America.

In 1718, the French began indigo production in Louisiana— where one name for indigo mud was *mal*, 'evil.' Shortly thereafter, cultivation in Virginia was joined by the Carolinas, Georgia, and Mississippi. Indigo exports from Jamaica and the Spanish colonies fell off, replaced by sugar cane. By 1776, indigo was mainly a North American export crop on par with rice and tobacco.

After 1776, English buyers understandably looked to India for the product, and American indigo production fell off rapidly. Following the invention of the cotton gin, cotton cultivation in the American South became immensely more profitable; as the WPA guide to Mississippi noted: "[E]nthusiasm for indigo disappeared." This ramping-up of cotton cultivation then demanded even greater imports of Africans; and the lands of the southern Indian nations were put squarely in the sights of an economic system now best thought of as utterly insane.

The horrible history of indigo production was quickly forgotten. The language moved on, too. By 1807, *a fit of blue devils* had become *the blues.*

By then the Indigenous and African peoples of the United States were consigned to their appalling fates; their destinies linked forever to the heedless Europeans who controlled the continent and whose own destiny would be to drift across it endlessly. The so-called wilderness they presumed to tame, the fortunes they strove to create, and the people they aimed to control would inevitably deny them any promise of rest short of the one guaranteed by the grave. By naming some of that restless sadness the blues, the language came to reflect the feelings of inner disorder that seem to exist at-large in the land, strange disruptions and wild harmonies we still struggle to understand.

The New World

In the end I saw that the forces that had created the guitar were the same which formed my family, the people who had, one way or another, forged my history in the first place. I decided that they needed an accounting too, if only briefly, not as beings radiant with intimate power, which is the proper subject of memoir, but as actors in history, as participants or witnesses themselves. Necessarily connected to this idea is the recognition that the ultimate subject of a fugitive history may be the fugitive history writer himself, and that something autochthonous largely molds us all.

The Genesee River passes through the center of Rochester, New York, over a broad and flat rock basin, in a trough about one hundred yards wide. Most of the year the water runs in shallow sheets around and under occasional snags of debris between shelves of stone and the spectral trunks of whole trees, stuck between the city's vaulted arch bridges.

But in the spring, when rains melt the snow for a hundred miles south of town, the Genesee is a fierce, chaotic thing, as it descends some two hundred feet within city limits to reach Lake Ontario. Even those familiar with the river's early spring course through town cannot look down on that yearly flood, unbound in fury, without a deep, native unease.

The water takes two distinct drops, the first a smooth settling of perhaps ten feet near the main library, the second, a quarter-mile further down, into a limestone chasm a hundred feet deep that forms the High Falls around which Rochester was founded and quickly grew.

The opening of the Erie Canal in 1825 made Rochester the nation's first frontier boomtown. The grain and saw mills along the river sent Genesee valley flour and lumber east to New York City and west to the Indiana wilderness. A Romanesque stone arch aqueduct vaulted the canal over the river a couple hundred yards above the High Falls, an engineering marvel of the new republic, mentioned with something like awe in both *Moby Dick* and *Leaves of Grass*.

Rochester was famous for being the town where civilization had replaced wilderness overnight. The historian Paul E. Johnson quotes a visitor, Nathaniel Parker Willis, who commented that the town's falls were "the only instance in the known world of a cataract turned, without the loss of a drop, through the pockets of speculators."

The new city had ten thousand residents by 1829, with nearly as many passing through every year, working the canal or heading west. A year earlier, the most famous man in the country, a hard-drinking daredevil named Sam Patch, the nation's first entertainment celebrity, died performing a stunt there: a jump into the falls gorge on Friday, November 13.

In 1826, Patch was a thirty-year-old mill worker from Pawtucket, Rhode Island, who, at a bridge-raising across the Passaic Falls in Paterson, New Jersey, leapt from the cliff there after first taking up a collection. Famous for nothing more than that, he was fearless by way of an innate sense of balance and regular applications of strong drink. Patch's true talent, though, lay in self-promotion. He had handbills printed with American eagles rampant and the words "There's no mistake in Sam Patch!" He also coined a motto that might be the country's first advertising slogan: "Some things," he said, "can be done as well as others." Patch, in fact, was good to the last drop.

He was in Rochester that November fresh from an engagement at Niagara Falls, where he made two jumps from an eighty-four-foot platform on Goat Island. By then a hardened celebrity, he was traveling the western frontier with a pet bear and drinking heavily. In Rochester, his leap was to be from the cliff at the middle of the falls. His first jump on November 6th didn't draw much of a crowd, so Patch ordered a twenty-five-foot tower built at the spot and advertised another show for the following Friday, vowing it would be his last. He spent the next week drumming up business at taverns and in the press. The thirteenth was a typical mid-November day in western New York, with gray low skies and cold, but eight thousand people, equal to the whole population of the city, came to watch.

Some said later that the platform shook a bit when Patch climbed it, others that the shaking was all Sam's. He first tossed over his pet bear as a kind of test, which was successful. He then gave a short and by all accounts incoherent address, which few were able to hear over the sound of the water, though close auditors said he compared himself to Napoleon.

Then he jumped.

Patch started all his leaps knees-to-chest then straightened, entering the water feet first. That day he pitched from his vertical posture almost immediately and, arms and legs flailing, hit flat on his back with a pop audible over the roaring falls. He vanished instantly. People waited for him to surface; he didn't. Spectators recalled departing without a word, unwilling to look each other in the eye.

Some reckoned Patch planned it all and was hiding in a cave behind the falls. Newspapers across the northeast reported sightings, but the body turned up the following March, several miles down river, frozen in ice. An autopsy revealed his shoulders were dislocated when he hit the river and that he'd probably died instantly. He was buried nearby. "Sam Patch," his marker read, "Such is Fame." Not long after, Nathaniel Hawthorne came to Rochester to meditate upon Patch's feats and call him a hero. Edgar Allan Poe, in New York, compared him to a frog.

The critic Edmund Wilson, with family roots in northern New York, observed that something about living so far removed from the Puritan Protestant social structures of the Atlantic seaboard unleashed a certain mania.

In 1824, a millennial Jew, Mordecai Noah, proposed to build a Jewish homeland, a city called Ararat, on Grand Island in the Niagara River. This was considered no more improbable than the canal set to open the following year, though, after a big kickoff party in Buffalo to promote the new Jewish state, Noah went back to New York, never to return.

The same period saw an impressive assortment of utopian/ socialist, radical Quaker, and anti-masonic settlements between the Hudson and Lake Erie. From the free-love Oneida Community (named for the local Iroquois tribe) to celibate Shaker villages, one would be hard-pressed to find a landscape more haunted by visions and populated by visionaries anywhere else in the country.

The countryside around Rochester underwent an eruption of religious mania as commerce in the city grew exponentially in the two decades after the canal opened. The Spiritualist movement, which accounted for seance communication with great spirits and the souls of the dead, was founded nearby, as was the Mormon Church.

Near Buffalo, a Seneca named Handsome Lake based a new Iroquois religion, named Longhouse for where meetings were held, on a series of redemptive visions that merged Indigenous and Quaker beliefs. Rochester was ground zero for the first evangelical revival in the new republic, a movement that created broad pubic support for the abolition of slavery (Frederick Douglass, striking out on his own from Boston, moved to Rochester in 1847 and published his *North Star* newspaper there); the city was a terminus for the Underground Railroad, from which fleeing slaves embarked on boats to Canada. Women's suffrage was another local radical cause (Susan B. Anthony was a neighbor of Douglass's), as was the temperance movement, perhaps the least popular of the local campaigns (Buffalo, a sink of frontier sin, remained immune to the cause), but a powerful one nevertheless.

The zeal was also reflected in new commerce: the manufacture of furniture, clothing, shoes, and, with German immigration in the 1840s, lenses. Cabinet makers and lens grinders made Rochester an early locus of camera making. There were fifteen camera and film companies there in 1879 when George Eastman, a clerk at the Rochester Savings Bank, perfected a means of mass producing dry plate film. He invented roll film shortly after that, which soon led to both photography for the masses and motion pictures—therefore life as we know it today.

The land from the Genesee west to the Maumee River in Ohio had been once the control of the Seneca Nation, the westernmost of the Iroquois confederation, which ran the fur trade across the Great Lakes. British allies during the Revolution, the main Seneca towns were destroyed by the Continental Army in two years of fighting, and their land was forfeit in a 1797 treaty that left them two large reservations, one bordering the new town at Buffalo Creek, the other east and south across the Pennsylvania border.

The Seneca managed to survive the social pathologies that mainly obliterated the five other Iroquois nations, in large part thanks to the Longhouse religion, which combines enduring practices of Native spirituality with a code of behavior and meeting practice gained from Quaker missionaries. Another factor in Seneca survival was their successful resistance to removal to Indian territory. In 1838, as the five southern tribes were forced from their land, the Buffalo Creek reservation was sold to the expanding city, with the understanding that the Seneca remove themselves to their Cattaraugus reservation.

By then, land values in western New York, overpriced by speculators, had collapsed. Farmland in Ohio and Indiana was flatter and more fertile; settlement moved westward and the Seneca were able to hold on to what they had. In following years, just as Mohawk riveting crews adapted to industrial life, Seneca men took perilous blue-collar jobs. Part of the old Buffalo Creek reservation became the enormous West Seneca rail yards, and Seneca men hired on as train brakemen on the lines radiating from it.

For the Seneca, the Genesee falls were the dwelling of the Stone Throwers, a clan of the Djogeon, the Great Little People, who guided the natural world. The falls dwellers "are terribly strong," Edmund Wilson writes in *Apologies to the Iroquois*, "and can hurl rocks and uproot trees." Other Djogeon

> care [for] the plants: they wake them up in the springtime, they see that the flowers bloom and they turn the

fruit so that it gets the sun. The third live in caverns, and their special task is to guard all the entrances to the underworld and prevent the white buffalo that live there from breaking out and wreaking havoc on earth.

In the late 1950s, the Seneca were fighting against further government annexation of their treaty lands, the combined assaults of a state power plant near Niagara Falls, and a federal dam project that would flood a large portion of the Cattaraugus reservation. Wilson went to report on their plight and in 1961, interested in the Longhouse religion, he attended a performance of the so-called Dark Dance, a new year ceremony, in a private home on the reservation in Salamanca, New York.

A group of about fifteen people, he wrote, sat in a circle of chairs in a lightless kitchen, and sang to the Great Little People, inviting them into the room.

When the Little People enter the room, its occupants are heard to shift their feet. The visitors, in the darkness, are stumbling over their legs. The Little People sing in their own language, which nobody understands.

The effect, Wilson says, is

extraordinary . . . at first even frightening. The singing fills up the room, as if something had opened out that was larger than those who released it, and that had some kind of independent existence, embodying some projection of the human spirit which has survived through uncounted centuries . . . which was now still alive in this shabby old house, rising up and renewing itself, taking over and animating the darkness.

The songs are varied and addressed to specific charms, which have been bestowed by the Little People and also by various animals, and these have been passed on from person to person, each one, before he dies, appointing the next possessor. The charms need to be present at the dance and must be sung to, because, "like [the Great Little People], if neglected, they may become angry."

Though part of the Longhouse religion, the Dark Dance is very old, based on the tale of an Indian boy who while hunting encounters two little men trying to shoot a squirrel. Their tiny arrows can't reach it, so the boy kills the animal and gives it to them with two others he has.

The grateful Little People bring the boy to their village, where he's treated to a feast of squirrel and corn soup and a dance:

> They burned sacred tobacco and then covered up the fire. In the dark they sang songs to the beat of the drum, and they told the boy to learn them. He stayed for several days and the same thing took place every night.

The lad learns the ceremony and is bidden by the Little People to repeat it when he gets home so that they can come visit him. They also tell him that the Seneca should throw tobacco into the river gorges when they hear the sound of the Little People's drums.

The boy returns to his village, but it is now overgrown by the forest and everyone gone. He eventually finds his people, but they do not recognize him; they have grown strangely older.

One point on which Wilson is uncharacteristically quiet is the strong resemblance between the Seneca tale and that of our old friend Washington Irving's "Rip Van Winkle." Like the Seneca boy, Rip is out hunting squirrels, leaving his little village on the Hudson to go tramping into the Catskill wilderness. There he hears a strange voice call his name and sees a short old man, dressed in the antique Dutch fashion, who leads him to a party of similarly dressed short men playing ninepins in a glen nearby. Rip is made to serve the wordless company from a keg, which, as the day wears on, he drinks from himself, eventually falling asleep.

Waking, he finds the men gone, the path to their bowling green now a running stream; in addition, his rifle is rusted over and his dog gone. Returning to his village, Rip finds that his house is a ruin; everything has changed. He meets a number of people, none of whom he knows. His beard, he discovers, has grown a foot.

In a passage that brilliantly judges the American scene, Irving writes:

> The very village was altered—it was larger and more populous. There were rows of houses which he had never seen before, and those which had been his familiar haunts had disappeared. Strange names were over the doors—strange faces at the windows—every thing was strange.

Furthermore, "[t]he very character of the people seemed changed. There was a busy, bustling, disputatious tone about it." Rip looks in vain for old friends. Then "[t]wo tavern politicians bustled up to him, and drawing him partly aside, inquired 'on which side he voted?' Rip stared in vacant stupidity."

His predicament is finally resolved when he recognizes his grown daughter and, before identifying himself, asks what became of her father. It's twenty years, she says, since he went away with his gun and has not been heard from since. "His dog came home without him—but whether he shot himself, or was carried away by the Indians no body can tell." Note that, though set in a broad comedy, Irving offers a glimpse of two abject perils of frontier life: suicide and Indian kidnapping.

Story over, Irving can't resist a final word to say that Rip's tale was true, and not taken from a German myth. Then, in a postscript to the end note, he tips his hand: "The Indians considered the [Catskills] the abode of spirits." In so many words Irving, who was familiar with Native folk tales of the Hudson Valley, tells his readers that Rip's story is not European, but American, one from the wilderness of spirits, Indians, and lost explorers.

The story of the young hunter and the Great Little People, whose single night is that of a human year, became Irving's satire on progress and a portrait of the fundamental strangeness of change. Where the Indian myth shows the wanderer returning to mainly familiar surroundings with new insights into an eternal cycle taught by the sacred beings he met on his way, the American sleeper awakens to a harsh new world—and his enchanted captors barely spoke to him at all.

Fleeta Jemison, a descendent-daughter of Mary Jemison, the girl kidnapped by Indians and adopted by the Seneca, was born about 1920 on the Cattaraugus rez in Salamanca and eventually sent to Rochester by an aid agency to work as a maid. For a while she was a housekeeper living in the maid's room at my great-aunt Inez's home, which is where we became friends.

She had an easy laugh, a soft, round face with a flat, broken-looking, pug nose, bright Eurasian eyes, which tended to squint behind her cat-eye frame glasses, a tattoo (a black-ink heart and the initials RS on her right forearm), and spoke with the flat nasal drawl of western New York in cadences of reservation English.

Married several times, she stayed at my great-aunt's house until Inez died, in 1964, eventually working for my mother and grandmother, and living in a shabby apartment building near downtown. Her ancestor Mary was born to Scotch or Irish parents—when recalling her life story at eighty, Mary was not sure where they came from—on a ship sailing to America in 1742. The Jemisons landed in Philadelphia and moved west to farm. Mary was captured in 1758, during the French-Indian War. Jemison, also spelled Jimmerson, passed down, like all Seneca names, by matrilineal descent.

Mary outlived two husbands, both respected warriors, gave birth to eight children, and lived on a vast tract of land the tribe deeded her on the Genesee south of Rochester. Though her sons fell prey to violence and alcoholism—one going crazy and murdering another—Mary was highly esteemed by her settler neighbors. One of the wealthy ones hired a schoolmaster to take down her story. That he rendered it in the polite voice of a modest scholar does not take away from the vividness of Mary's story or the emotion with which it was told.

"I was fortunate in falling into their hands," Mary Jemison said of her Seneca sisters, "for they were kind, good-natured women; peaceable and mild in their dispositions; temperate and decent in their habits, and very tender and gentle towards me." I can say that ran in her family. Fleeta was unfailingly sweet tempered, sympathetic to the troubles of children and adults, and stalwart towards troubles of her own, which centered mainly around alcohol.

Inez's home was a short walk from the Council Rock, a flat-topped, car-sized boulder left by the glaciers. Once the meeting point for Seneca deliberations and oratory, it has been moved across a busy street away from any pedestrians, and is today an obscure municipal landmark with a bronze plaque. Before its relocation, Fleeta, in her white uniform and apron, and I would take walks to the rock which I would then climb on. Whatever thoughts she had about visiting such an important, if not sacred, landmark of her overwhelmed nation, she kept to herself.

When I was about eight, having a succession of pet box turtles, Fleeta gave me a rock that closely resembled a turtle's shell, a turtle rock she called it, which I've kept ever since; a smooth gray stone the span of an adult's hand, shaped like a mushroom cap nipped off at both ends, with irregular cracked hexagons across its surface. Though clearly not a petrified turtle, neither does it appear to be fashioned by hand.

If it had a ceremonial or totemic function, Fleeta never said. There are several turtle rocks, of different sizes and colors but all resembling turtle shells, in the Rochester museum's collection, apparently formed in ancient riverbeds and scattered by glaciers around western New York. According to the museum display, they were props for storytelling, a pastime the Seneca allowed only in winter, when the world was asleep.

Fleeta left our lives as quietly as she first appeared. She waitressed at a burger joint until retiring and moving back to Salamanca in the late seventies. I can't recall the last time I saw her. My mother kept in touch occasionally by phone. "When are you going to stop drinking that stuff?" Mom asked her once.

"When they stop makin' it," Fleeta told her. They stayed in contact around ten years, until about the time, I learned much later from one of her nieces, Fleeta died.

It's possible, though, that I did see her again, in a dream so vivid it had all the marks of a brief visit from the dead. Though I recognized her instantly, in the dream Fleeta looked prettier and younger than I'd ever known her, and held the turtle rock tenderly to her right cheek. "It's lonely," she said. I woke up as if slapped.

By then my oldest possession, the turtle rock had settled to the bottom of a bookshelf in my Minneapolis apartment, a neglected paperweight and bookend. Leaping out of bed, I put it on a windowsill where it had a view of the sky and trees. It may still be lonely, but it is no lonelier now than me, and Fleeta has not come back to explain any more of its needs. I think her visit that morning was meant to encourage other steps too. Be that as it may, it was not long after the resurrection of the turtle rock that I got my first guitar, that mythic descendent of the turtle, and began to learn to play.

There's a Kodak color snapshot I took of my father holding a guitar on Christmas Day, 1967. It was in my grandmother Dolly's living room and Dad is dressed in a suit and tie, sitting in his father-in-law's rather baronial, high-backed armchair. The cheap acoustic guitar was a present to one of my sisters. It looks like he is forming a G chord, and he regards the camera with a merry squint. He might be singing, his mouth in goofy smile that always indicated mild teasing.

It's easy to see that his intention was mockery, a Republican gentleman's amiable raillery regarding a common-enough figure at the time, the folk singer. (While mainly a fan of big band music and Lawrence Welk's TV show, Dad was also fond of singing "The Happy Wanderer" and "Goodnight, Irene," the latter presumably picked up from the Weavers' 1950 hit single.) Interestingly enough, he holds the guitar in a correct classical posture, balanced on his right knee, pointed upright.

Though we had a small electric organ for a time when I was young, I don't recall my father playing it much, and it wasn't taken in the move to our new house. I certainly never saw him pick up a guitar again. But once I started playing, so many years ·later as to be another lifetime, I began to wonder if the photo might have pictured him with something he'd wanted but never got to have.

Exactly when his father, Alfonso Gioia, came from Valledolmo, Sicily is not clear. The eldest of five sons and a daughter, Alfonso's 1950 newspaper obituary says it was 1895, when he was fourteen or fifteen. His brother Antonio's 1957 obituary puts the date of his arrival in 1887. A year younger than Alfonso, he would have been six. The 1970 obit of their youngest brother, Samuel, (b. 1890) states he arrived with his parents about 1892.

A short, error-filled Who's Who–type biography of Alfonso (which gave him Samuel's wife and children) from 1925 says he came to America with his parents in 1894, "settling in Chautauqua County, New York. There the father purchased a farm, becoming one of the prominent agriculturalists of that locality."

There are likely several reasons for this hazy accounting of recent family history, the chief one being that there was little desire to recall Sicily with any longing, or consider a departure as anything more than an escape. (As late as 1998, when I told Uncle Nino of my plans to see the old hometown, he made it sound like a dumb idea. "What do you want to go *there* for?" he said. A frequent Italian traveler with his wife, he never laid eyes on the place.)

Along with the desire to forget Sicily was the associated need to romanticize the American arrival. The story of Alfonso's New World progress, selling newspapers and shining shoes, the official version given me for decades, becomes somewhat less stereotypical, though probably no less difficult, if his father owned land.

For the sake of clarity, then, let's say that in 1892, Oratzio Gioia journeyed from Sicily to eventually purchase a farm near Fredonia, New York. His sons worked a number of local industrial and agricultural jobs as they grew up. Oratzio died in 1908. In 1910 (this date is certain), Alfonso and Antonio were in the wholesale fruit business when a Fredonia businessman named Bellanca, from another Valledolmese family, loaned them money to start a macaroni company.

In 1914, they purchased pasta machines in Buffalo from that notable American success, Carmelo Gugino, who then brokered the marriage of his sister Nanetta to Alfonso, a rising young man. In early 1918, the A. Gioia & Brother macaroni company (note the useful ambiguity in the business name) relocated to Rochester, whose Italian community was larger than Buffalo's, where my father was born that November.

In the twenties, Alfonso, following Carmelo's example, opened a bank to handle savings accounts and wire money transfers to Italy. "He ran a bank through the Depression," Dad said once, "and nobody lost a dime!" Alfonso also bought a farm with an apple orchard west of town, and was for a period before World War II Honorary Italian Council for western New York.

In 1940, the two brothers, who'd been business partners for twenty-five years, had a dramatic and bitter falling out. Antonio paid Alfonso for the factory and the family brand name, deducting from the agreement an amount he considered his by way of salary. Alfonso, incensed, felt he was being robbed, though declined to take his brother to court. He instead satisfied himself by simply considering Antonio dead.

The next year, Alfonso founded Bravo Macaroni (the name, of course, is Italian for Brave), incorporated as Alfonso Gioia & Sons, and competed with his brother for ten years before Antonio took the Gioia company to Buffalo. Alfonso died of a heart ailment, after what was supposed to be a routine operation, less than a year later.

After serving in the Army during the war, Dad worked as a salesman at Bravo, covering the route between Rochester and Boston, and lived with his parents—the last unmarried son. It's not clear if he ever considered not working for Alfonso. By the time he left for Cornell, he had already spent summers working on the farm, milking cows, haying, plowing, and pruning apple trees. For the rest of his life he kept the broad forearms and upper body strength that farm work gives. At college he was ROTC, and, graduating in 1941, was in uniform when the war began and stayed that way for the duration.

An armored division recon lieutenant in North Africa, and then a member of the latest (perhaps last) army to invade Sicily, and carry on into Italy, France, and Austria, Joe finished the war with captain's bars, along with a Purple Heart, and a Silver Star earned in Tunisia at El Guettar—pronounced, yes; *guitar*—action in which his outfit, the 601st tank destroyers, also won a Presidential unit citation. (El Guettar was the first American victory of the Second World War. A. J. Liebling's limpid and moving eyewitness account of the battle forms the last chapter of his war book, *The Road Back to Paris*.)

One suspects Dad's immediate postwar years passed happily enough. His job got him away from home on a regular basis and likely offered the sorts of entertainment familiar to traveling salesmen everywhere. He said he went to a lot of movies, though there was surely more to it than that. He was a young veteran, with money and good looks. He was also a very good card player—often sending money home to his mom from Army games—and fond of horse racing and dice; in short, a man's man, one who enjoyed the company of women who could smoke, drink, and laugh at racy jokes; the sort of woman who was the exact opposite of his mother and, of course, mine.

His bachelor idyll ended when his father died. Alfonso's friend and lawyer, Frank D'Amanda, handled the estate and, presumably noting the presence of an unmarried son living with his widowed mother, went on to introduce the now not-so-young Gioia son to Rosalie Scinta, his not-so-young niece, a school teacher also living with her parents.

It is hard judging at this remove the precise levels of love, need, cultural logic, and expectations that combined to make my parents' marriage. While Uncle Frank had been a friend of Alfonso's, let's note that ten years earlier, before the war, Dad would not have been considered suitable for my mother; from a nice family certainly, but Sicilian, you know, and a little rough around the edges. But time moved on, and it was late for both. Looked at one way, my father married his lawyer's niece. Considered another, they were made for each other.

While I do not think Joe was an unhappy man, he kept a silent reserve, an interior Sicilian landscape which he never ventured far from for very long. When I think of him being happy, I tend to picture the way he looked holding that guitar Christmas Day at Dolly's.

He was not tall, about five feet six, with a pleasant, handsome face that was certainly beguiling when he smiled. Rarely, though, did he smile while at the factory; in fact, he could rapidly ease into yelling fits of abrading intensity if he found something that displeased him.

The Bravo Macaroni factory stood in a warehouse district near what had been the Erie Canal's western course through the city, a big four-story brick building, with window bays large enough for seven men to stand upright in, painted an industrial maroon. As the brother in charge of production, Dad woke up early every morning to unlock the building in time for the few men working the night shift to punch out at seven a.m. For the rest of the day, he presided over the works with a gruff energy, striding up and down stairs and across the floors dressed in an unvarying uniform of dark gray flannel pants, button-down Oxford shirt, white or buff blue, sleeves rolled to his elbow, brown wing-tip shoes, and a dark tie.

Needless to say his standards were very high, and his employees, many of whom had worked for Alfonso, bore his rages with the resigned acceptance that Italians have developed to a skill rivaling balance. (Among Sicilians, yelling is first a familial bond.) There was, indeed, something operatic about his storms, which, if the target didn't speak English, could unfold in Italian with equal skill. When he was really going, Joe would shake both hands next to his head, his fingers wide, as if distributing greater rays of fury from his temples. If it wasn't focused on you, and all within earshot felt uneasy at least, it was a marvel to behold.

It's clear to me now that the factory was my father's larger, more perfect family: demanding and loyal, while tractable in ways that his real family could never be. An abiding respect for Alfonso could still be felt there twenty years after he died. Growing up around such a place made it hard for me afterwards to work at anything that did not offer, beyond a paycheck, greater returns in dedication and pride.

This bias has proved to be something of a liability for me, but Dad never knew another way to live. He had been raised through hard times by an autocratic, self-made man. Duty defined his life, and he approached nearly everything he did with a scouring thoroughness, an ingrained impatience with delay, and an abiding scorn at anything less than a full effort on the part of others.

We never really got along, he and I, a consequence of our very different upbringings. Our best times together were those few occasions when we traveled, father and son in unfamiliar surroundings, when we could be the companions we were not at home. At right angles to the faintly provincial, regular-guy image Dad presented to his many collegial, clubmen friends, he was an observant, worldly man in his own right, conversant in French and fluent in Italian, who wrote letters, which I found after Mom died, with a succinct clarity and ease.

The time came to sell Bravo in the mid-seventies. Macaroni by then was a mainstream American food, drawing corporations into what had been an exclusive enterprise of regional families. Their aging, center-city rust-belt plants were a distinct disadvantage against new competition. Gioia and Bravo were sold the same year to the same multinational. Bravo production moved, for a while, to Buffalo. The Gioia cousins, after decades of silence, their fathers long dead, became friends again.

Old-timers at the factory made no secret of the betrayal they felt. One woman, part of a crew of ladies who, dressed in white uniforms, weighed and boxed those larger, fragile pasta varieties meant for stuffing and baking—the Large Shells and Manicotti—by hand, told Dad bluntly, in Italian, that Alfonso would have been ashamed. The building was donated to a charity and has been ever since a depot for secondhand clothing and furniture.

By then I was on my way to being a writer, living hand-to-mouth in New York City and measuring success in $300 assignments. Joe never approved of, or really understood, the choice. Likewise, I don't think he was above feeling jealousy for how I managed to escape the overwhelming demands of family. This was not due to any great skill on my part. The forces that had gripped him so tightly had simply vanished over time. There were periods when we barely spoke.

Our petty antipathies were finally set aside during his last illness. A year after putatively successful surgery for intestinal cancer, the disease returned at the base of his spine, where it was inoperable and increasingly painful. Nearly seventy-three, Dad met his final months in bed at home with optimism, equanimity, and increasing doses of morphine. I would come up from New York every couple weeks. There were no great father-son talks or grand transmissions of advice. Just small talk we'd had no room for earlier. "I faced death *many* times," he said once, I guess to reassure me. After surviving Kasserine, Salerno, and the Anzio beachhead (where everyone who made it out did so by way of brute luck), dying in bed of cancer was no big deal.

When the time came for our last goodbye, he was unconscious from morphine and I was overwhelmed with sorrow. All I could do finally was to kiss his cheek and whisper in his ear that I was proud of him.

Some will find it sad that I didn't mention love, but the reader should understand that love in our family was a ferocious given, something that bound us together and set us apart from others. Dad knew I loved him; what he did not know three days before he died was what I thought of him.

I was not expecting an answer, but his voice drifted up from far away. "I always tried," he whispered without opening his eyes, "to hold up my head."

Dolly, increasingly blind and disconnected from the world, had not been told that Dad was ill, for fear of upsetting her. The morning he died, she had minor surgery in Boston, where she then lived with her daughter and son-in-law; reviving from the anesthetic the next day, she saw my Aunt Carlotta at her bedside.

"Joe's happy now," Dolly told her.

For Dolly's family, the D'Amandas, her gallant and high-strung parents, brothers, and sisters, the past was not something to be shunned, but rather a powerful, albeit indistinct realm, the source of an identity rather separate from other immigrant families.

The father, Luigi D'Amanda, was a professional portrait photographer in Rochester, that very photographic city, and for that the family passed down hundreds of pictures, not only snapshots but also an archive of starkly beautiful large-camera photos of his wife and children that Luigi made over the years. While just a handful of photographs document the Gioias, the D'Amandas recorded an impressive chronicle of their lives—beautiful clothes, nice cars, lovely homes, and festive occasions.

None of them were very tall. (Luigi stood at five feet; his sons Frank and Chris about five two.) They compensated for that with upright, martial postures, which mainly drew attention to how well they dressed. This military bearing might have come from Luigi's father, Christoforo, a veteran of Garibaldi's army who had a great beard, Dolly said, and told the children terrifying stories of the capture of Palermo. (He died in Rochester when she was eight.) Perhaps it predated even him. "Sit up straight, dear," Dolly would say. "Posture is very important."

What one mainly notices in their pictures now is an immense pride, in the tilt of their heads, their confident expressions and gallant poses. Only occasionally do their faces betray dark and wistful moods, hinting at a certain emotional toll beyond the camera's gaze.

Its nature may be measured between the opposing personalities of their parents. Luigi was an artist no less attached to wine, women, and song than his contemporary Carmelo Gugino (with whom Luigi must have been acquainted by reputation at least). Charlotte, their mother, demanded discipline and sacrifice, hard work and high professional accomplishment.

Luigi D'Amanda and Charlotte Carlucci were from different regions in Italy, and met in New York City. Luigi came to America with his parents and brother from Siginiano, a mountain village in the district of Salerno, about twenty miles due east of Naples. Charlotte was the daughter of a pharmacist, Rocco Carlucci, who emigrated to New York with his wife and three children from Rome in 1886, a rare example of an established businessman who relocated his trade to America.

He opened a shop at 86 Mulberry Street, the first of two in New York City, and sent his sons to medical school. The Carluccis brooked no nonsense in taking their place in the world. Rocco's sons, Joseph and Francis, were among the first Italian immigrants to earn medical degrees in the United States. (A great-grandson, another Francis, was secretary of defense.)

Luigi and Charlotte started their family in Williamsburg, Brooklyn, and came to Rochester in 1896 with their daughter Clementine, known her whole life as Dolly, who was three, and son Christopher, not quite two years younger. Portrait photographs of them before their marriage show two darkly attractive young people. Charlotte had a long neck, black hair, which she wore up, and a fiercely intelligent gaze; Luigi, seen in a tandem portrait with his younger brother Rafaele, had the posture of a cavalry rider and the clothes of a gentleman. His occupation on their 1889 marriage license is listed as shoemaker; his age, twenty-one; Charlotte's, seventeen.

Dolly was born four years later, in their home on Marcy Avenue, the address remembered in the sworn testimony of a cousin sent to Manhattan, probably to Mulberry Street, to fetch the midwife for her delivery. (For some reason Dolly did not have a birth certificate, and the cousin's sworn testimony, made almost fifty years later for her war work in the Red Cross, is the only official record.)

She was the first surviving child. A boy, probably born three years before her, died in an accident, the story goes, when a nurse carrying him fell down a flight of stairs. Any official notice of his death, like Dolly's birth, is also missing from city records.

Williamsburg in 1893 was one of two main locations of American shoe manufacturing. The other, for a few more years anyway, was Rochester. Though an online search of the *Brooklyn Eagle* archive did not turn up anything regarding the death of Dolly's infant brother, it did reveal a notice of incorporation by Luigi and his father-in-law of the Brooklyn Shoe Company, a year before the young family moved upstate.

Whether or not Luigi intended to follow the shoe trade there, he soon purchased the studio and business of a portrait photographer, one Cimeruta, from the man's widow. The studio was on North Street, in the Italian Seventh Ward, and there Luigi thrived, demonstrating an artistic skill at posing the human form and lighting his portraits in the chiaroscuro technique of Italian Renaissance painting—brilliant faces and clothing rising out of dark backgrounds. He was soon a peer of the established professional photographers in town.

Three more children were born: Francis, Helen, and, fifteen years younger than Dolly, Inez. By then, Luigi had published the first Italian weekly newspaper in western New York, and would shortly become president of the local professional photographers association.

Dolly was a schoolteacher, the rest of her siblings bound for professions. Chris became a surgeon, Frank studied law at Harvard, Helen and Inez became teachers too. My grandfather Anthony Scinta, fresh from the Buffalo medical school and with a new practice in Rochester, one day saw Dolly walking with Helen and asked who they were. He presented himself at the family's threshold soon after, asking to be introduced. Sicilian or not, the new doctor was one of the community's most eligible bachelors, and the introduction was made. Dolly could have sent him away, of course, but she claimed to have fallen in love immediately.

There is a beautiful photograph of them on their wedding day, made in Luigi's photo studio, a posed family portrait of three generations of D'Amanda's. The whole family surrounds the stout-chested doctor, as they did for the rest of their lives.

Luigi, in his mid-forties, his hair combed back and his mustache waxed to a short handlebar, stands at the far left of the back row next to his tired-looking wife. He has probably just stepped into the frame after arranging the group and is closely watching his assistant at the camera. Several relatives, including Luigi's brother Rafaele, fill out the back row, which ends with the boys, Chris and Frank, standing with a foppish, teenage reserve, in white tie for the first time in their lives. Helen sits far left in the front row, dressed in a pinafore with a large white bow at the back of her head. At the other end, leaning on Anthony's knee, stands Inez, about four years old, in a dress and petticoat, regarding the camera with the same wariness as her father.

Anthony sits four-square next to his bride, who is the center of the group. At her right hand is Domenica, her widowed grandmother in a long black dress, who sits impassively, hands on knees. Anthony is stolid and ill-at-ease in white tie, in some contrast with his dandified brothers-in-law. He grips his knees with gray-gloved hands and blinks during the long exposure, making his eyes appear ghostly, as if covered by gauze. But it is Dolly, in her white gown and long veil, who reveals the most. Everyone else sits or stands at the poised attention characteristic of nineteenth-century portrait photos, but she moves slightly during the long moments of the exposure, caught in the act of leaning towards her new husband, her faintly blurry white figure and sleepy dark eyes enacting a promise of tenderness and love towards the reserved Sicilian taking her, in name at least, from her extravagant clan. They were married for over sixty years.

Anthony left Valledolmo at age five, in 1894. His passage to Buffalo was very likely the hardest of all my relatives. According to the ship manifest at Ellis Island, he made the trip with one Luigi Costanza, his father's cousin. The boy's mother, Rosalie, had just died, and Costanza, who carried a single valise for the two of them, was entrusted with bringing the young boy to a father whom he probably barely knew—if, that is, he remembered him at all.

In the time I knew Anthony, when he was on either side of eighty, he still maintained his practice of general medicine and making house calls. He wore dark, boxy suits, in contrast to his wife's beautifully tailored brothers, and a small white carnation, which Dolly ordered in boxes of a dozen and pinned to the lapel of his jacket every day. His plain suits and prized cigars, the hard, black ones favored by Italian workingmen, were, in a way, perfect foils with which to subtly rankle his in-laws. Another was a chronic, casual lateness in arriving to family events, where he was expected to bring the bread from the bakery near his office, a tardiness due, of course, to his many patients.

My grandfather insisted upon living the life of the city even as, in the 1960s and '70s, it vanished around him. He kept his office on Lyell Avenue as what had been an Italian neighborhood changed to black, then Hispanic. Though he had the ingrained and broadly sentimental racial prejudices of his generation, he remained until he retired a doctor to the poor.

Every Saturday, he would stop at the barber's for a shave, then proceed to his favorite restaurant downtown, where, once I turned thirteen, we met regularly for lunch. He would order a gin martini and a London broil, and greet a retinue of well-wishers—retired cops, old reporters, lawyers, politicians, and former patients—from his table.

He had been a crusading city councilman during the worst years of the Depression, a rare Italian Democrat (his brother-in-law Frank was another) in a Republican town, leading a reform campaign. A surviving scrapbook of newspaper clippings details his causes: municipal takeover of the trolley company, meat inspection and pasteurized milk, free books for public school students, free eye exams for kids, construction of a new main public library, protecting a shelter for homeless men. One banner headline reads "Councilman Scinta Charges 'Flagrant Waste' by Kelly in Welfare Department." A year later he took on what he called "chiseling" in the city's coal program for the poor.

Reading the clippings, you get the idea that Anthony took the matter of reform rather more seriously than his fellow Democrats. One of the last headlines in the book reads "Scinta Aids GOP Asking Tax Probe." He returned to private life soon after. By the seventies, he was a Nixon man, though his favorite president remained Teddy Roosevelt.

When my grandfather mentioned the past, it wasn't to talk about his voyage to America, Mr. Costanza, or either of his parents, but rather to recall medical school at the University of Buffalo, the pranks played by student doctors, and how they idolized their professor, the great surgeon Roswell Park, or how, when he was twelve, he went to shake President McKinley's hand at the Pan American Exposition, and how McKinley died because Roswell Park was out of town that day.

He mentioned dope peddlers who trolled the streets with full hypodermics looking for new customers, and how he played first base for an amateur ball club, without mentioning that a lot of club games at the time were certain to end in brawls. Even as a slightly stooped old man, Anthony had a barrel chest, likely from assisting his stonemason father when he wasn't in school.

His features as a young man were dark and fine, very much at odds with his robust frame. In the picture taken on the occasion of his graduation from medical school, Anthony has the extravagant handsomeness of a corsair, bespeaking his Arabic ancestry.

In Dolly's family he was, quite simply, a Sicilian, an Arab, among Romans. In dozens of family snapshots made through the twenties and thirties, Anthony cultivates the same placid plainness of the wedding picture, distinct from the vivid family he had married into. Dolly probably loved that about him most of all.

Though their father was an artist of no small status, there was no question whatsoever of the D'Amanda children—or grandchildren for that matter—following his example. All were directed to professional careers and, for the women, marriage to professional men.

Each of them as adults, however, exhibited a fine artistic sense of their own. Chris's remarkable skills as a surgeon were frequently compared to those of an artist. Frank was a passionate gourmet cook back when such a thing was almost unheard of for a man. Inez, the youngest, and so probably the most indulged, came the closest to being a true artist, keeping a studio where she sculpted small intriguing figures in stone and bronze.

The fundamental tension between their parents' competing views of the world, between duty and creativity, was made corrosive by Luigi's dedicated and open philandering. He was a charming, old-world monster, utterly lacking what might be called American middle-class morality—someone far more at home in Belle Époque Naples than Republican western New York. Luigi clearly didn't care what anyone thought, most especially his wife, who, one gathers, grew to despise him. For Luigi and Charlotte, divorce was, of course, out of the question.

Luigi died suddenly, following a series of small strokes, in December 1934. He was sixty-one. The Crash of 1929 and following Depression had been bad enough for business, but in the late twenties, as his last assistant told me sixty years later, Luigi built a new studio which still made exposures by way of a second-floor skylight. He remained a natural-light photographer, one who captured his relatively long exposures without a shutter, removing the lens cap and counting the moments necessary for the shot before replacing it with a flourish of his hand. Younger photographers were switching to more reliable photo flood lights, and much faster exposures, in walk-in storefront studios far more convenient for elderly and overweight customers.

As Luigi's business trailed off, one of his mistresses presented him with a son younger than several of his grandchildren. The last photographs of him show a man looking far older than his years. Around the same time his Buffalo contemporary Carmelo Gugino was patenting his new jazz guitar, Luigi gave up the ghost. A statue of a weeping girl, dressed in a long, high-waisted gown of the Romantic period, marks his grave.

Freed from the libertine at last, Charlotte undertook a campaign to erase his influence among his descendants, emphasizing their duty to her and to lives of almost unrelenting accomplishment at the cost of any personal wishes. I was born six months after she died and see in retrospect an effort by Luigi's children, especially Dolly and Inez, to form, perhaps in a compensatory way, a kind of ideal ninteenth-century Italian gentleman out of me.

Siginiano was—and still is—a sparsely populated nest of snug stone houses set in a mountain cleft. According to Dolly, the D'Amandas had a castle there, a charming tale I never much believed until, on a chilly and bright February day in 1999, I saw that there was indeed a ruined Norman tower and keep that loomed above Siginiano's three or four streets, fenced off as a hazard next to the village dump. It commanded a strategic, vanishing-point view of the broad valley that was—and, judging by the autostrada running through it, still is—the main thoroughfare between Naples and Bari on the Adriatic coast.

Though close to Naples as the crow flies, there was something inexpressibly forlorn about Siginiano that winter day, feeling more like a frontier outpost than a typical village of the Italian south. The surrounding peaks rise around it like walls, and in winter it can't get more than a couple hours of direct sunlight each day. Even now, Siginiano is not easy to reach, and until the early twentieth century must have felt as remote as the moon.

Its Norman keep was probably knocked apart by Napoleon's army, which did a lot of that sort of thing when it invaded in 1805, or maybe it was reduced by earthquake. Beginning in the fifteenth century, it would have been an outpost of the Spanish crown. The D'Amandas—as the Gioias—had been Spaniards, logically, Frank once told me, from a place called Amanda.

Another colorful story of Dolly's was that the d'Amandas (Luigi democratically capitalized the *d'* in America) fled Spain for Italy after an ancestor had his head cut off and hung from a bridge. The mystery only deepened after I looked through an atlas of Spain and did not find an Amanda anywhere.

The Muslim advance into Sicily anticipated their conquest of Spain a half-century later, the Moorish kingdom of Grenada lasting for nearly eight hundred years. In 1469, the Catholic monarchs Isabella of Castile and Ferdinand of Aragon (a kingdom which mainly comprised the southern Italian peninsula, Sicily, Sardinia, and Corsica) married, an act which combined their armies. In 1492, after a twenty-year war, their forces captured Grenada, the last Moorish stronghold, along with its unfortunate sultan Muhammad XII, who then accompanied his subjects on their wholesale migration to North Africa. Some Moors elected to stay, many converting, and for a time were left alone. Sephardic Jews, whose communities thrived under the Moors, were not so lucky.

In March 1492, after two decades of increasing legal restrictions and state-sanctioned violence, Ferdinand and Isabella commanded the Sephardim to convert to Christianity within four months or forfeit their estates and quit the kingdom. "Some Jews accepted baptism, but those forced into exile were far more numerous," notes Nicholson Adams. "Conservative estimates put the number of exiles at 165,000, converted 50,000, lives lost in carrying out the decree 20,000."

A Spanish monk gave an eyewitness account of the Hebrew diaspora that, absent a couple of specific religious details, might well have described the expulsion of the American Indian nations to Oklahoma:

> They were abandoning the land where they were born. Small and large, young and old, on foot, atop mules or dragged by wagons, each one followed his own route toward the chosen port of departure. They stopped by the side of the road, some collapsing from exhaustion, others sick, others dying. There was not a person alive who could not have pity for these unfortunate people. Everywhere along the road they were begged to receive baptism, but their rabbis told them to refuse while urging the women to sing and play tambourines to keep their spirits up.

Soon enough, even those Jews and Muslims who had accepted conversion in 1492 were deemed unfit for residence. Many *conversos* were, according to Adams, "rich and powerful, holding high positions in the state or in the Catholic clergy itself." The Inquisition now suspected them of the heresy of insincerity. More probably, "some men were haled in front of the Inquisition because their estates were coveted." Though the persecution was conducted by the Church, the crown gained all confiscated property. "This feature must have greatly pleased Ferdinand, who was in constant need of money to pay for his wars." Many conversos were guiltier of being rich than of being bad Catholics. The Sephardim scattered to Portugal, Holland, Greece, Turkey, North Africa, Italy, and, eventually, the New World.

With Spain unified, finding new trade routes to India was the next project for the crown. Columbus was there to present his westward plans (and is supposed to have witnessed the Moors' surrender). Spain's will-to-power would soon have a new focus.

> With the expulsion of the Arabs (and . . . Jews), Spaniards had finally attained what they had been fighting for for more than seven centuries. During that time they had developed a formidably brutal and efficient military culture that suddenly found itself redundant. Now . . . they looked around for other lands to conquer.

Barely thirty years after Columbus's first voyage, Francisco Lopez de Gomara wrote that "The conquest of the Indies began when that of the Moors was over."

Long after Dolly died, at ninety-nine (presumably; lacking a birth certificate, no one was ever sure), and after my visit to Siginiano, I began to consider the tale of our ancestor's head in the light of Spanish history. She gave no year to the event, and, lacking an Amanda in Spain, the bridge in question was impossible to find.

It seemed likely that the execution and public exposure of the remains occurred because our ancestor was a Moor or Jew. That the d'Amandas ended up in the Italian south, instead of, say, North Africa, argues in favor of Sephardic origin. To be sure, my relatives did not harbor any customs to identify themselves as crypto Jews in the twentieth century, no secret prayers or lit candles. Though Dolly's two brothers despised priests (and Chris could be quite vocal in his hatred of the Church), that was not an uncommon feeling among men of the Italian south, where the Roman Curia had been a bastion of political repression for centuries.

Luigi and Charlotte's marriage certificate in the New York City archives revealed that they were not married by a priest; rather, a Manhattan alderman performed a civil ceremony at his home in Greenwich Village. A subtler hint of a Sephardic past was in the maiden name of Luigi's mother, which called to mind Siginiano's lonely remove. She was Domenica DeLuna, namely— of the Moon.

As part of their conversion, Spanish Jews were made to give up their Hebrew surnames for Christian ones, often taking place names reflecting where they were from, or perhaps such fanciful locales as the moon. But, again, with no place called Amanda in Spain, my suspicions reached a dead end.

But then one evening, when checking *fides* in a friend's Latin dictionary, it dawned on me to look up *amanda* as well. And there it was, where it had always been, the collective noun of the verb *amandare*, meaning 'to exile, to send away.' For centuries, Latin speakers would have known the d'Amandas as, quite literally, "the Exiles." The name might also be a pun, *amanda* being also an adverb of *amare*, 'to love,' meaning 'lovable,' which in itself is no small survival skill. Were those ancestors, notwithstanding the headless one, so charming? Luigi and his children certainly had that quality in abundance. It might explain how the Exiles ended up in that Italian castle.

Traditionally, converso families, even if practicing Christians, married among each other. The circumstantial evidence regarding Charlotte's Hebraic ancestry is rather more solid. Like money-lending, the apothecary trade was one of the few that Italian Jews were allowed to practice. Rome's Jewish ghetto was legally abolished when the Papal States were assumed into the Kingdom of Italy in 1870; it was largely torn down in 1885. Whatever Rocco Carlucci's religious identification, he opened his pharmacy in New York, a Sephardic refuge for two centuries, the following year.

Once established in the New World, it is inconceivable that he would have allowed his seventeen-year-old daughter to marry just anyone, no matter how charming. It is far more likely that the marriage was arranged. Perhaps Rocco felt there was something simpatico about the young man, even if it was only his family name.

To give some idea of the familial thrall into which I was born, that emotional grip Charlotte had on her descendants, I'll relate another dream—one of the first I can recall—from when I was not much older than three.

In it I have fallen down the stairs of my parents' house (which happened at least once in real life), fetching up on a landing overlooking the front door. Standing in the doorway, staring at me, is Charlotte—whom I recognize from a framed photograph on my mother's dresser—with my great aunts Helen and Inez on either side of her. No one speaks, the only sound the pulse of blood in my ears. After several apparently evaluative moments, the women turn and leave. It doesn't seem outlandish to me to think of Charlotte returning to size up the first of her descendants to be born after she died, one she had no hope of influencing directly. Visitation or not, there was no mistaking her stern look of appraisal. My young self understood, at the very least, that I had been born among people with high expectations. That said, it was decades before I learned about Charlotte's own first-born son, and how he died in a fall down a flight of stairs, at about the same age I was when I had that dream.

Rosalie, my mother, was Dolly and Anthony's middle child. She was quickly drafted into the service of Luigi's camera, appearing at eighteen months old, a chubby baby in a paper crown and a long gown of stars and stripes—very likely illustrating the nascent hopes of the new Armistice. In the pictures that follow, we see a cheerful girl with long black curls and bright smile.

She attended private school and graduated from the University of Rochester with a degree in English literature and, like all the D'Amanda women, an intention to teach. The war intervened and she joined the Red Cross, serving as a recreation nurse at Halloran Hospital on Staten Island, where the medical ships unloaded.

Rec nurses organized games and activities for severely wounded patients. Simply put, Mom's job for almost four years was to cheer up men and boys blown to physical and mental bits fighting in Europe. Like other vets, she never said much about her experience, ever let on how hard it must have been, or what she thought about it, other than to say a couple times how sad some of the boys were.

I suspect that, besides a shared cultural background, this is another basis of my parents' marriage: that Mom found one last soldier—five years after the war ended—and understood the same restlessness or anger she'd seen in all the others, one last GI in need of some kindness and understanding.

With the advent of the Second World War, Rochester, like Buffalo, Cleveland, and Detroit, became a destination for the southern black diaspora, drawn earlier to Chicago and New York. Unlike those larger, more industrial cities, Rochester offered little to the rural newcomers outside of domestic work and railroad jobs. Work at Kodak, by far the city's biggest employer, was understood to be for life, but required a high school diploma. This did not discourage further migration.

Between 1940 and 1960, the city's African American population doubled almost three times. Eventually, thirty thousand black people, ten percent of the city's population, lived mainly in the Seventh Ward, the former Italian ghetto—a neighborhood of small factories and shabby houses near the New York Central train yard—and the Second, a neighborhood near the west bank of the river with what remained of Rochester's first mansions, now divided into apartments and boarding houses.

The great Delta blues guitarist Son House moved to Rochester from Mississippi in 1943, shortly after his recordings with Alan Lomax, ones made in a shack so close to a rail line that trains can be heard roaring by on three of the songs. In Rochester, he worked as a porter for the New York Central, became a Baptist deacon, and, at his wife's bidding, gave up playing the blues until he was found living in the Second Ward by two young blues fans in 1964.

That same year, on a Friday night in July, white police officers at a Seventh Ward block party used undue force arresting a drunk they said was harassing women. Several bystanders objected. There'd been a riot in Harlem two weeks earlier, and in Rochester that night things went out of control very fast. The next night, the rioting picked up in the Second Ward. The fighting in both neighborhoods lasted three nights.

While there were but five fatalities (four of them coming when a police helicopter malfunctioned and crashed into a boarding house), over six hundred people were arrested, and white-owned ghetto stores were devastated. In spite of the best municipal intentions in the wake of the disaster, it took years to address its causes, and solutions have been few since, which is not a story unique to my hometown. Downtown shops, movie theaters, and restaurants closed, buildings were demolished for parking lots. All the places I visited on those Saturdays I had lunch with my grandfather have been gone now for decades.

But my family's central tragedy in that riot year was Inez dying from a stroke at fifty-three. The youngest, most stylish, outgoing, and artistic member of that very stylish, outgoing, and artistic family, died first. It was as if a light had been switched off, and the possibility of future light taken away, as if we were exiles once more, now with nowhere to go. Mom, for whom Inez was more sister than aunt, never really recovered from the loss, and, as her relatives grew old and died, gradually descended into the sort of depression that relies a great deal on the tender recollection of a happy, radiant past.

The raising of children in most Italian clans is a matter for women; Joe had very little say in how I was brought up, and he knew it. While Inez lived, my sisters and I were mainly her project. We spent weekends at her house filled with art books and objects collected in her European trips; everything in it seemed connected to something far away. She read to us, gave puppet shows, and took me, being the oldest, frequently to the art gallery and, especially, the museum, with its dark and beautiful galleries dedicated to western New York's Indigenous past.

After Inez died, the project slowed (gone were the intended Italian lessons) but was not forgotten. Rosalie and Dolly strove to form me in ways to produce an individual congruent with a certain worldly ideal they held high—a gentleman, like Luigi, or Chris and Frank, a gifted, thoughtful citizen of the world, at lofty odds with contemporary conventions of American life, and certainly not what Dad might have wanted for an American son.

He wasn't without influence, though. When, at nine, I was picked on after transferring to a new school, Rosalie's alma mater, Joe's solution was to take me for boxing lessons from an old club fighter he knew at a storefront gym near downtown. This horrified Dolly. Most summers, beginning when I was fifteen, I worked in the Bravo shipping room with men considerably less fortunate than myself. The first experience gave me a very respectable left jab, the second left me ambivalent towards the basic assumptions of white collar life.

While I think Joe was genuinely disappointed by our separate lives, by the time I was a teenager we were so unlike that to become closer would have required an enormous dislocation for both of us. It had been made clear that certain work, even running a factory, was, somehow, inappropriate for me. Better to be a doctor, a lawyer, or a professor, or to write books—most of all, to be a gentleman, for whom culture signified more than economy.

Dolly's final glimpse of Joe, happy at last, was by no means her first instance of second sight. Once she told me how a glowing hand had appeared in a cloud above her bed the night her brother Frank died, a voice telling her he was gone. Anthony, whom she survived for more than fifteen years, somehow remained a companion after death. She revealed such visions only occasionally, but no one who knew her well questioned her deeply intuitive mind. More than once, in her nineties, she would exclaim to me, apropos of nothing in particular, "Oh, it would be so nice, dear, if you played the guitar." Whether she'd seen the need after reviewing my life to come, or if this was just one more attempt to form what she considered a well-rounded gentleman, is hard to say. At the time I could only agree that, yes, it would be.

Eventually, I came to the guitar in no small attempt to account for that same landscape of loneliness that belonged to my father once I discovered it in myself. I also wanted to justify, in my own way, a century of familial striving as thoroughly as possible, to become serious about what would have struck most of my ancestors as a frivolous pursuit. We don't know what we carry with us until we reach for other things. It so happened that, just like Uncle Carmelo, I ended up with a guitar.

Looking back, it's easy to draw undue connections, or—perhaps more accurately—create strange connections, between the confusing lines of one's own life and the longer dangling threads of history. This is how people live and make sense of anything, I guess; the successful associations are the ones that endure. The only thing that prevents these provisional constellations of fugitive and recollected events from being fantasies is how thoroughly they intersect with the lives of others—to what other folk suffered and how they prevailed. Their stories should lend credence to our own.

For all their wanderings, all the people to whom I belong gathered together for a time at a particular place in the New World. While their descendants have now mainly scattered, those Gioias, Scintas, and D'Amandas, native and Italian-born, rest now in the great Catholic necropolis on a western rampart of the Genesee River gorge, about halfway between the High Falls and Lake Ontario; Luigi reclines next to Charlotte, Dolly beside

Anthony, Alfonso with Nanetta, Rosalie alongside Joe. None of them trouble my sleep much, though a shade resembling my father will visit from time to time, usually to criticize, though occasionally to praise.

Acknowledgments

First thanks must go to Jim and Lucia LaVilla-Havelin, dear friends who know Rochester, and a few of the people in these pages; and to Barbara Cyrus, Gerald Duff, and Kevin Martin for their early, perceptive, and greatly encouraging reading of my long first draft. Kevin especially gave the work the enormous, and uncalled-for, benefit of his exceptionally thorough skills as an editor, an invaluable gift.

To my family: my sisters, Tina Zabkar and Carlotta Boeschenstein, whose support and forbearance allowed me to speak aloud about those who dwell in our hearts; my aunt Carlotta Ames, for whom words cannot express my love and thanks for all she's done my whole life through (although I can tell you she's more fun than anyone I know).

My dear cousins: Louis and Allis D'Amanda, gentle, loving, and kind, have given me a home in Rochester whenever needed; Louise Yamada (the other author in the family) has been my generous big sister as long as I can remember (and is nearly as much fun as her cousin Skip); Carlotta D'Amanda awakened me to the life of the mind long ago. Her enthusiasm, regard for others, and profound love of, and dedication to, the City of New York represents the best of what our ancestors brought to America. Chris and Elisabetta D'Amanda were always happy to listen, offer ideas, and make dinner.

Profound thanks to my uncle Nino Gioia, and his wife Gloria, who started the ball rolling; to Jessica Gugino, my BU J-school classmate, who shared her father's memoir and led me to our cousins; to Frank Gugino, and his wife Rosalie, who fed me really well in West Seneca and shared priceless stories and pictures of his grandfather Carmelo; to Frances Valvo, and her son Nick, in Auburn, for another fine meal, and the wonderful stories about her father Natale; and to Rosalie Krajci, who gave me a deeper understanding of the Gugino family, especially her aunt Nanetta, and who, with husband Tom, took me on a memorable tour of the Mark Twain landmarks near their Elmira home. In Buffalo, Richard Gioia was always ready to pay for dinner (and Dylan tickets) and talk about old family dramas. Getting to know him was one of the distinct pleasures of the ride.

I am deeply grateful for the broad and sheltering shelves of the Harold Washington Main Public Library in Chicago, and its many branches, notably at Logan Square. The Buffalo/Erie County downtown library likewise was a site of profound discovery. Without these great institutions this book could not exist.

Also the library of the City of New York, 42nd St. Branch; the Brooklyn Heights division of the Brooklyn/Kings County library; the main branch of the Rochester/Monroe County library; and the library at Kenyon College all provided needed quiet and research material. Chicago's magnificent Newberry Library let me handle an original edition of the 1901 Buffalo Indian Congress *Libretto*, then made a copy for me to take home. With no advance notice, Mary Robinson at the McCracken Research Library, Buffalo Bill Historical Center in Cody, Wyoming, kindly allowed me time to fill in several blanks about Col. Fred Cummins. Scott Freilich in Buffalo and Dave Stutzman in Rochester were crucial sources of knowledge regarding the Gugino guitar works.

To my great teachers: Robert Daniel at Kenyon, who believed in a clear rhetoric; David Milch at Yale, who defined the responsibility of a writer; and Jim Higgins at Boston University, who encouraged me to listen to the voices of the dispossessed—my debt is indelible.

It is my great fortune to have had lessons from some awfully fine guitarists. In Minneapolis, Ed Cohen gave me my first; the second came from Alan Estavez. Farther along, Paul Metsa demonstrated a thing or two. Joel Paterson, simply Chicago's best, not only showed me the basic blues licks but gave me a bargain on his blond Gibson J-185. Jim Becker, an astonishing musician, has been an ocean of patience and a steady font of instruction. If I'm a player, it's thanks to him.

Jen Schalliol, Quentin Hardy, and Michael Tarbox, another inspiring guitarist, reviewed early drafts and helped clarify several fine points. Jen Phillis was a big help with Latin. John Hayes not only gave the manuscript the benefit of his great knowledge of guitar lore and folk music, but was the one who suggested thirteen years ago that we go catch the "Art of the Guitar" show at the Boston MFA; the earliest stirrings of this book started that afternoon. David McCormick believed in this work early on and brought it to the attention of many. James Peltz at SUNY Press gave it a home.

However, with all said and done, no one helped more as I went along than Rachel Cline, whose love, confidence, understanding, and support sustained this work's long transit from a series of odd and disparate ideas to the book you hold in your hands. This is for her.

Permissions

Excerpts from "Seneca New Year's Ceremonies" from APOLOGIES TO THE IROQUOIS by Edmund Wilson. Copyright © 1959, 1960 by Edmund Wilson. Reprinted by permission of Farrar, Straus and Giroux, LLC.

Quotes from Black Indians: a hidden heritage by William Loren Katz. Copyright © 1986 by Ethrac Publications Inc. Reprinted by permission of Simon & Schuster.

Quotes from Deep Blues by Robert Palmer reprinted by permission of Penguin Books.

Excerpt from The Earth Shall Weep, copyright © 1998 by James Wilson. Used by permission of Grove/Atlantic, Inc.

Brief excerpts from pp. 47, 75 from ESCAPING THE DELTA: ROBERT JOHNSON AND THE INVENTION OF THE BLUES by ELIJAH WALD Copyright © 2004 by Elijah Wald. Reprinted by permission of HarperCollins Publishers.

Quotes from In Search of the Blues by Marybeth Hamilton used by permission of The Perseus Books Group.

Quotes from INVISIBLE REPUBLIC: BOB DYLAN'S BASE-MENT TAPES by Greil Marcus. Copyright © 1997 by Greil Marcus. Reprinted by permission of Henry Holt and Company, LLC.

Excerpt from The Land Where the Blues Began—Copyright © 1993 by Alan Lomax. Reprinted by permission of The New Press. www.thenewpress.com

Quotes from Moanin' at Midnight by James Segrest and Mark Hoffman reprinted by permission of Random House, Inc.

Brief excerpts from pp. 133-4, 264 from THE MYTH OF THE NEGRO PAST by MELVILLE J. HERSKOVITS Copyright 1941 by Melville J. Herskovits, renewed © 1969 by Melville J. Herskovits. Reprinted by permission of HarperCollins Publishers.

Quotes from Red River Blues by Bruce Cook used by permission of Judith Aller.

Quotes from The Roots of the Blues by Samuel Charters reprinted by permission of Marion Boyars Publishers.

Passage from Shadow and Act by Ralph Ellison reprinted by permission of Random House, Inc.

Quotes from The Sixth Grandfather, edited by Raymond J. DeMallie reprinted by permission of The University of Nebraska Press.

Notes

26   *Italian books offer a number of dances* Turnbull, 44

26   *and with a thousand gestures and body movements* Grunfeld, 106

27   *The guitar passed from hand to hand* Irving, *Alhambra,* 13

27   *Now break forth from court* Irving, *Alhambra,* 53

28   I am indebted to Frederick Grunfeld's *The Art and Times of the Guitar* and Harvey Turnbull's *The Guitar from the Renaissance to the Present Day* for their excellent presentations of early guitar history.

29   *Its splendid music makes it difficult* Turnbull, 32

30   *One sixteenth-century observer declared* Grunfeld, 109

32   *A good guitar* Bilger, *The New Yorker,* 14 May 2007, 86

33   *composed by one Antonio Maggio* Wald, 16

34   *Eddie could lay down rhythm and bass parts* Hadlock, 249

34   *Southern blues deliverances soon replaced the more ordered measures* Hadlock, 249

36   Stuart Isacoff's *Temperament: The Idea That Solved Music's Greatest Riddle* was invaluable in my understanding of the elder Gallilei's achievement.

36   *that the series of overtones resonating above a string's fundamental musical tone,* and following, Isacoff, 196–97

38   *uniquely constructed from the entire carapace of a tortoise* Kuronen, 31

38   *Apollo the god of archers* Grunfeld, 6

38   *plays such a ravishing tune* Grunfeld, 35

38   *the Hebrew* kinnura . . . *the Chaldean* quitra Grunfeld, 37

39   *a grisly chronicle of mass executions* Robb, 99

40   *the nurse at whose breast* Robb, 54

40   *on a colossal scale*; and *For the most part* both Norwich, 50

40   *soon became one of the major trading centers of the Mediterranean* Norwich, 52

41   The Norman chronicle here owes a great debt to John Julius Norwich's *The Normans in Sicily.*

42   *We had a youth in our company* Walen, 32

45   I am especially grateful to Mark Goldman's *City on the Edge* for its descriptions of Buffalo's Pan-American Exposition.

45   *shot a broad ray in quick bursts through the damp air* This is visible in an Edison newsreel film now at the Library of Congress.

46   *the analogy between it and the ascent of man from savagery to civilization* Moses, 146

48   My understanding of the Italo-American experience at the Pan relies mainly on the University of Buffalo's terrific online study beginning at http://library.buffalo.edu/libraries/exhibits/panam/immigrants/italians.html

52   *shortly thereafter agreed to shut the Bozeman Trail posts* Eastern public opinion was moved greatly in favor of the Sioux following Red Cloud's address at Cooper Union in New York City, a damning account of his government treaty negotiations delivered after his visit to Washington. see: Josephy, 395

53   *five dollars* "Chief Geronimo Has Learned The Game Of Graft"
      Buffalo Courier 2 September 1901

59   *inscribed on the face of a button not as large as a dime Buffalo
      Times*, 1 September 1901

59   *McKinley had been eager to get to Buffalo all summer* The fol-
      lowing account of McKinley's tragic visit, his funeral, and the
      trial and execution of Leon Czolgosz is mainly based on Eric
      Rauchway's *Murdering McKinley.*

60   *I don't know how it was, but it came* Rauchway, 7

61   *either the blessing or sanction of the Indian Bureau* Moses, 145

61   *A picturesque figure stood in front of the stand* "Inspiring Scenes
      On President's Stand" *Buffalo Times*, 5 September 1901. (A
      sub-headline reads: "Kinetoscope Views Were Taken.")

61   *largest pyrotechnical display ever seen* "Gorgeous Display Of
      Pain's Fireworks" *Buffalo Times*, 5 September 1901

62   *At sunset the exposition grounds were illuminated* Goldman, 8

62   *threw its gleaming light upon the party* "Crowds of Yesterday
      Largest Yet Recorded" *Buffalo Times*, 6 September 1901

62   *sold two million tickets* Moses, 137

62   *All of the Indians on exhibition Buffalo Courier*, 26 August 1901

63   *Word of this traveled quickly through the desolated reservations
      of the Far West* "Historian James C. Olson has speculated that
      the Sioux heard about the new Indian messiah from the Sho-
      shones in Wyoming, who were once mortal enemies until Red
      Cloud reconciled with them during the 1880s." Larson, 265

64   *great lights and signal fires shone from the bluffs* Larson, 274

65   *woman with an infant in her arms* Pritzker, 944

65   *A Thunder-being nation I am I have said* DeMaillie, 273–74

66   *an Indian marvel who defies electricity* "Great Time At Indian Congress" *Buffalo Times*, 30 August 1901

67   Mitchell's essay in Wilson, E., *Apologies,* 13–14

68   *Recollecting the event three weeks later* "Czolgosz Was Twice Noticed" *Buffalo Times*, 30 September 1901

68   Though contemporary reports called the music a Bach sonata, organist William Gomph's daughter told an interviewer in 2001 that her father was playing *Träumerei,* which strikes me as eerily apt; see: http://library.buffalo.edu/libraries/exhibits/panam/music/organ/organ.html

69   *A whisper began to pass from mouth to mouth* Leary and Sholes, 114

71   *for being widely unexpected* Though the death was announced suddenly, Rauchway observes that "Conspicuously absent among the reactions to William McKinley's murder was any significant expression of surprise." Many thought he deserved what he got and some, like the moral crusader Carrie Nation, said so out loud. "Even Americans who did not share the excitability of the yellow press had a sense that violence was in the offing." Rauchway, 171

71   *[A] delegation of sixty-five braves*; and *The rainbow of hope is out of the sky* both in "Remains Leave In State Today For Washington" *Buffalo Courier*, 16 September 1901

72   *There was a terrible flash of lightning* "A Dramatic Story Of Abner M'Kinley Getting News" *Buffalo Times*, 8 September 1901

73   *Pandemonium broke loose* "Lights Of The Pan-American Go Out Forever From Electric Tower As Buglers Sound 'Taps'" *Buffalo Courier* 3 October 1901

73   *after the shooting of the president*; and *Electric light bulbs were jerked from their posts* both Goodman, 18

73   *Police on the grounds could not handle the fierce mob* "Amid Wildest Scenes The Dream City's Lights Glimmer And Die Out" *Buffalo Times*, 3 November 1901

75   *The Red men and the squaws marched to the very center* "Indians Defeated In Fierce Battle" *Buffalo Courier* 3 November 1901. The account notes that all of the braves were given rifles to shoot blanks with except Geronimo, who was not trusted to handle the prop responsibly. Even so, as the above headline reflects, the fight was reported to have appeared quite real to spectators.

75   *a beautiful diamond stud* "Amid Wildest Scenes The Dream City's Lights Glimmer And Die Out" *Buffalo Times* 3 November 1901

77   *since the turn of the century* Powers, 18

79   *seven cars trimmed in black* "Remains Leave In State Today For Washington" *Buffalo Courier* 16 September, 1901

81   *Maybelle Carter's playing on* "Cannonball Blues," "Years later, Maybelle would tell Mike Seeger that [Esley] Riddle [a black friend] had taught her how to play the blues licks in "The Cannonball." But Riddle always demurred . . . 'You don't have to give Maybelle any lessons,' Riddle remembered thirty years later. 'You let her see you playing something, she'll get it. You better believe it.'" Zwonitzer and Hirshberg, 132–33

83   Peabody, 148

84   Peabody, 152

85   *A lean, loose-jointed Negro* Handy, 74

86   *To hear the blues as a west African import* Davis, 38

86   *Even W.C. Handy goes on to allow* Davis, 28

87   *If Scott Fitzgerald can be taken as an authority* from *The Great Gatsby*, Chapter VIII: "For Daisy was young and her artificial world was redolent of orchids and pleasant, cheerful snobbery and orchestras which set the rhythm of the year, summing up the sadness and suggestiveness of life in new tunes. All night the saxophones wailed the hopeless comment of the *Beale Street Blues* while a hundred pairs of golden and silver slippers shuffled the shining dust."

87   *includes whooping, or sudden jumping into falsetto range* Palmer, 28

87   *Muddy was a vigorous twenty-six-year-old* Palmer, 3

90   *some two thousand of them by one estimate* Certainly, a generous one which counts 1,000 Cherokee who stayed in North Carolina's Smokey Mountains in 1835 with local government knowledge, and an unknown number who kept to the deeper reaches of Tennessee and Virginia. For the eastern Cherokee see: Perdue and Green, 128

91   *Even now, deer, bears, panthers, wolves, and deadly snakes are not infrequent* Newton, 113

91   *emigrated to Louisiana where they intermarried* Mississippi WPA Guide, 58

92   *refused to leave Mississippi* MS WPA, 59

92   *as high as seven thousand* Wallace, 81

92   *in the deeper reaches of the Yazoo delta* Perdue and Green, 127

93   *as the twentieth century has drawn to a close* Oliver, 5

93   *And while there is no disputing* Cook, 30

93   *There are no African retentions* Cook, 49

93   *Don't start me to lyin'* Cook, 50

94   *understood, finally, that in the blues I hadn't found a music* Charters, 127

94   *In one of the groups*; and *an older boy in a wildly colorful costume* both Charters, 67–68

95   *In the early years of Mardi Gras* Baum, *The New Yorker* 9 January 2006, 53

95–96   *incomprehensible words or phrases*; and *from one of the languages* both Charters, 69

96   *black hail cloud, still standing yonder watching* Neihardt, 132

97   *He was a really great man* Words of Roebuck Staples read by John Sinclair on *Jas. Mathus and his Knock-Down Society Play Songs for Rosetta*, Mammoth Records, 1997

97   *The local record company scout, Henry Spier* Spier also discovered Big Chief Henry's Indian String Band. Wardlow, 146

97   *Different [players] from different places* Segrest and Hoffman, 20

97   *Patton heard the young man* Segrest and Hoffman, 19

98   *The Indian boy learns the legendary history* Burton, 6

99   *indicated a talent for music* Handy, 7

100   *Patton was the best guitarist in the Delta* Segrest and Hoffman, 18

103   *an old woman carrying a small bundle* Wilson, J., 166

103   *If either parent was of Indian decent* Calt and Wardlow, 44

103   *By such niceties in nomenclature were a people allowed to vanish* see Miles in Brooks, 147

104   *Several times have I assembled the urchins to join in sacred song* Cooper, 738

104   *The so-called settlement of America* Wilson, J., 75

105   *military alliances kept settlers off Indian lands* Wallace, *Long,* 24

106   *Left to themselves the Cherokees would become* Wallace, *Long,* 64

107   *Census figures recorded* Numbers for those transported are far more exact than for those who stayed; accepted totals are at http://en.wikipedia.org/wiki/Indian_removal#Aftermath

107   *approximately one thousand Cherokee* Tennessee WPA Guide, 42

108   *By 1900, over twenty thousand blacks were given some form of tribal recognition* "Researching Black Indian Genealogy of the Five Civilized Tribes" http://www.african-nativeamerican. com/1IntroPage.htm

108   *ministered to in part by Indian friends* Fletcher, 8

109   *Indian songs I have discovered travel far* Fletcher, 9

110   *taken apart or modified* Fletcher, 12

110   *Music is no mere diversion for the Indian* Burton, 5

110   *As a child I had not heard the Pipe of Pan* Handy, 14

111   *The most distinctive feature* Nettl, 173–74

112   *Men and women dance as partners* Densmore, 99

113   *A man, when accepting the gift of a horse* Fletcher, 52

114   *the blue falsetto yodels of Jimmie Rodgers, Robert Johnson, Tommy Johnson* Wardlow notes that Tommy Johnson and Ishmon Bracey "played for Jimmie Rodgers in Jackson, Mississippi on at least one occasion. Rodgers, who was appearing at the King Edward Hotel, heard them performing on the street in front of the hotel and invited them to the roof where he allowed them to play for his audience. Bracey said. 'He was struck by that yodel of Tommy's and asked us if we had recorded.'" 65

116   *The half Cherokee Andrew Baxter* Bastin, 38–39

119   *slender boats* Epstein, 69

120   *fifteen hundred Indian slaves* Berlin, 68

120   *the final extinction of Indian slavery* Johnston, 26

120   *In 1854 Father William, a priest of the Catholic Church* Johnston, 28

120   *In 1843* Johnston, 29

120   *always was and is the sinke of America; and Europeans and Africans who could not or did not* both Maynor in Brooks, 330

121   *It had become clear to any who cared to look* Katz, 127

121   *1743—Cambridge* and following, Southern, 32–34

122   *1734—Runaway, the 26th of June last* Johnston, 28

122   *In the blacks' quarter* Southern, 63

122   *returned to England, horrified by the abject state of the Negroes and Indians* Epstein, 28

122   *Among the objects from America was* Epstein, 49

123   *There are also songs* Nettl, 165

124   *Listen! A voice is calling you!* Neihardt, 137

127   I have drawn details of Rodgers's life from *Jimmie the Kid* by Mike Paris and Chris Comber, and Nolan Porterfield's *Jimmie Rodgers.*

130   *the only numbers the old bluesmen wanted to play together* Johnny Shines sang and played guitar with Robert Johnson and later recalled their repertory: "And the country singer, Jimmie Rodgers, me and Robert used to play a hell of a lot of his tunes, man." Wald, 118

130   *I was inspired by the records of Jimmie Rodgers* Segrest and Hoffman, 22

131   Accounts of Ralph Peer, the Bristol Sessions, and the Carter Family are given in Porterfield, Paris and Comber, and Zwonitzer and Hershberg.

135   *A boy came in there by the name of Jimmie Rodgers* Paris and Comber, 35

139   *He'd just go in* Zwonitzer and Hirshberg, 128

139   *He always was in the deepest study* Zwonitzer and Hirshberg, 59

139   *There is no uniform key for a song* Fletcher, 11

140   The story of "Black Jack David" is told by Leslie Nelson-Burns at http://www.contemplator.com/child/johnnyfa.html

142   *The shoes I had on when at home they took off* Dickenson, 70

143   *an Indian went behind us with a whip* Seaver, Chap. II

143   *an Indian took off my shoes and stockings* Seaver, Chap. II

143   *The next morning, the Indians led us off* Seaver, Chap. II

143   *immediately set up a most dismal howling* Seaver, Chap. III

144   *Down across the Middle West* Wallace, *Long*, 37

145   *opened a window on a closed-off world* Escott, 3

146   *so strangely demanding* Marcus, *Invisible*, 165

147   *As a small boy* Marcus, *Invisible*, 161

147   *It is an imp that disorganizes* Marcus, *Invisible*, 173

149   *through which [the departed spirit] might reenter* Morgan, 176

150   *You cannot dance to it* Maynor in Brooks, 328

150   *[T]o meet the demands of the rhythm of the music* Fletcher, 12–13

151   *Never had a beard* Wald, 112

153   *now considered responsible for the sale of more guitars than anyone else* In the judgment of Hank Snow and Ernest Tubb. Porterfield, 363

158   *Herskovits published a survey* Miles in Brooks, 144

159   *That in most of the New World* Herskovits, 133–34

160   *Far greater attention must be given* Herskovits, 264

161   I am greatly indebted to Marybeth Hamilton's *In Search of the Blues* for its very complete treatment of the lives of John and Alan Lomax, and their fraught relationship with Huddie Ledbetter.

162   *Lomax cultivated a portrait of benevolent master* The two men starred in a *March of Time* newsreel which recreated their prison meeting, "and a *Life* magazine profile was titled 'Bad Nigger Makes Good Minstrel.'" Wald, 232

162   *That Leadbelly grew increasingly truculent* Hamilton, 121

163   *filled the archive's shelves* Hamilton, 149

164   *steeped in the politics of the Popular Front* Hamilton, 170

164   *the melancholy dissatisfaction* Lomax, ix intro.

165   *It came in the sudden emergence* Lomax, 233

165   *[I]t is a blues only by the loose definition* Wald, 75

166   *recorded Delta-style hollers in other regions* Wald, 296 fn.

166   *very similar songs* Lomax, 233

166   *Senegalese slaves were prized* Lomax, 234

166   *a TV program about the origins of the Delta* Lomax, 234–35

168   *insistence on an occult, Gothic America* Marcus, *Granta* 76 (Winter 2001), http://www.granta.com/Archive/76/American-Folk

170   *The humorous costume* Kahn, 264

171   *I want to tell you about my uncle Tom* Miles in Brooks, 139; also typescript facsimile of report of interviewer Beulah Sherwood Hagg, # 30309, pg. 27 Arkansas slave narrative project.

171   *My father wuz a full-blooded African* Hilegas and Lawrence, 1415

173   *There was nobody around the place but Indians and Negroes* Baker and Baker, 315

173   *I never did get along good with those Creek slaves* Baker and Baker, 84

173   *I belong to a full-blood Creek Indian* Baker and Baker, 108

174   *He was a white man that married a Cherokee woman* Baker and Baker, 493

174   *When I was 20 years old* Baker and Baker, 104

174   *The Creek man that bought her* Baker and Baker, 172

175   *I can make an old fiddle talk* Baker and Baker, 84

176   *De chicken dance is de "Tolosabanga"* Baker and Baker, 111

176   *No, in them days I didn't know nothin'* Oakley, 42

176   *Well, they used to have several names for them* Oakley, 42

176   *Jigs and reels* Wald, 47

177   *Up 'til then, the blues was only inside me* Russell, 48

178   *[E]verybody knows how provoking it is* Irving, *History,* 136

179   *Indigo leaves exuded a strong, unpleasant odor* Pettit, 27

180   *Long-term exposure to the chemicals* Ross, at http://www.leeric. lsu.edu/le/special/indigo.htm

180   *Because it was thought* Mattson, at http://www.lib.umn.edu/ bell/tradeproducts/indigo

180   *[E]nthusiasm for indigo disappeared* MS WPA, 95

184   My understanding of the settlement of Rochester and the Sam Patch phenomenon were aided greatly by the books of Paul Johnson, *A Shopkeeper's Millennium: Society and Revivals in Rochester, New York, 1815–1837* and *Sam Patch, the Famous Jumper.*

184   *mentioned with something like awe* "For many tourists, the aqueduct was the aesthetic high point of a stopover at Rochester. Travelers on the Canal passed between tall stone buildings at either end of the aqueduct, then suddenly found themselves in the open and high above the rapids." Johnson, *Patch*, 131

184   *the only instance in the known world* Johnson, *Patch*, 149

185   *The critic Edmund Wilson* In *Upstate: Records and Recollections of Northern New York*, 15

186   *Frederick Douglass* Douglass, born in rural Maryland of mixed African, Native, and European ancestry, left an account of something resembling the blues in his 1855 memoir, *My Bondage and My Freedom*, cited in Oakley, 19: Slaves would "make the dense old woods, for miles around, reverberate with their wild notes. These were not always merry because they were wild. On the contrary, they were mostly of a primitive cast, and told a tale of grief and sorrow. In the most boisterous outbursts of rapturous sentiment, there was ever a tinge of deep melancholy."

187   *Seneca men hired on* Wallace, *Long*, 58

187   *are terribly strong* Wilson, E., *Iroquois*, 205–06

188   *When the Little People enter the room* Wilson, E., *Iroquois*, 208–09

189   *if neglected, they may become angry* Wilson, E., *Iroquois*, 210

189   *They burned sacred tobacco* Wilson, E., *Iroquois*, 206

190   *The very village was altered* "Rip Van Winkle" in Irving, *History*, 769–85

192   *I was fortunate in falling into their hands* Seaver, Chap. III

194   *settling in Chautauqua County, New York History of Genesee Country*, vol. 4, 703

199   *by way of brute luck* My father *never* told battle stories, and it was only from Uncle Nino, many years after Joe died, that I heard about the day at Anzio, where Joe spent three months in the winter of 1944 under conditions comparable to the worst of World War One. Sitting in the back of a truck with some of his men, Dad recognized a young priest from Rochester in a passing jeep, hopped out, and ran to say hello. While they were talking, an incoming shell hit Dad's truck, killing all aboard. The same priest married my parents seven years later. It should surprise no one that Joe was a devout Catholic.

202   My Spanish ancestry is not cryptic; Inez, Alfonso, and Carlotta are all family names.

208   *Some Jews accepted baptism* Adams, 92

208   *They were abandoning the land where they were born* in Bass

209   *rich and powerful* Adams, 93

209   *some men were haled in front of the Inquisition* Adams, 94

209   *With the expulsion of the Arabs* Wilson, J., 30

210   *his home in Greenwich Village.* 110 Leroy Street

212   *and understood the same restlessness or anger* The strangest I ever saw my father behave was during our one family trip to Italy, when we visited the papal summer palace, Castel Gan-

dolfo, for a summer audience with Pope Paul VI. South and slightly east of Rome, Castel Gandolfo had been along Joe's route out of Anzio with his Army unit to the city twenty-four years earlier. Next day we were racing up the autostrada to Switzerland. Joe was seething, and did not stop driving, or say much of anything, until we reached the Alps hours later.

212   *a destination for the southern black diaspora* One who came to Rochester from Mississippi was William Tucker, hired by my grandfather to work loading and unloading trucks at the Bravo factory. Bill was a tall, wiry, very dark-skinned man of few words, who laughed easily and wore a gray-green twill shirt and matching cap to work every day. According to my Aunt Concetta, on his first day at the company, Bill was the target of some pretty dumb remarks. Next day at lunchtime he took a tomato from his sack and, in full view of the shipping room crew, placidly used a long, very sharp knife to remove the skin from the fruit in one flowing red strip.

Italians are connoisseurs of symbolic acts, and this one was very impressive. Mr. Tucker worked at Bravo for over 36 years.

213   *That same year, on a Friday night in July* My account of Rochester's 1965 riot is based on a scrapbook of contemporary articles on the subject from *The Times-Union* and *Democrat and Chronicle* newspapers on file in the reference division of the Central Library of Rochester, and Sanford Horwitt's *Let Them Call Me Rebel: Saul Alinsky, His Life and Legacy.*

214   *its dark and beautiful galleries* The extensive collection of Native American artifacts at Rochester's Museum of Arts and Sciences was founded with the collection of Lewis Henry Morgan, the local lawyer who successfully defended the Seneca's rights to Cattaraugus and began the serious study of U.S. Anthropology with his book, *League of the Iroquois,* published in Rochester in 1851.

Arthur C. Parker added to Morgan's collection and shaped it into the present displays of Iroquois village life. A paternal great-nephew of Ely Parker—Grant's aide-de-camp who had assisted Morgan before going to engineering school—Arthur was a trained archeologist, collected tribal folklore, published a translation of the Code of Handsome Lake and a biography of his uncle Ely. He became director of the Rochester museum in 1925, where he stayed for 26 years.

In retirement, he was an advocate for Indian rights and died at his home in Canandaigua, N.Y., once the site of a large Seneca town, on the same day, and several hours after, I was born up in Rochester, 25 miles away.

214   *an old club fighter* Ossie Sussman, "The Jewish Buzzsaw," a tough lightweight who sacrificed a professional career for Army service in World War Two. See: http://youtu.be/Gwmy-idk3524

Bibliography

Acton, Harold. *The Bourbons of Naples*. London: Prion Books, 1998.

Adams, Nicholson. *The Heritage of Spain*. New York: Henry Holt, 1952.

Ashton, Anthony. *Harmonograph*. New York: Walker & Company, 2003

Bacon, Tony. *The History of the American Guitar*. New York: Friedman/ Fairfax, 2001.

Baker, T. Lindsay, and Julie P. Baker, eds. *The WPA Oklahoma Slave Narratives*. Norman: University of Oklahoma Press, 1996.

Baraka, Amiri. *Blues People: Negro Music in White America*. New York: William Morrow, 1999.

Barry, John M. *Rising Tide*. New York: Touchstone, 1997

Bass, Howard. Liner notes. *Songs of the Sephardim*. Troy, New York: Dorian Discovery, 1993.

Bastin, Bruce. *Red River Blues*. Urbana: University of Illinois Press, 1986.

Batey, Rick. *The American Blues Guitar*. Milwaukee: Hal Leonard, 2003.

Baum, Dan. "Deluged." *The New Yorker*, 9 January 2006.

Berlin, Ira. *Generations of Captivity: A History of African-American Slaves*. Cambridge, MA: Belknap Press of Harvard University Press, 2003.

Berton, Pierre. *Niagara: A History of the Falls*. Toronto: McClelland & Stewart, 1994.

Betts, Lillian. "The People at the Pan-American." *The Outlook*, 14 September 1901, panam1901.bfn.org/documents

Bilger, Burkhard. "Struts and Frets." *The New Yorker*, 14 May 2007.

Boggs, Dock. " 'I Always Loved the Lonesome Songs.' " *Sing Out!*, July 1964.

Brayer, Elizabeth. *George Eastman: A Biography*. Baltimore: Johns Hopkins University Press, 1996.

Briggs, John W. *An Italian Passage: Immigrants to Three American Cities, 1890–1930.* New Haven, CT: Yale University Press, 1978.

Brookes, Tim. *Guitar: An American Life.* New York: New York: Grove, 2005.

Brooks, James F., ed. *Confounding the Color Line: The Indian-Black Experience in America.* Lincoln: University of Nebraska Press, 2002.

Brown, Dee. *Bury My Heart at Wounded Knee.* New York: Holt, Reinhart & Winston, 1970.

Calloway, Colin G., ed. *Our Hearts Fell to the Ground.* Boston: Bedford/ St. Martin's, 1996.

Calt, Stephen, and Gayle Wardlow. *King of the Delta Blues: The Life and Music of Charlie Patton.* Newton, NJ: Rock Chapel Press, 1988.

Campbell, Garth. *Johnny Cash: He Walked the Line.* London: J. Blake, 2003.

Cash, Johnny. *Cash.* New York: HarperSanFrancisco, 1997.

Chapman, Richard. *Guitar Music, History, Players.* London: Dorling Kindersley, 2000.

Charters, Samuel B. *The Roots of the Blues.* New York: Perigee, 1981.

———. *The Country Blues.* New York: Da Capo, 1975.

Cohen, John. "The Folk Music Interchange: Negro and White." *Sing Out!,* January 1964.

Connell, Evan S. *Son of the Morning Star.* New York: Perennial Library/ Harper & Row, 1984.

Cook, Bruce. *Listen to the Blues.* New York: Da Capo, 1995.

Cooper, James Fenimore. *The Leatherstocking Tales.* Vol. 1. New York: Library of America, 1985.

Cummins, Frederick T. *Historical Biography and Libretto [of the] Indian Congress.* Buffalo, NY, 1901.

Dash, Mike. *The First Family.* New York: Random House, 2009.

Davis, Francis. *The History of the Blues.* New York: Da Capo, 2003.

Dawidoff, Nicholas. *In the Country of Country.* New York: Pantheon, 1997.

DeMallie, Raymond J., ed. *The Sixth Grandfather.* Lincoln, NE: Bison Books, 1985.

DeMarce, Virginia Easley. " 'Verry Slitly Mixt': Tri-racial Isolate Families of the Upper South—A Genealogical Study." *National Genealogical Society Quarterly,* March 1992.

Densmore, Frances. "Cheyene and Arapaho Music." *Southwest Museum Papers.* Los Angeles, 1936.

Dickinson, Alice. *Taken by the Indians: True tales of captivity*. New York: F. Watts, 1976.

Dickson, Jean. "Mandolin Mania." *Western New York Heritage* 8, no. 3. Cheektowaga, New York.

Doty, Lockwood Richard, ed. *History of the Genesee Country*. Vol. 4. Chicago: S. J. Clarke, 1925.

Douglass, Frederick. *Narrative of the Life of Frederick Douglass*. Garden City, NY: DolphinBooks, 1963.

Dylan, Bob. *Chronicles*. New York: Simon & Schuster, 2004.

Ellison, Ralph. *Collected Essays*. New York: Modern Library, 1995.

Epstein, Dena. *Sinful Tunes and Spirituals*. Urbana: University of Illinois Press, 1981.

Escott, Colin. *Lost Highway: The True Story of Country Music*. Washington: Smithsonian Books, 2003.

Federal Writers' Project (Works Progress Administration). *Mississippi: A Guide to the Magnolia State*. New York: Hastings House, 1946.

Federal Writers' Project (Works Progress Administration). *New York: A Guide to the Empire State*. New York: Oxford University Press, 1940.

Federal Writers' Project (Works Progress Administration). *Tennessee: A Guide to the State*. New York: Hastings House, 4th printing 1959.

Fletcher, Alice. *A Study of Omaha Indian Music*. Lincoln, NE: Bison Books, 1994.

Fox, Austin M. *Symbol and Show: The Pan-American Exposition of 1901*. Buffalo: Western New York Wares, 1987.

Frazier, Ian. *Great Plains*. New York: Farrar, Straus & Giroux, 1989.

Freilich, Scott, "Oddball Guitars," *20th Century Guitar Magazine*, March 2001.

Goldman, Mark. *High Hopes: The Rise and Decline of Buffalo, New York*. Albany: State University of New York Press, 1983.

Grunfeld, Frederick V. *The Art and Times of the Guitar*. Toronto: Macmillan, 1969.

Gura, Philip F. *C. F. Martin and His Guitars*. Chapel Hill: University of North Carolina Press, 2003.

Guralnick, Peter. *Last Train to Memphis: The Rise of Elvis Presley*. Boston: Little, Brown, 1994.

———. *Lost Highways*. Boston: Back Bay/Little, Brown, 1999.

———. *Searching for Robert Johnson*. New York: Dutton, 1989.

Hadlock, Richard. *Jazz Masters of the Twenties*. New York: Collier Books, 1974.

Hamilton, Marybeth. *In Search of the Blues*. New York: Basic Books, 2008.

Handy, W. C. *The Father of the Blues*. New York: Da Capo, 1991.

Hart, Lavinia. "The Exhibit of Human Nature." *The Cosmopolitan*, September 1901. panam1901.bfn.org/documents/.

Hart, Mary Bronson. "How to See the Pan-American Exposition." *Everybody's Magazine*, October 1901. panam1901.bfn.org/documents/.

Hartman, Robert Carl. *Guitars and Mandolins in America*. Hoffman Estates, IL: Maurer, 1984.

Herskovits, Melville. *The Myth of the Negro Past*. Harper & Bros, New York, London, 1941.

Hill, Raymond C. *A Great White Indian Chief*. Frederick T. Cummins, 1912.

Hillegas, Jan and Ken Lawrence, eds., *The American Slave: A Composite Autobiography, vol. 9, Mississippi Narratives pt. 4*. Westport, CN: Greenwood Press, 1977.

Horwitt, Sanford D. *Let Them Call Me Rebel: Saul Alinsky, His Life and Legacy*. New York: Alfred A. Knopf, 1989.

Howe, Daniel Walker. *What Hath God Wrought*. New York: Oxford University Press, 2007.

Irving, Washington. "The Alhambra," in *Works*, vol. 5. Bedford, Clarke, Chicago, n.d.

———. *History, Tales, and Sketches*. New York: Library of America, 1983.

Isacoff, Stuart. *Temperament: The Idea That Solved Music's Greatest Riddle*. New York: Alfred A. Knopf, 2001.

Johnson, Paul E. *A Shopkeeper's Millennium: Society and Revivals in Rochester, New York, 1815–1837*. New York: Hill and Wang, 2004.

———. *Sam Patch, the Famous Jumper*. New York: Hill & Wang, 2004.

Johnston, James Hugo. "Documentary Evidence of the Relations of Negroes and Indians." *The Journal of Negro History*, January 1929.

Josephy, Alvin M., Jr. *500 Nations*. New York: Alfred A. Knopf, 1994.

Kahn, Ed. "Hillbilly Music: Source and Resource." *Journal of American Folklore*, July–September, 1965.

Kallen, Stuart A. *Native Americans of the Great Lakes*. San Diego: Lucent Books, 2000.

Kasson, John F. *Amusing the Million*. New York: Hill & Wang, 1978.

Katz, William Loren. *Black Indians: A Hidden Heritage*. New York: Atheneum, 1986.

Kuronen, Darcy. *Dangerous Curves: The Art of the Guitar*. Boston: MFA Publications, 2000.

Lampedusa, Giuseppe Tomasi di. *The Leopard*. London: Collins & Harvill, 1960.

Lankford, George E., ed. *Bearing Witness: Memories of Arkansas Slavery: Narratives from the 1930s WPA Collections*. Fayetteville: University of Arkansas Press, 2003.

Larson, Robert W. *Red Cloud*. Norman: University of Oklahoma Press, 1997.

Laux, Wilma. *Village of Buffalo 1800–1832*. Buffalo, New York: Buffalo and Erie Co. Historical Society, 1960.

Leary, Thomas, and Elizabeth Sholes. *Buffalo's Pan-American Exposition*. Charleston, SC: Arcadia, 1998.

Lepore, Jill. *The Name of War: King Philip's War and the Origins of American Identity*. New York: Vintage, 1999.

Lomax, Alan. *The Land Where the Blues Began*. New York: New Press, 2002.

Long, Cathryn J. *The Cherokee*. San Diego: Lucent Books, 2000.

Louisiana Writers Project (Works Progress Administration). *Louisiana: A Guide to the State*. New York: Hastings House, 1941.

Lovett, Laura L. " 'African and Cherokee by Choice': Race and Resistance under Legalized Segregation." In Straus, *Roots and Relations*.

Marcus, Greil. *Invisible Republic: Bob Dylan's Basement Tapes*. New York: Henry Holt, 1997.

———. "American Folk." *Granta* 76 (Winter 2001).

Mattson, Anne, "Indigo in the Early Modern World." University of Minnesota. James Ford Bell Library. 2010. http://www.lib.umn.edu/bell/tradeproducts/indigo.

Maynor, Malinda "Making Christianity Sing." In Brooks, *Confounding the Color Line*.

McKee, Jessee O. *The Choctaw*. New York: Chelsea House, 1989.

McMurtry, Larry. *Crazy Horse*. New York: Viking/Penguin, 1999.

———. *Oh, What a Slaughter: Massacres in the American West, 1846–1890*. New York: Simon and Schuster, 2005.

Merrill, Arch. *The White Woman and Her Valley*. New York: Stratford, 1961.

Miles, Tiya. "All in the Family? A Meditation on White Centrality, Black Exclusion, and the Intervention of Afro-Native Studies." In Straus, *Roots and Relations*.

———. "Uncle Tom Was an Indian." In Brooks, *Confounding the Color Line*.

Miller, Lee. *Roanoke: Solving the Mystery of the Lost Colony.* New York: Arcade, 2000.

Mitchell, Joseph. "The Mohawks in High Steel." In Wilson, *Apologies to the Iroquois.*

Morgan, Louis Henry. *League of the Iroquois.* Secaucus, NJ: Citadel, 1975.

Moses, L. G. *Wild West Shows and the Images of American Indians.* Albuquerque: University of New Mexico Press, 1996.

Neihardt, John G. *Black Elk Speaks.* Lincoln: University of Nebraska Press, 2004.

Nelson, Paul. "'Jug Band! Jug Band!'" *Sing Out!,* 1963.

Nettl, Bruno. *Folk and Traditional Music of the Western Continents.* 3rd ed. Englewood Cliffs, NJ: Prentice-Hall, 1990.

Newton, Elsie Eaton. "The Country of the Yazoo Delta." *The Southern Workingman,* February 1907.

Norwich, John Julius. *The Normans in Sicily.* London: Penguin, 1992.

Oakley, Giles. *The Devil's Music.* New York: Da Capo, 1997.

Obermeyer, Brice. "Lessons from Salt Creek: Maintaining Tribal Identity among the Black Indians of the Five Civilized Tribes." In Straus, *Roots and Relations.*

Oliver, Paul. "Introduction: Yonder Come the Blues." In *Yonder Come the Blues: The Evolution of a Genre.* Cambridge: Cambridge University Press, 2001.

———. "Savannah Syncopators." In *Yonder Come the Blues: The Evolution of a Genre.* Cambridge: Cambridge University Press, 2001.

———. *The Story of the Blues.* Boston: Northeastern University Press, 1997.

Palmer, Robert. *Deep Blues.* New York: Penguin, 1981.

Parker, Arthur C. *Seneca Myths and Folk Tales.* Lincoln, NE: Bison Books, 1989.

———. *The Code of Handsome Lake, the Seneca Prophet.* Ohsweken, Ontario: Iroqrafts, 2000.

Parkman, Francis. *France and England in North America.* Vols. 1 and 2. New York: Library of America, 1983.

Paris, Mike, and Chris Comber. *Jimmie the Kid.* New York: Da Capo, 1977.

Peabody, Charles. "Notes on Negro Music." *Journal of American Folk-Lore* 16 (July 1903).

Percy, William Alexander. *Lanterns on the Levee.* New York: Alfred A. Knopf, 1941.

Perdue, Theda, and Michael D. Green. *American Indians of the Southwest*. New York: Columbia University Press, 2001.

Pettit, Florence. *America's Indigo Blues*. New York: Hastings House, 1974.

Porterfield, Nolan. *Jimmie Rodgers*. Urbana: University of Illinois Press, 1992.

Powers, Thomas *The Killing of Crazy Horse* New York: Alfred A. Knopf, 2010.

Powers, William K. *War Dance*. Tucson: University of Arizona Press, 1990.

Pritzker, Barry M. *A Native American Encyclopedia*. New York: Oxford University Press, 2000.

Rauchway, Eric. *Murdering McKinley*. New York: Hill & Wang, 2004.

Rawick, George P., ed. *The American Slave: A Composite Autobiography*. Vol. 9, *Mississippi Narratives*, edited by Jan Hillegas and Ken Lawrence. Wesport, CT: Greenwood, 1972.

Robb, Peter. *Midnight in Sicily*. New York: Vintage, 1999.

Rosecan, Stephen. "Some Notes on Early Eighteenth-Century Contact between Choctaws, the Louisiana French, and Africans." In Straus, *Roots and Relations*.

Ross, Gary Noel. "Mysterious Dye—Indigo." *Louisiana Environmentalist*, May-June, 1995.

Runciman, Steven. *The Sicilian Vespers*. Cambridge: Cambridge University Press, 1992.

Russell, Tony. *Blacks, Whites, and Blues*. New York: Stein and Day, 1969.

Rydell, Robert W. *All the World's a Fair*. Chicago: University of Chicago Press, 1984.

Sallis, James. *The Guitar Players*. Lincoln, NE: Bison Books, 1994.

Sanders, Ronald. *Lost Tribes and Promised Lands*. New York: Harper Perennial, 1992.

Schmidt, Paul William. *Acquired of the Angels*. Metuchen, NJ: Scarecrow, 1991.

Seaver, James E., *A Narrative of the Life of Mrs. Mary Jemison*. Project Gutenberg EBook, November, 2004 [EBook #6960] http://www.gutenberg.org/cache/epub/6960/pg6960.html.

Segrest, James, and Mark Hoffman. *Moanin' at Midnight*. New York: Pantheon, 2004.

Souter, Chelsea. "Outside the Box: Black Indian Identity in the United States." In Straus, *Roots and Relations*.

Southern, Eileen, ed. *Readings in Black American Music*. New York: Norton, 1971.

Speck, F. G. "The Negroes and the Creek Nation." *Southern Workman*, January, 1908.

Straus, Terry, ed. *Race, Roots and Relations: Native and African Americans*. Chicago: Alabatross, 2005.

Terkel, Studs. *And They All Sang*. New York: New Press, 2005.

Toqueville, Alexis de. *Democracy in America*. New York: Library of America, 2004.

Tosches, Nick. *Country*. New York: Da Capo, 1996.

———. *Where Dead Voices Gather*. Boston: Back Bay/Little, Brown, 2001.

Turnbull, Harvey. *The Guitar from the Renaissance to the Present Day*. New York: Scribners, 1974.

Van Ronk, Dave, with Elijah Wald. *The Mayor of MacDougal Street*. Cambridge: Da Capo, 2005.

Wald, Elijah. *Escaping the Delta*. New York: Amistad, 2004.

Walen, Richard F. *Truro: The Story of a Cape Cod Town*. Bloomington, IN: Xlibris, 2002.

Wallace, Anthony F. C. *The Long Bitter Trail*. New York: Hill & Wang, 1993.

———. *The Death and Rebirth of the Seneca*. Vintage Books, New York, 1972.

Walton-Raji, Angela. *Black Indian Genealogy Research*. Bowie, MD: Heritage Books, 1993.

Wardlow, Gayle Dean. *Chasin' That Devil Music*. San Francisco: Miller Freeman Books, 1998.

Wilder, Alec. *American Popular Song*. New York: Oxford University Press, 1972.

Williams, Jay. "Heathens, Savages, Africans, Indians and War Captives: Stereotypes of Past and Present Peoples." In Straus, *Roots and Relations*.

Wilson, Edmund. *Apologies to the Iroquois*. New York: Farrar, Straus & Cudahy, 1960.

———. *The Fifties*. New York: Farrar, Straus & Giroux, 1986.

Wilson, James. *The Earth Shall Weep: A History of Native America*. New York: Atlantic Monthly Press, 1999.

Wolff, Kurt. *The Rough Guide to Country Music*. London: Rough Guides, 2000.

Yans-McLaughlin, Virginia. *Family and Community: Italian Immigrants in Buffalo*. Ithaca, NY: Cornell University Press, 1977.

Zwonitzer, Mark, and Charles Hirshberg. *Will You Miss Me When I'm Gone?: The Carter Family and Their Legacy in American Music.* New York: Simon & Schuster, 2002.

Index